SUBMARINE
WARFARE TODAY

CHRIS CHANT

Published in 2005 by Silverdale Books
an imprint of Bookmart Ltd
Registered Number 2372865
Trading as Bookmart Ltd
Blaby Road
Wigston
Leicester LE18 4SE

ISBN 1-84509-158-2

Produced by
Amber Books Ltd
Bradley's Close
74-77 White Lion Street
London N1 9PF
www.amberbooks.co.uk

Project Editor: Tom Broder
Design: Colin Hawes

PICTURE CREDITS:
Photographs courtesy of US DOD, IWM, US National Archives.

Previously published in a different format as part of the reference set *War Machine*.

Printed in Italy

SUBMARINE
WARFARE TODAY

Contents

Introduction

Submarine technology has come a long way since the first torpedoes were used in anger during the American Civil War, but the strategies and tactics used in modern submarine warfare have changed little since the days of the Cold War between the West and the Soviet Union. In the 1950s the Americans and Russians began to explore the concept of the nuclear-powered ballistic missile submarine, a vessel capable of remaining submerged for lengthy periods. Armed with nuclear-tipped missiles, they would be the ultimate nuclear deterrent: almost impossible to detect, and able to respond to any surprise nuclear attack on the home country.

The US Navy first merged the new technologies of ballistic missiles, smaller thermonuclear weapons, inertial guidance systems and nuclear weapons into a single weapon system in 1960. The first Fleet Ballistic Missile (FBM) submarine was armed with the Polaris A1 missile. The Soviet Union was quick to respond, deploying the Hotel-class nuclear ballistic submarine. The ballistic missile submarine race was on, and it would later be joined by Britain, France and China.

By the 1980s, the missile submarine (SSBN) had become an awesome weapon of destruction, capable of carrying up to 16 missiles, each with multiple warheads, that could rain nuclear destruction on targets 4600km (2500nm) from their launch point. Just one of a missile's warheads can destroy 60 per cent of a major city. Today, despite the end of the Cold War, the SSBN remains a key asset for the small number of navies – and governments – which they serve.

For nearly three decades until the 1990s, NATO and Warsaw Pact submariners played a potentially deadly game of cat-and-mouse in the depths of the world's oceans – the tools of their trade being nuclear attack and hunter-killer submarines (SSNs), packed with weaponry and sensors. Their targets: the SSBNs and naval task forces of the other side. Many of the lessons learnt by both sides during this time have subsequently been incorporated into modern submarine design and tactics.

The development of nuclear attack submarines in the United States and the Soviet Union also began in the 1950s, but the designs followed different paths; the Americans concentrated on anti-submarine warfare (ASW) and the Russians on a multi-mission role, encompassing both ASW and surface attack with large anti-ship cruise missiles. Later, the Americans also adopted a multi-mission capability, with the deployment of submarine-launched weapons like Sub-Harpoon and Tomahawk, designed for anti-ship and land attack; in recent years this facility has been used successfully to attack key targets with heavy anti-aircraft defences in both Afghanistan and Iraq.

It was thought by some that the advent of the nuclear submarine would mean the demise of diesel-powered boats, craft which had carried the submarine through all the stages of its development since World War I. The United States Navy, for example, decided to go all-nuclear; its last three diesel-electric boats, known today as SSKs, were built in the late 1950s. The Russians, on the other hand, never lost faith in the SSK, and continued to develop it alongside their nuclear types. European navies also continued to build SSKs; after their retirement, many of these boats found their way into service with other navies around the globe, and today most of the world's active navies operate diesel-powered submarines, which are significantly cheaper to operate than their nuclear brethren.

As you will discover, this book provides a detailed survey of the submarines that patrol the seas, the tactic they use to avoid detection, the awesome weaponry they carry, and, finally, the dedicated ASW helicopters and maritime aircraft that have the difficult task of finding these elusive craft.

The 'Los Angeles'-class submarine USS Albuquerque surfaces in the Atlantic Ocean while participating in exercise Majestic Eagle in 2004.

Ballistic Missile Submarines

Cold War sub patrol

The shield protecting both East and West from the horrors of nuclear conflict during the years of the Cold War was to a large extent provided by constant patrols by the respective navies' submarine forces.

Above: The Royal Navy's initial SSBN, the four-ship 'Resolution' class, was built by stretching the hull of a 'Valiant'-class attack submarine for the carriage of 16 Polaris A3 missiles. Each weapon carried three 200-kT MIRVS, all aimed around the same target. Unlike their US counterparts, the Royal Navy's Polaris fleet remained in service until after the end of the Cold War.

The nuclear-powered ballistic missile submarine, or 'SSBN' (Sub-Surface/Ballistic/Nuclear) is beloved of Hollywood film directors. Movies such as *The Hunt for Red October*, *Crimson Tide* and *K-19* have illustrated how things can go dramatically wrong on vessels armed with unimaginable levels of destructive power. The reality, both during the Cold War and after, was invariably more mundane. These submarines, with their arsenals of long-range nuclear-tipped missiles, would quietly patrol for weeks, sometimes months on end, trying to avoid detection by other submarines, surface ships or Anti Submarine Warfare (ASW) aircraft. Their crews would conduct endless practice missile launchings, hoping that they would never need to do their job for real. SSBNs have several advan-

tages. The reactors provide power for vastly extended periods, unlike conventional diesel-electric engines. The air supply in the boat is continually regenerated and filtered, eliminating the need for surfacing. The only limit to the SSBN's endurance is the food supply and crew stamina.

To avoid detection, SSBNs would follow complex courses and manoeuvres to disorientate any surveillance. Sometimes these boats would be accompanied by hunter-killer submarines and surface combatants to provide a secure cordon around the vessel. Communications to and from the SSBNs were few.

Right: USS Georgia enters port at New London, Connecticut, in February 1984. Unlike its Soviet contemporary, the 'Typhoon', the 'Ohio'-class SSBNs were not equipped to operate through weak spots in the polar ice.

They normally consisted of short bursts, in the orders of one-tenth of a second, of Exceptionally Low Frequency (ELF) 'flash' radio traffic. Should they ever be detected, SSBNs were fitted with countermeasures such as decoys and acoustic homing torpedoes for self-defence.

Entry into service

The first ballistic missile submarine to enter service was the Soviet diesel-electric 'Zulu' class. These boats were constructed in the early 1950s. Initially, a single boat was converted to launch the R-11FM (SS-N-1b 'Scud-A') ballistic nuclear missile. Five boats were then converted following successful trials. Each carried two R-11FMs, later replaced with the R-13 (SS-N-4 'Sark'), with a range of 650 km (404 miles) and a 5-megaton (MT) warhead.

The 'Zulu' vessels were later followed by the diesel-electric 'Golf'-class boats. However, these boats were easy prey for the US Navy's anti-submarine force. The range of the R-13 missiles forced the 'Golfs' to operate close to the continental US. Fifteen 'Golf'-class boats entered service between 1960-62. Some 13 of the vessels were later converted to deploy the R-21 (SS-N-5 'Sark') – a revolutionary missile for the Soviet navy in that it could be fired while the submarine was submerged, unlike previous Soviet SLBMs.

The first SSBN to enter service with the US Navy was the USS *George Washington*. This boat was effectively a stretched 'Scorpion'-class nuclear submarine. The hull was lengthened to allow for two rows of eight Polaris A1 missiles to be installed. Polaris A1 had a range of 2600 km (1,615 miles) and a single 500-kiloton (kT) warhead. The USS *George*

Washington was launched on 15 November 1960, a mere three years after its keel was laid down. The rapid completion of the boat was seen as a managerial and technical triumph for Rear Admiral W. Raborn, who led the project. However, the range of the Polaris A1 meant the boats had to be based at forward locations such as Holy Loch in Scotland, Rota in Spain and Guam in the Pacific Ocean.

The seminal 'George Washington'-class nuclear-powered boats would see the introduction of several now-standard procedures for American SSBNs. For

instance, each boat was served by two crews, designated 'Blue' and 'Gold', one of which was at sea, while the other was on shore, preparing to relieve the Blue crew on its next mission.

The 'George Washingtons' were followed by the 'Ethan Allen' class. Completed between 1961-63, these vessels were similar to their predecessors, but were designed specifically to serve as SSBNs.

In 1962, the Royal Navy deployed its first SSBN, after the UK signed an agreement with the US to purchase four Polaris missile submarines.

Left: As the most potent Western SSBNs of the Cold War, the 'Ohio' class were originally fitted with 24 missile launch tubes for the Trident I SLBM.

The first boat, HMS *Resolution*, was completed in 1967. The Polaris missile bodies were constructed in the US, while warheads and some command and control systems were designed and built in the UK.

Missile conversions

During the same year, the US completed the service induction of the 'Lafayette'-class SSBN. Thirty-one boats entered service. The first eight boats were fitted with the Polaris A2, the rest of the class were fitted with the Polaris A3, the most modern variant. Between 1979-83, 12 'Lafayettes' were converted to deploy the Trident C4 SLBM. The first vessel to receive the conversion, the USS *Francis Scott Key*, began its first deterrence patrol on 20 October 1979.

In 1972 the Soviets announced a new, major SSBN. Known as the 'Yankee' class, it was armed with 16 R-27 (SS-N-6 'Serb') missiles. However, the R-27, with a range of 2,400 km (1,491 miles) and 3000 km (1,864 miles) for models one and two respectively, meant that the boats would have to get close to the US coastline, and therefore closer to US anti-submarine activities, if they were to strike targets deep in the US. However, this gave the Soviets a major advantage, as flight times of the missiles would be around four to five minutes, leaving little time for warning.

The Soviets followed the 'Yankee' class with the 'Delta' class. Most of the 'Deltas' deployed 12 R-29 (SS-N-8 'Sawfly') missiles, with a 7800-km (4,846-mile) range. Later,

Right: The sonar room of the 'Lafayette' boat USS Ulysses S. Grant in 1969. SSBNs can be fitted with very large sonar arrays, as their nuclear reactors generate so much electricity.

the 'Delta III' class would deploy the R-29R (SS-N-18 'Stingray') with a range of 8000 km (4,971 miles). The 'Deltas' were essentially designed to be a first-strike weapon. They would pierce the relatively thin ice in the Arctic and fire their missiles for a crippling nuclear strike against the US.

During the same year, the US began the development of the Trident I SLBM, based on the previous Poseidon SLBM. In 1981, Trident was deployed on the massive US 'Ohio'-class SSBNs. These boats deployed 24 missiles. The first eight boats, entering service between 1981-86, were armed with the Trident I missile. The remaining boats, completed between 1988-97 were fitted with Trident II.

The Soviet response to the 'Ohios' were the 'Typhoon'-class SSBNs. These vessels would each deploy 20 R-39 (SS-N-20 'Sturgeon') missiles. These boats were designed to stay beneath the waves for over a year. They would be used to deliver a blow against the US once it was beginning to recover from a nuclear war. Unlike previous Soviet and American SSBNs, the missiles of the 'Typhoon' are equipped forward of the sail. Due to the long period that the vessel was expected to stay away from port, and submerged, crew areas were lavishly furnished with saunas and even a swimming pool. Six 'Typhoons' were completed between 1977-89.

While some land and air units charged with nuclear delivery belonging to the world's nuclear powers were downsized or eliminated at the end of the Cold War, the US, UK, France, Russia and China show no signs of dismantling their SSBN forces. Such vessels continue to provide a powerful message of stealthy deterrent, and an important badge of national prestige, providing future filmmakers with dramatic settings for many years to come.

US SLBM RANGE: STRATEGIC REACH

Although Poseidon could not strike as far as Polaris A3, it made up for this by carrying 10 kiloton-yield MIRVs (a maximum of 14 was possible, but outlawed under the SALT I agreement) rather than the three of its predecessor. Polaris A3 passed from US Navy service in 1983, but was retained by the Royal Navy until after the Cold War. Trident I, development of which began in 1972, was based on the Poseidon C3 missile but added a third stage for increased range.

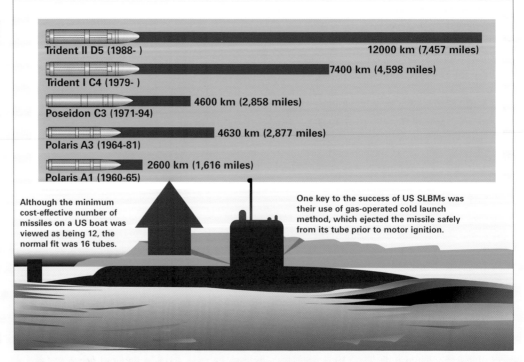

Trident II D5 (1988-)   12000 km (7,457 miles)

Trident I C4 (1979-)   7400 km (4,598 miles)

Poseidon C3 (1971-94)   4600 km (2,858 miles)

Polaris A3 (1964-81)   4630 km (2,877 miles)

Polaris A1 (1960-65)   2600 km (1,616 miles)

Although the minimum cost-effective number of missiles on a US boat was viewed as being 12, the normal fit was 16 tubes.

One key to the success of US SLBMs was their use of gas-operated cold launch method, which ejected the missile safely from its tube prior to motor ignition.

Cold War missile submarines
Soviet and US developments

The concept of the missile-armed submarine is not new. Both the US and Soviet navies made use of captured World War II German technology in the post-war years, but it was in the 1950s that the modern conception of the nuclear-powered, nuclear missile-armed submarine arose.

In March 1946 the US Chief of Naval Operations ordered the conversion of two fleet submarines, USS *Cusk* and USS *Carbanero*, to launch two air-breathing Loon missiles derived from the German V-1, and thus initiated the US sub-launched strategic missile programme. At the same time as the first successful Loon launch in March 1947, development of two long-range submarine bombardment missiles was in progress. The Rigel missile was cancelled in 1953, but in the previous year the fleet submarine USS *Tunny* had been converted to carry two Regulus I missiles, fired from the surfaced vessel. A further unit, USS *Barbero*, was converted along the same lines, and two new conventional units, USS *Grayback* and USS *Growler*, were completed as missile launchers, each with capacity for four missiles.

Nuclear power

With the advent of nuclear propulsion, USS *Halibut*, a conventional boat ordered as a Regulus carrier, was reordered in 1956 with nuclear propulsion and the ability to carry five missiles. This was to have been followed by a class of larger nuclear boats each with four supersonic Regulus IIs. This missile was cancelled in 1958 and the submarines

*Above: **O**ne of the first launches of Polaris A3, in 1964, signalled the culmination of the astonishing scientific and industrial achievement which marked the Polaris programme. In the space of five years the US had built 41 boats and established a major strategic advantage.*

Left: The follow-on class to the six Soviet 'Whiskey Twin Cylinder' conversions was the 'Whiskey Long Bin' type. This involved lengthening the hull and inserting a section into the sail to carry four SS-N-3c 'Shaddock' strategic cruise missile container-launchers at a fixed angle of 15°. A total of six boats was built.

reordered as attack units. Regulus II had fallen foul of the Polaris ballistic missile. Evolved in the mid-1950s, this new type of underwater-launched missile required a projected force level of 30 submarines to be on station from a 45-50 unit total. To accommodate the interim Polaris A1 a conversion programme began in the late 1950s to install a 16-missile section abaft the fin in five 'Skipjack' attack submarines to produce the 'George Washington' SSBN class. As these vessels were being launched, five 'Ethan Allen' vessels, designed as SSBNs, were laid down. These were in effect ballistic missile versions of the 'Thresher' SSN making use of that type's machinery-silencing techniques and deep-diving hull materials.

Equipped with the Polaris A2 SLBM they were followed by the larger 31-strong 'Lafayette' and 'Benjamin Franklin' SSBN classes, the last 23 of which were commissioned carrying the Polaris A3. The first Pacific Fleet SSBN went on patrol at the end of 1964 so the five Regulus I boats were phased out after seven years of patrols in the area. The 41

Polaris vessels were completed between 1959-64, marking one of the major industrial and military achievements of the Cold War.

In the Soviet Union Admiral Gorshkov became navy commander-in-chief in 1956 with a directive to build new missile submarines. The Soviets already had an SLBM programme based on captured German technology, culminating in September 1955 when a conventionally armed R-11FM missile was launched from a converted 'Zulu' conventional submarine. This was followed by five 'Zulu V' conversions (1954-58, each with two such missiles), and 23 boats of the 'Golf' class (1958-62, three missiles each) which carried the surface-launched SS-N-4 missile. In order to offer alter-

COLD WAR WARRIOR: 'OHIO'-CLASS SSBN

Much larger than its predecessors, the 'Ohio' is armed with the Trident missile system. The D5 missile in that system was for the first time accurate enough to allow submarines to attack 'hard' targets. With 24 missile tubes for initially the Trident I and then the Trident II as it became available, the 'Ohio' is the West's largest SSBN and is currently the only such type in US Navy service.

native strategic submarine systems the Soviets designed and built the SS-N-3c surface-launched nuclear cruise missile, tested in 1957 on the 'Whiskey Single Cylinder' conventional submarine. This was followed by six 'Whiskey Twin Cylinder' (1959-60, two SS-N-3c each) and six 'Whiskey Long Bin' (1961-65, four SS-N-3c) conversions.

As these entered service the Soviets introduced nuclear-powered classes using a common design basis. The SSBN class was the 'Hotel I' (eight built 1958-62, three SS-N-4 each) while the SSGN was the 'Echo I' (five commissioned 1960-62, six SS-N-3c each). The latter was the only nuclear-powered class equipped with strategic cruise missiles before the Soviet navy lost its strategic role in the early 1960s and the new land-based Strategic Rocket Forces assumed the task. Apart from deploying the submerged-launch SS-N-5 missile on seven 'Hotels' to give the 'Hotel II' subclass and on 14 'Golfs' to give the 'Golf II' variant, the Soviet navy did not match the massive American SSBN build-up until reassigned the strategic role as a primary task. Soviet military intelligence obtained plans of the 'Ethan Allen' class and British long-range sonar details, and when the 'Yankee' SSBN entered service in 1967, it was similar in appearance to the US class and equipped with a new long-range low-frequency sonar of the type required for SSBN operations.

In a programme matching American SSBN construction, the USSR built 34 'Yankee' units between 1964-74 for use off both US coasts. These had to transit long distances through enemy-controlled waters to their patrol areas, so the Soviets designed new long-range SLBMs that could be fired from waters adjacent to the USSR and still hit US targets. To accommodate these they enlarged the 'Yankee' to give the 12-tube 'Delta I' and the 16-tube 'Delta II', both armed with the SS-N-8 missile. With MIRVing of submarine-launched missiles the Soviets produced the 'Delta III' variant with 16 SS-N-18s.

As the first 'Delta' series was introduced the US began to deploy Poseidon MIRV-equipped SLBMs aboard their last 31 SSBNs. Its follow-on, the longer-range Trident, required a new submarine design with more missile tubes for greater cost effectiveness. As an interim measure 12 Poseidon-equipped units were converted to carry the Trident I SLBM, while the result of the new design programme was the 'Ohio' class. The Soviet counterpart to the 'Ohio' was the 'Typhoon' class, which entered service in 1981. With 20 missile tubes forward of the fin for the SS-N-20, the vessel was designed for operations under the Arctic ice, a capability unmatched in the West.

Above: A 'Yankee I' SSBN runs on the surface. The Soviets kept several units of this type off each coast of the US to provide a minimum-warning attack on time-sensitive targets such as Strategic Air Command bomber bases in the event of a nuclear war.

Right: The first Soviet SSBN class was the 'Hotel' type. Reconfigured in the 1960s to carry the SS-N-5 missile, these boats were subsequently phased out and were either scrapped or converted to other roles such as submerged naval command posts.

SSBNs
Death from the deep

Lurking stealthily beneath the surface of the world's oceans, nuclear-powered ballistic missile submarines carry the ultimate threat of destruction.

The history of nuclear missile submarines is interwoven with the Cold War rivalry between the USA and the USSR. After World War II, the outermost Soviet defensive line consisted of a huge force of submarines intended to deter or to intercept hostile task forces. After a period of instability

also being studied. After some unsuccessful attempts with V-2 missiles towed in watertight containers, the Soviets decided to install vertical launch tubes in the conning tower of the submarine itself. Between 1956 and 1958, a number of 'Zulu' class boats were modified to take two tubes, each about 2.25 m (7 ft) in

The Polaris missile brought about a revolution in strategic warfare. Developed in under four years, it was the West's primary strategic deterrent for two decades from 1960.

Left: The mighty 'Typhoon' ballistic missile submarine – known to its Russian users as Akula or Shark – is the largest submarine ever built.

following Stalin's death in 1953, Nikita Khrushchev took power in February 1955. He quickly initiated a crash programme of submarine development. By August 1958, the first of the 'November' class of nuclear-powered submarines had been commissioned, and ways of giving the submarine an offensive strategic role were

diameter, in the aft part of the fin. The missiles needed to be fired from the surface, and their range was only 563 km (350 miles).

Polaris

Meanwhile, the USA had been engaged in more cautious submarine development. The first sub-launched strategic weapons were solid-fuel, low-

trajectory cruise missiles. However, in an astonishing display of scientific, economic, engineering and financial muscle, the US Navy developed the Polaris system in less than four years. By 1960, the first of the 'George Washington' class was in service, armed with sixteen Polaris A-1 ballistic missiles: These were solid-fuelled, could

be launched under water, and had a range of some 2253 km (1,400 miles). By 1965, a fleet of 41 had been commissioned.

The Soviets were unable to deploy a similar submarine until 1967, when the first of 34 'Yankee' boats was commissioned. It is believed that the Soviets based the design on stolen US plans. It was fitted with 16 SS-N-6 'Sawfly' single-stage liquid-fuel missiles in hull-mounted tubes placed aft of the conning tower.

From the beginning of the 1970s, both navies concentrated on the development of larger and larger submarines to carry even longer-range missiles. In 1980 the four Soviet 'Delta' class designs were joined by the first of the 'Typhoon' class – at 171 m

BOOMERS: UNDERWATER DETERRENT

Early submarine-launched missiles were not very accurate. However, the development of advanced guidance systems means that the current generation of missile submarines, known as 'Boomers' to the US Navy, can be used against specific targets with devastating accuracy.

01 MISSILE ALERT

1. Silent waiting
SSBNs creep along at 5 kt (9km/h; 6mph) or less to avoid being detected. If new orders are necessary, ELF (extremely low radio frequency) messages can penetrate deep under water, alerting the submarine.

2. Firing orders
The submarine cautiously approaches the surface, scanning for enemy radar and making a periscope check of the waters around. If all is clear, it will raise its radio mast to receive instructions via satellite.

02 UNDERWATER LAUNCH

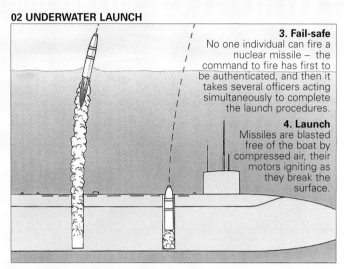

3. Fail-safe
No one individual can fire a nuclear missile – the command to fire has first to be authenticated, and then it takes several officers acting simultaneously to complete the launch procedures.

4. Launch
Missiles are blasted free of the boat by compressed air, their motors igniting as they break the surface.

03 MID-COURSE

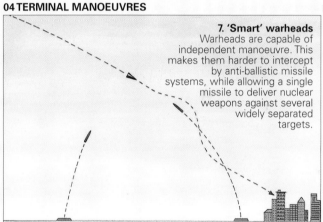

6. Navigation
Modern strategic missiles use a combination inertial guidance and automatic star sights to ensure that their warheads are released at exactly the right point.

5. Into space
The multi-stage missile blasts the warload into a sub-orbital path, accelerating to several thousand miles per hour.

04 TERMINAL MANOEUVRES

7. 'Smart' warheads
Warheads are capable of independent manoeuvre. This makes them harder to intercept by anti-ballistic missile systems, while allowing a single missile to deliver nuclear weapons against several widely separated targets.

(561 ft) and up to 40,000 tons, these were the largest submarines in the world.

Meanwhile, the Americans had replaced Polaris with Poseidon, and then in 1976 began to build the 24 missile 'Ohio' class (170.7 m/560 ft; 18,700 tons). Smaller than the Typhoon, they are much more quiet, and are even more deadly. They carry the D5 Trident 2 missile, which is as accurate as any land-based missile.

Other navies

The Royal Navy began operations with four Polaris boats of the 'Resolution' class in the late 1960s. They have been replaced by the larger 'Vanguard'-class vessels (148 m/486 ft; 15,000 tons), which carry 16 Trident 2s. The

French, who withdrew from NATO in 1966, went ahead with the development of their own nuclear submarines and ballistic missiles. *Le Redoutable* (128 m/420 ft; 9,000 tons), commissioned in 1971, deployed 16 M1 missiles of a size and range similar to the Polaris A-2. The 'Triomphant' class (138 m/453 ft; 14,200 tons) became operational in the 1990s, and will be upgraded to the M5, comparable with the Trident 2.

China completed one 'Xia' class boat in 1987. It carries 12 Chinese-manufactured JL-2 two-stage solid-fuel missiles, which have a range in excess of 6437 km (4,000 miles). A new missile submarine is currently under development.

Above: Crewmen manning ballistic missile submarines spend long, boring patrols at sea – but they must be ready to launch their awesome charges at a moment's notice.

With the ratification of the SALT agreements and the START process, the number of US and Soviet missile submarines has been decreased. However, it is noteworthy that even in the

new world order, defence cuts have rarely extended to submarines, and numbers of these vessels will continue to prowl the black depths of the world's oceans for the foreseeable future.

Chinese SSBNs Types 092 'Han' and 094

The Chinese navy's SSBN programme began in the 1970s but has yet to produce a functioning weapons platform. The sole Chinese SSBN, the **Changzheng 6**, is a modified 'Han'-class (NATO designation) SSN, laid down in 1978 and launched in 1981. Commissioned in 1987, the NATO designation is **'Xia' class**; to the Chinese it is the **Type 092**. Construction of both boat and intended missile system was a catalogue of disasters. The 'Xia' class is slow, noisy and its reactor unreliable. The JL-1 missile failed on its first live firings in 1985 and it took three years to achieve a successful test launch. The JL-1 (CSS-N-3) has a single 250-kT

warhead and its comparatively short range of 2,150 km (1,336 miles) would force the vessel to patrol perilously close to enemy shores. In fact, the 'Xia' class has never left Chinese coastal waters and seldom put to sea before a refit that lasted from 1995 to 2000. It emerged from dockyard hands with a new coat of black paint – replacing the previous steel blue – a bow-mounted sonar, re-designed missile casing that would allow for longer missiles and (presumably) new firing systems for a different missile, the JL-1A SLBM, which has a reported range of 2,800 km (1,740 miles).

It was reported that a second unit was constructed but lost

with all hands in an accident in 1985, but Chinese secrecy remains at Cold War levels. A solitary SSBN has little strategic value but whatever plans there might have been to extend the 'Xia' class have come to nought. Even if all systems are functioning, the boat's performance is poor by modern standards. The sole 'Xia'-class boat would not

survive long in wartime against western ASW platforms. A new class of SSBN, the **Type 094**, reportedly with 16 JL-2 (CSS-N-5 'Sabbot') SLBMs (8,000-km/ 4,971-mile range) is under construction with an estimated launch date of 2006. This new vessel may well be based on the hull of the new Type 093 SSN with an additional missile 'plug'.

SPECIFICATION	
'Xia' class (Type 092)	**Diving depth:** 300 m (984 ft)
Displacement: 6,500 tons dived	**Armament:** 12 JL-1A (CSS-N-3)
Dimensions: length 120 m (393 ft 6 in); beam 10 m (33 ft); draught 8 m (26 ft 2 in)	SLBMs, six 533-mm (21-in) bow tubes for Yu-3 torpedoes
Machinery: one pressurised watercooled reactor delivering 90 MW (120,643 shp) to one shaft	**Electronics:** 'Snoop Tray' surface search radar; 'Trout Cheek' hull-mounted active/passive search, Type 921A ESM
Speed: 22 kts dived	**Complement:** 140

'Le Triomphant' class New generation SSBN/SNLE

Ordered in March 1986 to replace the 'Redoutable' class, the **'Le Triomphant' class** are known to the French as SNLE-NGs (*Sous-marins Nucléares Lanceurs d'Engines-Nouvelle Génération*) or 'new generation' SSBNs. **Le Triomphant** was laid down at Cherbourg in 1989, launched in 1994 and entered service in 1997. Six boats were planned but this was reduced to four after the end of the Cold War, and the M5 SLBM, which was proving very expensive to develop, has been abandoned. The 'Triomphant' class will be armed with the cheaper M51 missile but the two vessels currently in service carry the M45.

A first submerged M45 launch was conducted by *Le Triomphant*

Left: **Le Triomphant** *undertook its first cruise in summer 1995, while* **Le Téméraire** *began trials in April 1998. The next vessel,* **Le Vigilant**, *began trials in December 2003, and the fourth and final boat (and the first to carry the definitive M51 SLBM),* **Le Terrible,** *is scheduled to enter service in 2010.*

in February 1995. Operated by two crews ('amber' and 'blue') *Le Triomphant* is France's primary nuclear deterrent – only one of the 'L'Inflexible' M4 class is still operational. The 'Triomphant' class submarines are significantly quieter than their predecessors: the primary objective of the design team was to reduce noise levels to the point that even the best acoustic sensors would have problems detecting and tracking the vessels.

The second of the class, **Le Téméraire** was laid down in 1993, launched in 1998 and commissioned in December 1999. **Le Vigilant**, laid down in 1997, entered service in 2004. **Le Terrible** was laid down in October 2000 and is planned to join the fleet in 2010. The M45 SLBM has a maximum range of 5,300 km (3,293 miles) and each missile has six MIRVs each carrying a 150-kT nuclear warhead. The 'Triomphant' class can launch SM39 Exocet anti-ship missiles from their torpedo tubes to attack surface targets, in addition to dual purpose L5 active/passive homing torpedoes. Between 2010-15 the class of four boats, beginning with *Le Terrible*, is to be equipped with the M51.

Below: **Le Téméraire** *was the second of the 'Le Triomphant'-class SSBNs, launched in August 1997 and commissioned in 1999. This boat and the name ship currently carry the M45 SLBM.*

SPECIFICATION	
'Le Triomphant' class	**Speed:** 25 kts dived
Displacement: 12,640 tons surfaced; 14,335 tons dived	**Diving Depth:** 500 m (1,640 ft)
Dimensions: length 138 m (453 ft); beam 12.5 m (41 ft); draught 12.5 m (41 ft)	**Armament:** 16 M45 SLBMs each with six 150-kT MIRVs, four 533-mm (21-in) tubes for 18 L5 torpedoes/SM39 Exocet missiles
Machinery: one pressurised water-cooled reactor delivering 150 MW (201,072 shp), two diesels delivering 700 kW (939 shp), one pump jet propulsor, one shaft	**Electronics:** Dassault search radar, Thomson-Sintra DMUX multi-function passive bow and flank arrays, towed array passive sonar
	Complement: 111

'Le Redoutable' and 'L'Inflexible' classes SSBNs/SNLEs

The first French SSBN (or more correctly *Sous-marin Nucléare Lanceurs d'Engine* or SNLE) **Le Redoutable** was authorised in March 1963, laid down in November 1964 and commissioned in 1971 after being employed for 2 1/2 years on trials as the prototype for the French naval deterrent known as the *Force de Dissuasion* in official circles. This vessel and its **'Le Redoutable' class** sister ship **Le Terrible** were initially equipped with the 2400-km (1,490-mile) range two-stage solid-propellant inertially-guided M1 SLBM that had a single 500-kT nuclear warhead and a CEP of 930 m (3,050 ft). In 1974 the third unit, **Le Foudroyant**, was commissioned with the improved 3100-km (1,925-mile) range M2 SLBM with a more powerful second-stage motor but carrying the same warhead and having a similar CEP. The

SPECIFICATION	
'L'Inflexible' class	**Armament:** 16 launch tubes for 16 M4 SLBMs (16 M45 SLBMs fitted in *l'Inflexible* in 2001), and four 533-mm (21-in) bow tubes for total of 18 L5 dual-purpose and F17 anti-ship torpedoes and SM39 Exocet anti-ship missiles
Displacement: 8,080 tons surfaced and 8,920 tons dived	
Dimensions: length 128.7 m (422 ft 3 in); beam 10.6 m (34 ft 9 in); draught 10 m (32 ft 10 in)	
Propulsion: one pressurised water-cooled reactor powering two steam turbines driving one shaft	**Electronics:** one surface search radar, one passive ESM system, one DLT D3 torpedo and Exocet fire-control system, one DSUX 21 sonar, and one DUUX 5 underwater telephone
Speed: 20 kts surfaced and 25 kts dived	
Diving depth: 350 m (1,150 ft) operational and 465 m (1,525 ft) maximum	**Complement:** 135

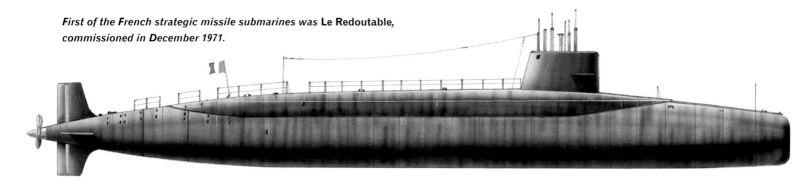

First of the French strategic missile submarines was **Le Redoutable**, *commissioned in December 1971.*

two previous vessels were then retrofitted with the M2 system during their normal overhauls. The fourth boat, **L'Indomptable**, was commissioned into service in 1977 with the vastly improved M20 missile that had the same range and accuracy as the M2 but carried a new 1.2-MT yield hardened warhead with what is believed to be chaff-dispensing penetration aids to confuse defending radar systems. The last vessel, **Le Tonnant**, was also completed with the M20 while the three units equipped with the M2 were subsequently brought up to the same standard. From 1985 the last four units built underwent yet another modification to carry the M4 SLBM that entered service aboard **L'Inflexible**. All five boats were also converted to carry the SM39 Exocet anti-ship missile and sonars of the **'L'Inflexible' class**. After the paying off of *Le Redoutable* in December 1991, the remaining submarines of the class were classified as the **'L'Inflexible' class SNLE M4**. The better streamlining of the M4 con-

version gave the boats a silhouette similar to that of *L'Inflexible*. The last such boat remaining in service was *L'Indomptable*, which received M4 missiles in 1989 and was decommissioned in late 2004. The similarly upgraded *Le Tonnant* was paid off into the reserve in 1999.

'L'Inflexible' class

Ordered in September 1978, the sole boat of the 'L'Inflexible' class, *L'Inflexible* is an intermediate design between the 'Le Redoutable' class and the 'Le Triomphant' class. *L'Inflexible* retains most of the external characteristics of the earlier class, but the internal fittings and sensors differ by taking advantage of the advances made in the propulsion system, electronics and weapons since the 'Le Redoutable'-class boats were constructed. The rationale behind this intermediate boat lay in the fact that France required three SSBNs to be continuously available, of which two were to be on patrol. In order to achieve this the French navy had to have six submarines in ser-

Above: **Le Foudroyant** *and its sister ships were designed and built in France without any help from the US, unlike the British Polaris boats, which required considerable design assistance.*

SPECIFICATION	
'Le Redoutable' class	**Diving depth:** 250 m (820 ft)
Displacement: 8,045 tons surfaced and 8,940 tons dived	operational and 330 m (1,085 ft) maximum
Dimensions: as 'L'Inflexible' class	**Armament:** 16 launch tubes for 16 M20 SLBMs, and four 550-mm (21.7-in) bow tubes for 18 L5 dual-purpose and F17 anti-ship torpedoes
Propulsion: one pressurised water-cooled reactor powering two steam turbines driving one shaft	
Speed: 18 kts surfaced and 25 kts dived	

vice, a number one more than the 'Le Redoutable' class total.

Laid down in March 1980, *L'Inflexible* achieved operational status in April 1985 and is due to remain in service until at least 2008, or possibly until 2010. Like all French missile submarines, *L'Inflexible* has two crews, *Bleu* (blue) and *Ambre* (amber), to crew the vessel in rotation in order to maximise the time spent on patrol between reactor-refuelling refits. French SSBNs

normally undertake patrols of two months' duration, with three months as the absolute maximum. All the French SSBNs are based at Ile Longue near Brest and have special protection when transiting to and from the port.

In April 2001 *L'Inflexible* conducted a successful test launch of the M45 SLBM, containing components of the new generation M51 missile with which it is planned to equip the 'Le Triomphant' -class SSBNs.

Left: France tries to maintain a minimum of two SNLEs on patrol at any one time, and submarines such as the **Le Terrible** *('Le Redoutable' class) were screened on departure and return by navy surface units, submarines and ASW aircraft in order to maintain security.*

'Golf' class SSBN

The **'Golf' class** is NATO's designation for the Soviet **Project 629**, a 22-strong class of conventionally powered submarines armed with nuclear missiles. Authorised in 1955, a year ahead of the 'Hotel'-class nuclear boats, the 'Golfs' carried the same SLBMs, the R-13 or SS-N-4. The first boat was launched at Severodvinsk in 1960 and another 14 followed there while seven were built at Komsomolsk-na-Amur for the Pacific Fleet. The boats were commissioned between 1959 and 1962 and served for upwards of twenty years. **K-36** and **K-91** were transferred to the Pacific Fleet; six spent their last years with the Baltic Fleet; and **K-113** was converted to a minelayer then stricken in 1974. The other vessels were decommissioned from 1980-91.

K-129 was lost with all hands some 66 km (600 miles) northwest of Hawaii on 11 April 1968 in circumstances that remain classified. The Soviets were unable to locate *K-129*, but the US did. By then, these were not the most modern boats in the Soviet fleet but *K-129* was carrying nuclear missiles and associated command equipment plus sonar and radar and communications systems that would amount to a major intelligence windfall. The recovery, codenamed 'Project Jennifer', was undertaken using a specially built 63,000-ton ship financed by Howard Hughes, the *Glomar Explorer*. The CIA and US Navy brought up the submarine in September 1974. The operation was conducted in great secrecy and many details remain unclear. Officially the whole boat was never raised because the crane snapped, leaving the US with a 11.6-m (38-ft) section of the hull and the mortal remains of eight Soviet submariners, who were subsequently reburied at sea. Tactical nuclear warheads from two torpedoes were recovered but the SLBMs fell back to the ocean floor. Exactly what coding equipment ended up in US hands was never confirmed.

'Golf' exports

Three 'Golf'-class submarines were supplied to China without nuclear missiles. One sank in an accident. Soviet specialists were withdrawn from China in 1960 as Sino-Soviet relations broke down, but China launched an SSBN almost identical to the 'Golf' in 1966. This remains in service and was used to test launch China's first SLBM, the JL-1 (CSS-N-3) in 1982. Refitted in 1995 for the JL-2 (CSS-N-5) missile, it has been used in trials for China's first submarine launched missile with global reach – the missiles have a range of some 12070 km (7,500 miles) – since 1999.

Above: Of the 22 'Golf I' boats with SS-N-4 missiles, 14 were refitted with SS-N-5 weapons (as 'Golf IIs') and a further boat was built to Project 629B standard as a testbed for new liquid-fuel and solid-propellant missile systems. A 'Golf II' is pictured.

SPECIFICATION	
'Golf' class (Project 629)	operational; 300 m (984 ft)
Displacement: 2,794 tons surfaced and 3,553 tons dived	maximum
Dimensions: length 98.4 m (32 ft 4 in); beam 8.2 m (26 ft 11 in), draft 7.85 m (25 ft 9 in)	**Armament:** ('Golf I') D-2 missile system with three R-13 (SS-N-4) missiles, or ('Golf II') D-4 missile system with three R-21 (SS-N-5 'Sark') missiles
Propulsion: three diesels delivering 4474 kW (6,000 shp) with electric motors driving three shafts	**Electronics:** one 'Snoop Tray' or 'Snoop Plate' surface search radar, one Herkules sonar, one Feniks sonar
Speed: 15 kts surfaced; 12.5 kts submerged	
Diving depth: 260 m (853 ft)	**Complement:** about 80

Above: 'Golf'-class boats carried their three missiles within upright launch tubes located directly behind the conning tower. Launches were conducted on the surface.

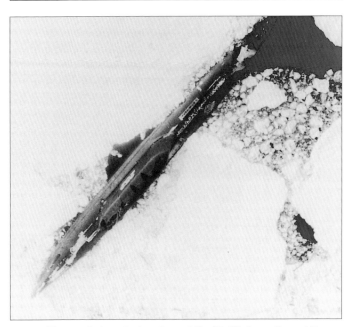

Above: The combat control system of the 'Golf' class allowed the flight path of the submarine's missiles to be automatically corrected as the boat's position changed, reducing launch time.

'Hotel' class SSBN

Assigned the NATO reporting name **'Hotel' class**, the Soviet Union's first SSBN was designated **Project 658**. The first of the class was laid down on 17 October 1958 and ultimately eight boats were completed, all at Severodvinsk between 1960 and 1962. All were decommissioned between 1988 and 1991. As built they carried three R-13 nuclear missiles (Western designation SS-N-4) positioned upright in the sail. Nearly 12 m (40 ft) long, the positioning of the missiles also necessitated a bulge in the submarine's keel underneath the rear part of the sail. By later standards the missile had a very short range, just 650 km (404 miles) so the submarines would have had to cross the Atlantic from their base in the Barents Sea in order to threaten America. The submarines had to surface to fire, and it took 12 minutes to launch all three missiles. From 1965-70 they were refitted with the R-21 system (SS-N-5 'Sark'); this had a range of 1400 km (870 miles).

K-55 and **K-178** had their SLBMs removed and served in the Pacific fleet until decommissioned. The others served with the Northern Fleet. **K-145** was given a major refit in 1969-70 just six years after it was commissioned. The hull was lengthened by 13 m (43 ft) and the sail enlarged to carry R-29 SLBMs (NATO designation SS-N–8 'Sawfly'). **K-40** was converted to a communications boat in 1977 (the Soviets lacked global coverage in HF stations and relied on command boats to relay orders).

K-19 became the most infamous Soviet nuclear submarine in history, known to submariners as 'Hiroshima' after successive reactor breakdowns irradiated two complete crews. The first disaster took place on 4 July 1961 when a leak in the reactors was detected. Several crew members entered the contaminated compartments to attempt repairs – knowing this would doom them to certain death. Repairs proved impossible, the crew was taken off and *K-19* was towed into port. Eight men died of radiation burns soon after and cancer rates among their comrades are horrendous. The reactor was replaced during 1962-64 but *K-19* caught fire while on patrol

Above: The 'Hotel' class was the first Soviet nuclear-powered ballistic missile submarine. The armament of SS-N-4 missiles was replaced by SS-N-5s on the 'Hotel II'.

off Newfoundland on 4 February 1972. More than 30 ships were involved in the rescue but fighting the fire cost the lives of 28 of its crew. A movie version of this grisly saga was released in 2002 (*K-19 Widowmaker*). The ill-fated submarine was finally decommissioned in 1991. The single **'Hotel III'** vessel refitted in 1969-70 for test of the new R-29 (SS-N-8 'Sawfly') SLBM carried six missile launchers.

SPECIFICATION	
'Hotel' class (Project 658)	maximum
Displacement: ('Hotel II') 5500 tons dived	**Armament:** ('Hotel I') D-2 missile system with three R-13 (SS-N-4)
Dimensions: length 114 m (374 ft); beam 9.2 m (30 ft 2 in); draft 7.31 m (24 ft)	missiles, or ('Hotel II') D-4 missile system with three R-21 (SS-N-5 'Sark') missiles
Propulsion: diesel electric	**Electronics:** one 'Snoop Tray' surface search radar, one Herkules sonar,
Speed: 18 kts surfaced; 26 kts dived	one Feniks sonar
Diving depth: 240 m (787 ft) operational; 300 m (984 ft)	**Complement:** 104

'Yankee' class SSBN

The **'Yankee' class (Project 667A Navaga)** was the first modern Soviet SSBN to be built. The design was apparently based on the plans of the US 'Benjamin Franklin' and 'Lafayette' classes

that were covertly obtained by Soviet military intelligence (GRU) in the early 1960s. A total of 34 units were built between 1967-74 at the shipyards in Severodvinsk and Komsomolsk, the peak year

being 1970 when 10 vessels were completed. The 'Yankees' were distinguishable from the later 'Deltas' by having a smaller rise to the 'turtle-back' missile compartment abaft the sail. In

1976 one unit was converted to a **'Yankee II' class (Project 667AM)** configuration in which the original 16 missile tubes were replaced by 12 larger units for the solid-propellant R-31 (SS-N-17 'Snipe') SLBM.

The 'Yankee II' also differed from the similar 12-round 'Delta Is' by having a sloping forward edge to the 'turtle-back' casing of the missile tubes.

In order to comply with the SALT agreement a number of 'Yankee I' SSBNs were deactivated as SLBM carriers. By mid-1984 10 had been so treated, a number being converted to SSNs by the complete removal of the ballistic missile section of the hull. These are now inactive.

SLCM conversion

Another was converted for the highly accurate RK-55 Granat (SS-N-21 'Sampson') cruise missile with a single 200-kT yield warhead and a range of 3000 km (1,865 miles). This **'Yankee Notch'** vessel now operates with the Northern Fleet. The 35 Granat SLCMs are launched from torpedo tubes.

During the early 1980s, three or four of 14 **'Yankee I'** boats, plus the sole 'Yankee II' in the Northern Fleet, were on station at any one time off the eastern seaboard of the US, with a further unit either on transit to or from a patrol area. Overlaps did occur, and these occasionally raised the number of boats on patrol. Of the nine 'Yankee Is' in the Pacific Fleet two were on permanent patrol off the western US seaboard with another on transit to or from the patrol zones. The forward-deployed 'Yankees' were assigned the wartime role of destroying time-sensitive area targets such as SAC bomber alert bases and carriers/SSBNs in port, and of disrupting the American higher command echelons as much as possible to ease the task of follow-up ICBM strikes.

Right: The 'Yankee I'-class boat K-219 suffered a launch tube decompression resulting in a fire in October 1986. The vessel was conducting a combat patrol east of Bermuda. The vessel surfaced but could not be towed and later sank.

Subsequently, NATO sources indicated that several of the 'Yankees' in each theatre had been switched to operate against theatre nuclear targets, with the submarines operating in sanctuary areas closer to the Soviet homeland. These vessels replaced the older 'Hotel' and 'Golf II' submarines in this role. Two 'Yankee' vessels operate in the research and development role, one undertaking sonar trials and the other taking part in underwater operations in support of the 'Paltus'-class auxiliary submarines.

A single boat was refitted in 1982 to test the Meteorit-M (SS-N-24 'Scorpion') supersonic cruise missile as the **'Yankee Sidecar'**.

Below: The 'Yankee I' class, with its armament of SS-N-6 missiles, formed the major part of the Soviet SSBN fleet in the early 1970s. 'Snipe'). The boat carried 12 of these weapons, each of which was equipped with a 500-kT warhead.

Above: With an increased displacement, the single 'Yankee II' was equipped with the Soviet's first solid-propellant SLBM, the the R-31 (SS-N-17 'Snipe'). The boat carried 12 of these weapons, each equipped with a 500-kT warhead.

SPECIFICATION	
'Yankee' class (Project 667A) **Displacement:** 7,700 tons surfaced and 9,300 dived **Dimensions:** length 132 m (433 ft); beam 11.6 m (38 ft 1 in); draught 8 m (26 ft 4 in) **Propulsion:** two pressurised watercooled reactors powering four steam turbines driving two shafts **Speed:** 13 kts surfaced and 27 kts dived **Diving depth:** 400 m (1,315 ft) operational and 600 m (1,970 ft) maximum **Armament:** ('Yankee I') 16 launch tubes for R-27 (SS-N-6 'Serb')	SLBMs, or ('Yankee II') 12 launch tubes for R-31 (SS-N-17 'Snipe') SLBMs, and (both classes) four 533-mm (21-in) and two 400-mm (15.7-in) torpedo tubes **Electronics:** one 'Snoop Tray' surface search radar, one low-frequency bow sonar, one medium-frequency torpedo fire-control sonar, VHF/SHF/UHF communications systems, one VLF towed communications buoy, one ELF floating antenna, one 'Brick Group' ESM suite, and one 'Park Lamp' direction-finding antenna **Complement:** 120

'Delta I' and 'Delta II' class SSBNs

The first 'Delta I'-class ballistic missile submarine was paid off in 1992, and a decade later all but a single vessel had been scrapped or laid up at operational bases in the North and the Pacific.

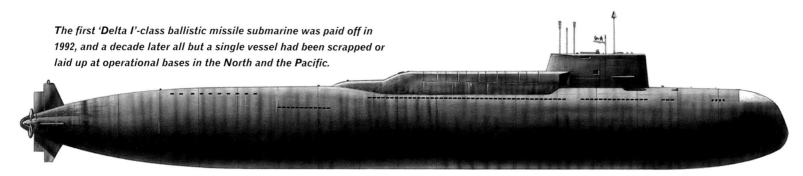

The **'Delta I'** SSBN or **Project 667B Murena** was a larger vessel than the previous 'Yankee' class. Built initially at Severodvinsk and then at Komsomolsk in the Soviet Far East, the 'Delta I' was the world's largest undersea craft when the first unit entered Northern Fleet service in 1972. The 18th and last of the class was completed at Komsomolsk and commissioned in 1977. Designated a ballistic missile submarine (*podvodnaya lodka raketnaya laylataya* or PLRK) by the Soviet Union, the class carried two parallel rows of six D-9 missile launch tubes for the R-29 (SS-N-8 'Sawfly') missile aft of the sail, which was set forward with diving planes on each side.

'Sawfly' missiles

Unlike its predecessor, the 'Delta I' with its long-range SLBMs was capable of mounting sustained patrols within the marginal ice seas of the Soviet arctic littoral, including the Barents and Norwegain seas. As a result they did not need to pass Western SOSUS sonar barriers before their targets were within range. Cold War tactics saw the 'Delta I' ships deployed in friendly waters, protected by Soviet naval 'bastions'.

Right: Only four 'Delta II'-class vessels were built at Severodvinsk between 1973-75. Their lengthened hulls were capable of carrying a load of 16 R-29D missiles.

The R-29 missiles themselves incorporated accurate Topol-B navigation and Cyclone-B satellite navigation. The 'Sawfly' missiles could be launched in a single salvo whilst the submerged vessel was moving at a speed of 5 kts.

'Delta I' SSBNs served with the 41st Division of Strategic Submarines with the Northern Fleet from 1973 (based at Yagyelnaya Bay) and with the 25th Division, Pacific Fleet, beginning patrols in 1976. Pacific Fleet vessels were originally based at Kamchatka, but were transferred to Pavlovsk in the early 1990s. Nine survivors were operational in 1991, and their decommissioning under

START-1 began in 1994. In 2002, a single 'Delta I', **K 447**, remained in Russian service.

Interim class

Between 1972-75 at Severodvinsk an interim batch of four **'Delta II'** (**Project 667BD** **Murena-M**) class units was constructed. These were essentially similar to the earlier design but were lengthened by 16 m (52 ft 6 in) to make possible the incorporation of a further four missile tubes. The 'Delta II' carried improved R-29D missiles and introduced several features to decrease noise levels, including a new hydroacoustic coating. The first vessel entered service with the Northern Fleet in September 1975. In accordance with START-1, decommissioning of the 'Delta II' began in 1996.

Below: The range of its D-29 'Sawfly' missiles allowed the 'Delta I' to maintain constant patrol in remote areas or remain on combat alert whilst moored at their bases.

'Typhoon' class SSBN

The 'Typhoon' does not need to submerge or even go to sea in order to launch its payload of up to 200 nuclear warheads: during the Cold War, targets in the continental US could be attacked while the vessel was moored at its Northern Fleet home base.

The **'Typhoon'-class** (**Project 941 Akula**) boats are the largest undersea vessels ever built, and are based on a catamaran-type design that comprises two separate pressure hulls joined by a single outer covering to give increased protection against ASW weapons.

The class was built specifically for operations with the Soviet Northern Fleet in the Arctic ice pack. The reinforced sail, advanced stern fin with horizontal hydroplane fitted aft of the screws and retractable bow hydroplanes allow the submarine to break easily through spots of thin ice within the Arctic ice shelf.

'Sturgeon' SLBM

The first unit was laid down in 1977 at Severodvinsk and commissioned in 1980, achieving operational status in 1981. To arm the 'Typhoon', design of a fifth-generation SLBM, the R-39

SPECIFICATION
'Typhoon' class

'Typhoon' class
Displacement: 23,200-24,500 tons surfaced; 33,800-48,000 tons dived
Dimensions: length 170-172 m (558-564 ft); beam 23-23.3 m (75-76 ft); draught 11-11.5 m (36-38 ft)
Propulsion: two OK-650 190-MW (254,750 shp) pressurised water-cooled reactors and two 37.3 MW (50,000 shp) steam turbines driving two shafts
Speed: 12-16 kts surfaced and 25-27 kts dived
Diving depth: 500 m (1,640 ft)
Armament: D-19 launch tubes for 20

R-39 (SS-N-20 'Sturgeon') SLBMs, two 650-mm and four 533-mm torpedo tubes for RPK-7 Vodopei (SS-N-16 'Stallion') and RPK-2 Viyoga (SS-N-15 'Starfish') or VA-111 Shkval respectively
Electronics: one surface-search radar, one ESM system, one low-frequency bow sonar, one medium-frequency torpedo fire-control sonar, VHF/SHF/UHF communications systems. One VLF towed communications buoy, and one ELF floating antenna
Complement: 150-175 (50-55 officers)

Right: Soviet doctrine envisaged the 'Typhoon' as a 'doomsday weapon', capable of emerging from the polar ice and launching a devastating second strike after an initial nuclear exchange. The high maintenance and manpower costs of these vessels is likely to result in their retirement in the medium term, although Russia is keen to maintain them as short term force multipliers.

Taifun (SS-N-20 'Sturgeon'), began in 1973. Six vessels were constructed between 1981-89, entering service to form part of the 1st Flotilla of Atomic Submarines, within the Western Theatre of the Northern Fleet, and based at Nyerpicha. Construction of a seventh vessel was not completed.

The R-39 allowed the submarine to fire the weapon from within the Arctic circle and still hit a target anywhere within the continental US. The 'Typhoons', were originally to be retrofitted with the improved R-39M (SS-N-28) missile.

Two vessels were decommissioned in 1997, and in 2002 only two remained in service, although it has been reported that three of the class will remain active in order to test the R-39M or the new Bulava SLBM, contravening the Co-operative Threat Reduction Program. However, the status of the R-39M, intended to arm the fourth-generation Borei-class SSBN, is uncertain.

SPECIFICATION

R-39 (SS-N-20 'Sturgeon')
Type: SLBM
Dimensions: total length 16 m (52 ft 6 in); length without warhead 8.4 m (27 ft 7 in); diameter 2.4 m (7 ft 11 in)
Payload: 2550 kg (5,622 lb)
Performance: range 8300 km (5,158 miles); CEP 500 m (1,640 ft) **Warhead:** up to 10 MIRVs of 200 kT each
Propulsion: three-stage solid-propellant rocket
Guidance: stellar-inertial

'Delta III/IV' class
Ballistic missile submarine

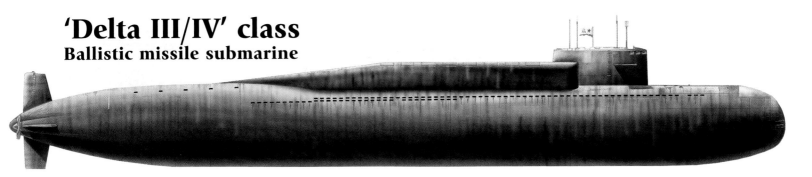

Although the Soviets were pioneers in firing missiles from submarines, their early systems were short-ranged. The 34 units of the 'Yankee' class, built between 1967 and 1974, were apparently based on stolen American plans for the 'Benjamin Franklin' class. These provided the foundation for the follow-on **'Delta'** class, an enlarged development of the 'Yankee' design. The first Deltas entered service in 1972, the original **'Delta I'** design being succeeded by the interim **'Delta II'** with 16 missiles rather than the original 12.

'Delta III'

These were followed from 1976 by the **Type 667 BDR 'Kalmar' class**, better known to NATO as the **'Delta III'**. These had a larger and longer 'turtle-back' abaft the sail. This housed R-29R missiles (NATO designation SS-N-18) the first Soviet sea-based multiple-warhead system. Fourteen submarines were built at Severodvinsk.

The 'Delta III' submarines which served in the Northern fleet formed a division and were based at Sayda and at Olyenya port. In the early 90s the ballistic missile submarines were transferred to Yagyelnaya. Pacific Fleet 'Delta IIIs' were based on Kamchatka.

Development of the **Type 667 BDRM 'Delfin'** or **'Dolphin' class**, known to NATO as the **'Delta IV'**, began on 10 September 1975. The first boat, *K-51*, was commissioned into Northern fleet in December 1985. Between 1985 and 1990, seven 'Delta IVs' were constructed by the Sevmashpredpriyatiye Production Association in Severodvinsk. The 'Delta IVs' were constructed in parallel to

At more than 16,000 tons submerged displacement, the 'Kalmar' class, known to NATO as the Delta III, were the largest submarines in the world when they entered service in 1976.

the 'Typhoon' class, in case the larger boats proved unsuccessful. The 'Dolphin' is a further modification of the 'Delta III', with an increased diameter pressure hull and a longer bow section. Displacement has increased by 1,200 tons and it is 12 m (39 ft) longer.

'Delta IV'

The 'Delta IV' is a strategic platform, designed to strike military and industrial installations and naval bases. The submarine carries the RSM-54 Makeyev missile (NATO designation: SS-N-23 'Skiff'). The RSM-54 is a three-stage liquid-propellant ballistic missile with a range of 8300 km (5,158 miles). The warhead consists of four to ten multiple independently targeted re-entry vehicles (MIRVs), each rated at 100 kt. The missile uses stellar inertial guidance for a CEP of 500 m (1,640 ft).

The submarine can also launch the Novator (SS-N-15 'Starfish') anti-ship missile or Mk 40 anti-ship torpedo.

SPECIFICATION

Type 667 'Delfin' or 'Delta IV' class
Type: Nuclear-powered ballistic missile submarine
Displacement: 13,500 tons surfaced, 18,200 tons submerged
Dimensions: length 166 m (544 ft 7 in); beam 12.3 m (39 ft 6 in); draught 8.8 m (29 ft)
Machinery: two pressurized water-cooled reactors powering two steam turbines delivering 44700 kW (60,000 shp) to two seven-bladed fixed-pitch shrouded propellers; 3 x 3200-kW (4,294-hp) turbo generators; two 800-kW (1074-hp) diesel generators; one 750-kW (1007-hp) auxiliary motor powering screw rudders bow and stern
Speed: c.14 kt (26 km/h; 16 mph) surface; 24 kt (44 km/h; 27 mph) dived
Patrol endurance: 90 days
Diving depth: 300 m (985 ft)

operational and 400 m (1312 ft) max
Weapons tubes: 16 missile and 4 x 533-mm (21-in) torpedo in bow
Weapons load: 16 x Makeyev RSM-54 Shtil (SS-N-23 'Skiff') nuclear ballistic missiles; 18 tube-launched weapons including RPK-7 Vodopei (SS-N-16 'Stallion') ASW missiles, and Type 65K, SET-65, SAET-60M 533-mm torpedoes
Electronics: one Snoop Tray I-band Surface Search radar; Skat-BDRM ('Shark Gill') LF active/passive sonar; 'Shark Hide' passive LF flank sonar; Pelamida passive VLF thin-line towed array sonar; 'Mouse Roar' active HF attack sonar; ESM/ECM; D/F radar warning; 'Brick Spit' optronic mast; Satellite/Inertial/ Radiometric navigation; satcom plus two floating aerials for VLF/ELF radio
Complement: 135

Above: Since 'Delta'-class boats remain a mainstay of Russia's nuclear deterrent force, they are kept in better condition than other nuclear submarines.

Left: Although the Russian navy is a shadow of its former self, it still maintains sufficent force to keep a minimum missile deterrent at sea at all times.

'Starfish' is armed with a 200 KT nuclear warhead and has a range of 45 km (28 miles).

The operational lifetime of these submarines was estimated to be 20–25 years, assuming normal maintenance schedules, but in the 1990s everything changed. When the START-1 treaty was signed in 1991, five 'Delta IIIs' served in the Northern and nine in the Pacific Fleet.

Russia is scheduled to dismantle one 'Yankee'-class, five 'Typhoon'-class and 25 assorted 'Delta'-class ballistic missile submarines by the year 2003.

By September 1999, US specialists had helped Russia to disassemble one 'Yankee'-class and six 'Delta'-class submarines, while the Russians had destroyed another five ballistic missile subs on their own using US equipment.

As of June 2000, the Russian Navy claimed that it operated five 'Typhoon'-class submarines, seven 'Delta IV'-class submarines, and 13 'Delta III'-class submarines, which between them carry 2,272 nuclear warheads on 440 ballistic missiles. With the chronic funding shortages affecting the Soviet navy, it is likely that many of these boats are of suspect seaworthiness.

However, the Russian navy reportedly believes that 12 nuclear ballistic missile submarines is the minimum necessary force structure for national security, and this force goal is likely to be maintained up until 2010 at least.

'R' class
Ballistic missile submarines

The missile compartment of the 'R'-class SSBN was based on a US Navy design, but the rest of the boat and equipment was British.

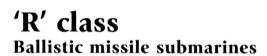

SPECIFICATION	
'Resolution' class	maximum
Displacement: 7,500 tons surfaced and 8,400 tons dived	**Armament:** 16 launch tubes for 16 Polaris A3TK submarine-launched ballistic missiles, and six 533-mm (21-in) bow tubes for approximately 16 tube-launched weapons
Dimensions: length 129.5 m (425 ft); beam 10.1 m (33 ft); draught 9.1 m (30 ft)	
Propulsion: one pressurised watercooled reactor powering two steam turbines driving one shaft	**Electronics:** one Type 1003 surface search radar, one type 2001 bow sonar, one Type 2007 sonar, one Type 2023 retractable towed-array sonar, one ESM suite, and an extensive communications outfit
Speed: 20 kt (37 km/h; 23 mph) surfaced and 25 kt (46 km/h; 29 mph) dived	
Diving depth: 350 m (1,150 ft) operational and 465 m (1,525 ft)	**Complement:** 135

Britain's initial nuclear-deterrent was carried by the RAF's V-bombers, but developments in radar and surface-to-air weaponry in the late 1950s and early 1960s made it clear that manned bombers were becoming increasingly vulnerable. In January 1963, the Defence Committee decided that the nation's deterrent should be carried in submarines.

In February 1963 the government announced that it was to order four **'Resolution'-class** nuclear-powered, Polaris missile-equipped 7,000-ton submarines, with an option on a fifth. The SSBNs would take over the nuclear deterrent role from the Royal Air Force's V-Bomber force from 1968 onwards.

The first two pairs of boats were ordered in May 1963 from Vickers Shipbuilding Ltd, Barrow-in-Furness, and Cammell Laird & Co. Ltd,

Birkenhead; the option on a fifth unit was cancelled in February 1965.

Missile boats

Although designed in the United Kingdom, the new missile boats incorporated a number of design features used on the contemporary 'Lafayettes' design. The lead ship, **HMS Resolution** (S22) was launched in September 1966 and commissioned in October of the following year. **HMS Repulse** (S23), followed in September 1968, with **HMS Renown** (S24), and **HMS Revenge** (S27), commissioning in November 1968 and December 1969.

Early in 1968 the *Resolution* sailed to Florida for missile launch trials, making the UK's first successful Polaris launch on 15 February. Four months later HMS *Resolution*, armed with Polaris A3P missiles, deployed on the first of more than 230 consecutive Polaris patrols by

the Royal Navy. As with French and American SSBNs, two crews (Port and Starboard) were used to maximise the time spent at sea, each patrol lasting around three months. When not aboard, the submarine crews took leave and underwent refresher training at the 10th Submarine Squadron base at Faslane on the Clyde.

All four boats underwent conversion in the 1980s, being fitted to carry the improved Polaris A-TK missile, which was

Right: HMS Renown heads for her home port at Faslane. The SSBN base became a focus for anti-nuclear protesters.

Below: In 1983 HMS Revenge became the second British SSBN to go on patrol with Chevaline. The new warheads were designed to penetrate Soviet ABM defences in place around Moscow.

fitted with the British-developed Chevaline MRV warhead.

Obsolete

In spite of these extremely costly improvements to the Polaris system, it had been clear as early as 1980 that the rapidly ageing **'R-class'** boats, together with potential improvements in Soviet anti-missile capability, meant that capability had to be

upgraded still further. In July of that year the British Government announced that it would acquire American-built Trident C-4 missiles, a decision modified in 1982 when it was announced that the Trident II system with the even larger D-5 missiles would be purchased.

As the 'V'-class boats entered service through the 1990s, their 'R' predecessors were retired.

'Vanguard' class SSBN

Above: The 'Vanguard' class is fitted with state-of-the art periscopes for both search and attack. TV cameras and infra-red technology aid reconnaissance.

Unlike its Polaris missile-armed predecessor, the 'Resolution' class, the British **'Vanguard'-class** nuclear powered ballistic missile submarine (SSBN) is a completely new design. It has, however, utilised several of the successful design features from previous SSBNs.

The 'Vanguard' class is the largest submarine type ever constructed in the UK, and the third largest type of vessel in Royal Navy service. However, it is cloaked in tight secrecy. Despite the ending of the Cold War and the downgrading of its strategic mission, details on 'Vanguard' weapon systems and patrols are still highly classified. All four of the boats, **HMS Vanguard**, **HMS**

Victorious, **HMS Vigilant** and **HMS Vengeance**, were built by Vickers Submarine Engineering Limited (now BAE Systems Marine) at its dockyard in Barrow-in-Furness, Cumbria. Such was their size that a special production facility, the Devonshire Dock Hall, had to be constructed. The boat's large hull was prompted by the Trident D5 Submarine-Launched Ballistic Missile (SLBM), of which it can deploy 16. However, the vessels patrol with a smaller

Right: This 'Vanguard'-class submarine is pictured being escorted out of port by a tug and a French naval Alouette III. The submarine will not return for several months.

complement of crew than that of the previous 'Resolution' class (132 as oppposed to 149).

Transition

The first major transition from Polaris to Trident occurred in 1996, when HMS *Victorious* was deployed on patrol with a complement of Trident SLBMs. Trident has since become the sole component of the UK's nuclear deterrent, following the decommissioning of the WE177 tactical nuclear gravity/depth bomb in 1998, as part of the UK Strategic Defence Review. Furthermore, the 'Vanguard'-class boats had their 'readiness to fire' changed from a matter of minutes to 'a matter of days' according to the UK Secretary of State for Defence.

The 'Vanguard'-class missile suite contains 16 tubes and is based on the 24-tube design which the US Navy deploys on its 'Ohio'-class Trident boats. The Trident missile system was built by Lockheed Martin, and is technically leased from the US. The Trident D5 is a MIRV (Multiple Independently-targeted

Re-entry Vehicle) system, and it is capable of deploying 12 warheads per missile.

Missile maintenance for the Trident missile system occurs in the US. However, the UK Atomic Weapons Establishment at Aldermaston undertakes all of the design, construction, installation and maintenance of the warheads.

Deployment

Each 'Vanguard'-class submarine can carry a maximum of 192 nuclear warheads, although the Royal Navy originally insisted that each boat would carry no more than 96, deployed across eight missiles. Since the Strategic Defence Review, this has been further reduced to 48 warheads per boat, spread across four missiles. Although the Ministry of Defence refuses to comment on how many missiles are deployed when a boat is on patrol, it has indicated that the complement of Trident missiles now only carries one warhead per missile, which is probably in the sub-strategic kiloton range. A single 'Vanguard'-class boat is on deterrence patrol

SPECIFICATION	
'Vanguard' class	(D5) 3-stage 12000-km (6,500 nm)
Displacement: 15,900 tonnes dived	range solid-fuel nuclear-armed
Dimensions: length 149.9 m	missiles. Each D5 can carry 12
(492 ft); beam 12.8 m (42 ft);	MIRV of 100-120-kT, sub-strategic
draught 12 m (32 ft).	warheads introduced in 1996
Machinery: (nuclear) one Rolls-	**Electronics:** Type 1007 I-band nav
Royce Pressurised Water Reactor;	radar, Type 2054 composite multi-
(conventional) two GEC turbines	frequency sonar suite including
developing 20.5 MW (27,500 shp)	Type 2046 towed array, Type 2043
Speed: 25 kts dived	hull-mounted active/passive
Torpedo tubes: four 21-in (533-mm)	search and Type 2082 passive
tubes	intercept and ranging
Missiles: 16 Lockheed Trident 2	**Complement:** 132 (14 officers)

Above: At least one 'Vanguard'-class boat is permanently at sea, providing the UK's nuclear deterrent. The submarines now perform a sub-strategic role.

at any one time, and a reserve boat is also available.

New systems

As well as having a new strategic weapons system, the Vanguard also features several other new systems. These include a Rolls-Royce nuclear Pressurised Water Reactor propulsion system, and new tactical weapons fit including Tigerfish and Spearfish torpedoes for short and medium defence. Tigerfish has a range of 13-29 km (8-18 miles) depending on the homing configuration, while Spearfish can hit targets up to 65 km (40 miles) away. The submarine also features a greatly improved Electronic Counter Measures (ECM) suite, and state-of-the-art attack and search periscopes. These are fitted with a TV camera and thermal imager as well as the traditional optical channel.

'Lafayette' class SSBN

Above: Underrated and underplayed, the 'Lafayette' was, for many years, backbone of the USN strategic missile submarine fleet and was a highly successful design.

The '**Lafayette' class** followed a successful series of US strategic submarines, which had begun with the 'George Washington' class, America's first strategic nuclear submarine. The 'Ethan Allen' class submarines followed the 'George Washington' class, the vessels being constructed between 1961 and 1963. However, unlike the 'George Washington' submarines, the 'Ethan Allen' class had the advantage of being designed as SSBNs from the start.

Nevertheless, both classes faced a distinct tactical disadvantage in having to operate close to Soviet shores. This so-called 'Moscow criteria' meant that the US Navy's ballistic missile submarines had to operate close to the USSR in order to

Above: An officer on the sail scans the horizon for hostile vessels and anti-submarine aircraft while his 'Lafayette'-class vessel carries out deterrence patrol.

Left: The 'Lafayette'-class submarines represented a formidable nuclear deterrent. This submarine displays 12 of its missile tubes. The 'Lafayette' class were the largest Western submarines completed during the 1960s.

Nevertheless, it set the standard and the ensuing Trident series still equips the US Navy SSBN fleet today.

Technically speaking, the 'Lafayette' class was divided into three separate classes, each group having only minor differences. The original 'Lafayette' class consisted of nine vessels; the modified **'James Madison' class** comprised 10 boats; and the **'Benjamin Franklin' class** was the largest, with 12 submarines. One vessel in the 'James Madison' class, the **USS Daniel Boone**, was the first ever fleet SSBN to visit Hawaii.

Modernisation

The 'Lafayette' class and its Poseidon missile system would eventually succumb to modernisation as the US Navy's 'Ohio' class came on stream deploying the Trident missile. The 'Lafayette' class would be an important platform for the Trident, with the USS *Daniel Boone* being the first boat to be converted to carry the Trident.

destroy targets in Moscow due to the range of their Polaris missiles. For example, Polaris A3, the model with the longest range, could still only hit targets at a maximum range of 4600 km (2,858 miles).

Construction

Construction of the **USS Lafayette** began in 1963, before the first 'Ethan Allen'-class vessel had been completed. Between 1963 and 1967, a total of 31 'Lafayette'-class boats were constructed. All of the vessels were fitted with Polaris

missiles, originally the Polaris A2 with a range of 2800 km (1,740 miles). However, in 1968, the **USS James Monroe** became the first submarine to receive the longer-range Polaris A3. Another four boats were planned although they were never constructed. Between 1970 and 1978, all of the vessels were converted to deploy the Poseidon SLBM system. Later on, between 1978 and 1983, 12 of these boats were converted to deploy the Trident C4 system. The first of these Trident vessels, the **USS**

Francis Scott Key, began its maiden patrol on 20 October 1979.

Although the Lafayette-class began its life deploying the Polaris missile, it was converted to take the Poseidon, for which the class had originally been designed. The Lafayette-class earned its place in Cold War history as the first SLBM to be fitted with Multiple Independently-targetted Re-entry Vehicles (MIRVs). Each MIRV contained a single 50-kT warhead. However, Poseidon proved to be a troubled system, being unreliable and prone to mechanical failure.

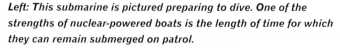

Left: This submarine is pictured preparing to dive. One of the strengths of nuclear-powered boats is the length of time for which they can remain submerged on patrol.

SPECIFICATION	
'Lafayette' class **Displacement:** 7250 tons standard surfaced; 8250 tons dived **Dimensions:** length 129.5 m (424 ft 11 in); beam 10.1 m (33 ft); draught 9.6 m (31 ft 6 in) **Machinery:** one pressurised-water cooled Westinghouse S5W reactor; two geared turbines developing 11186 kW (15,000 shp) **Speed:** 20 kts surfaced; approximately 30 kts dived **Torpedo tubes:** four 21-in (533-mm) Mk 65 (bow)	**Missiles:** first eight vessels fitted with Polaris A2 missiles, next 23 with Polaris A3 missiles, five vessels rearmed with Polaris A3 during 1968-70, vessels of class subsequently converted to carry Poseidon C3 in 16 tubes, from 1978-82 12 vessels fitted with Trident I/C4 missiles **Electronics:** Mk 113 Mod 9 torpedo fire control system, WSC-3 satellite communication transceiver, Mk 2 Mod 4 Ship's Inertial Navigation System (SINS) **Complement:** 140

'George Washington' class First-generation SSBN

On 28 June 1960 the **USS George Washington**, first of the eventually five-strong **'George Washington' class**, made the world's first successful test launch of a ballistic missile from a submerged submarine. The vessel launched two Polaris missiles, the second two hours after the first, while cruising off Cape Canaveral, Florida. Once the practicality of submerged launches had been demonstrated, the SSBN (nuclear-powered ballistic missile submarine) has been a key element in the concept and practice of nuclear deterrence. It is the proud boast of the SSBN fleets of the US Navy and Royal Navy that there were no fully confirmed detections of their boats by any potential enemy in some 40 years of operational patrols. The enormous difficulty in detecting and fixing the position of an SSBN means that the US, British, French and Soviet (now Russian) nuclear forces are constantly ready to retaliate against a nuclear strike on their homelands.

'Skipjack'-class SSN

The *George Washington* was actually laid down by Electric

Boat of Groton, Connecticut, as the *Scorpion*, a 'Skipjack'-class SSN, but the boat was cut in half during construction to allow the insertion of an an additional 39.64-m (130-ft) section to carry the vertical tubes required for the stowage and launch of 16 Polaris A1 ballistic missiles. These each carried a 600-kT warhead and had a range of 2200 km (1,367 miles). From the 'Skipjack' class the boats inherited the S5W reactor and six bow torpedo tubes, albeit with a reduced number of torpedo reloads.

Launched in June 1959, the *George Washington* sailed on its first operational patrol on 15 November 1960 as a member of Submarine Squadron 14. In 1966 the **Patrick Henry** (built by Electric Boat and launched in April 1960) was modified during a refit to carry the Polaris A3, an improved version of the Polaris A1 to deliver the 200-kT W58 warhead over the significantly greater range of 4360 km (2,709 miles) and in the process vastly enlarge the ocean areas in which the submarines could patrol but still be within range of their designated targets, and this missile soon became the core of

the missile armament carried by all of the 'George Washington'-class SSBNs.

In 1977 the **USS Abraham Lincoln** (built by Portsmouth Navy Yard and launched in March 1961) became the first SSBN to complete 50 patrols. But by this time newer SSBNs were entering service and the strategic arms limitation talks led to three of the class being converted to attack submarines. The *George Washington*, *Patrick Henry* and **USS Robert E. Lee** (built by Newport News of Norfolk, Virginia) had their Polaris missiles and associated systems (including the control room) removed in 1982, and at that stage were reclassified as SSNs even though they lacked sufficient torpedo stowage and the large bow sonars that would have made them effective in the attack submarine role. It is worth noting, though, that the 'George Washington'-class boats were quieter than the 'Skipjack' boats, though because of their greater

Above: The USS Robert E. Lee is seen November 1960. The volume of the missile compartment added to the 'Skipjack' design is readily apparent.

size somewhat slower. As it was, the Polaris missile tubes were filled with cement ballast as it had been decided that the boats were too old to warrant modification to carry the newer Poseidon C3 missile.

Final chapter

The *George Washington* was decommissioned in 1985 and scrapped in 1998. The *Robert E. Lee* was scrapped in 1991 and the *Abraham Lincoln* in 1994, while the **USS Theodore Roosevelt** (built by Mare Island Navy Yard and launched in February 1961) was decommissioned in 1981 and scrapped 1995. The *Patrick Henry* was decommissioned in 1984 and scrapped in 1997. Some consideration had been given to the revision of the boats to carry other weapons (each Polaris missile tube could carry eight cruise missiles, for instance), but nothing came of the various plans.

Left: The USS Theodore Roosevelt was the third of the 'George Washington'-class boats to be ordered but the fourth to be launched. This and the last two boats were based at Guam in the Marianas Islands.

SPECIFICATION	
'George Washington' class **Displacement:** 5,959 tons surfaced; 6,709 tons dived **Dimensions:** length 116 m (381 ft 8 /2 in); beam 10.5 m (33 ft); draught 8.1 m (26 ft 8 in) **Propulsion:** one S5W pressurised water-cooled reactor powering two geared steam turbines delivering 11185 kW (15,000 shp) to one shaft	**Speed:** 18 kts surfaced and 25 kts dived **Diving depth:** 180 m (700 ft) **Armament:** 16 Polaris A1 (later Polaris A3) submarine-launched ballistic missiles (SLBMs), and six 21-in (533-mm) torpedo tubes **Electronics:** BQS-4 sonar later replaced by BQR-19 sonar **Complement:** 112

'Benjamin Franklin' class SSBN

Above: The 'Benjamin Franklin'-class boat USS Mariano G. Vallejo, equipped with the Trident I C4 SLBMs each with eight re-entry vehicles.

Although actually two classes, the 12 **'Benjamin Franklin'-class** and 19 'Lafayette'-class submarines were very similar in overall appearance and in many physical and operational aspects. The main difference between the two classes was that the boats of the 'Benjamin Franklin' class were built with quieter machinery outfits than those of the 'Lafayette' class. An additional four boats were proposed for the FY65 shipbuilding programme so that there would be 35 submarines in these two related classes to complete the planned total of 45 SSBNs (including both earlier classes, the 'Ethan Allen' and 'George Washington' classes each of five boats) required for an SSBN force of five squadrons each of nine boats. The additional boats were cancelled by Secretary of Defense Robert McNamara.

The 'Lafayette'- and 'Benjamin Franklin'-class boats had a small diesel-electric arrangement for stand-by propulsion in the event of problems with the nuclear propulsion system, snort masts, and had an auxiliary propeller. The individual submarines that comprised the 'Benjamin Franklin' class were the USS *Benjamin Franklin*, USS *Simon Bolivar*, USS *Kamehameha*, USS *George Bancroft*, USS *Lewis and Clark*, USS *James K. Polk*, USS *George C. Marshall*, USS *Henry L. Stimson*, USS *George Washington Carver*, USS *Francis Scott Key*, USS *Mariano G. Vallejo* and USS *Will Rogers*.

The boats were built by the Electric Boat Division of the General Dynamics Corporation (six boats), Newport News Shipbuilding (four boats), and Mare Island Navy Yard (two boats), and were laid down between April 1963 and March 1965 for launch between August 1964 and July 1966, and commissioning between October 1965 and April 1967. The boats served with the Atlantic Fleet (from New London, Connecticut; Charleston, South Carolina; King's Bay, Georgia; and Holy Loch, Scotland) until decommissioned (or in two cases converted to SSN/special operations standard with provision for carrying, launching and recovering SEAL commando teams) between July 1992 and January 1999.

Armament

Completed with provision for the Polaris A3 SLBM, the boats were later converted to carry the altogether more capable Poseidon C3 missile with up to 14 re-entry vehicles (RVs) carrying W68 warheads and then the longer-range Trident C4 missile with up to eight RVs carrying W76 warheads.

Below: The 'Benjamin Franklin'-class SSBN USS Simon Bolivar underway off Hampton Roads, Virginia, at the beginning of the boat's sea trials in October 1965.

SPECIFICATION

'Benjamin Franklin' class
Displacement: 7,250 tons surfaced; 8,250 tons dived **Dimensions:** length 129.6 m (425 ft); beam 10.06 m (33 ft); draught 9.6 m (31 ft 6 in) **Propulsion:** one S5W pressurised water-cooled reactor powering two steam turbines delivering 11185 kW (15,000 shp) to one shaft **Speed:** 28 kts surfaced and 25 kts dived **Diving depth:** 350 m (1,150 ft) operational and 465 m (1,525 ft) maximum
Armament: 16 launch tubes for 16

Poseidon C3 or Trident I C4 SLBMs, and four 21-in (533-mm) tubes (all bow) for 12 Mk 48 ASW/anti-ship torpedoes
Electronics: one BPS-11A or BPS-15 surface search radar, one ESM system, one BQR-7 sonar, one BQR-15 towed-array sonar, one BQR-19 sonar, one BQR-21 sonar, one BQS-4 sonar, and extensive communications and navigation systems
Complement: 143

The last 12 units built to the 'Lafayette' SSBN design were officially designated as the 'Benjamin Franklin' class because they were completed with quieter propulsion machinery. Six boats were converted to carry the Trident I C4 instead of the Polaris A3 SLBM.

'Ohio' class SSBN

Designed in the early 1970s as successor to the 'Benjamin Franklin' and 'Lafayette' classes in the SSBN role, the lead boat of the **'Ohio' class**, the **USS Ohio**, was contracted to the Electric Boat Division of the General Dynamics Corporation in July 1974. As the result of an unfortunate series of problems both in Washington, DC, and at the shipyard, the lead vessel did not run its first sea trials until June 1981, and was not finally commissioned until November of that year, three years late. Production then improved, and the **USS Louisiana**, the last of these 18 'boomers', was commissioned in September 1997. The Atlantic and Pacific Fleets have 10 and eight boats with the Trident II D5 and Trident I C4 missiles respectively; the latter are being replaced from 1996

with the D5 weapon. The Trident I carries up to eight re-entry vehicles each with one 100-kT W76 warhead delivered over a range of up to some 7780 km (4,835 miles), while the larger Trident II carries up to a maximum of 14 but more typically eight RVs each with one 475-kT W88 warhead delivered to a classified range some hundreds of miles longer than that of the Trident I.

Each submarine carries 24 rather than the earlier standard of 16 SLBMs, is expected to have a 12-month reactor refuelling refit every nine years, and works a patrol period of 70 days followed by 25 days spent alongside a tender or jetty readying for the next patrol. Because of their longer-range Trident missiles, the 'Ohio'-class boats have patrol areas in

The mainstay of the American SSBN fleet, the 'Ohio' class carry the longer-range Trident II D5 SLBM that allows these submarines to operate in patrol zones close to the American coasts, where they can be protected more easily by other submarines, surface vessels and maritime patrol aircraft.

waters either close to the US or in the remoter parts of the world's oceans, making virtually impossible effective ASW measures, the more so as the boats are acoustically extremely quiet. Other than the *Ohio* and *Louisiana*, the 'Ohio'

class boats are the **Michigan**, **Florida**, **Georgia**, **Henry M. Jackson**, **Alabama**, **Alaska**, **Nevada**, **Tennessee**, **Pennsylvania**, **West Virginia**, **Kentucky**, **Maryland**, **Nebraska**, **Rhode Island**, **Maine** and **Wyoming**.

Below: Based on the streamlining of a fish, the clean shape and smooth contours of the 'Ohio'-class SSBN produce a boat that is fast. The shape is also designed for highly efficient and quiet cruising while underwater.

SPECIFICATION	
'Ohio' class **Displacement:** 16,764 tons surfaced; 18,750 tons dived **Dimensions:** length 170.69 m (560 ft); beam 12.8 m (42 ft); draught 11.1 m (36 ft 6 in) **Propulsion:** one S8G pressurised water-cooled natural-circulation reactor powering two geared steam turbines delivering 44735 kW (60,000 shp) to one shaft **Speed:** 20 kts surfaced and 25+ kts dived **Diving depth:** 300 m (985 ft) operational and 500 m (1,640 ft) maximum	**Armament:** 24 launch tubes for 24 Trident I C4 or Trident II D5 SLBMs, and four 21-in (533-mm) tubes (all bow) for Mk 48 anti-ship/submarines torpedoes **Electronics:** one BPS-15 surface search radar, one WLR-8(V) ESM system, one BQQ-6 bow sonar, one BQS-13 active sonar, one BQR-19 navigation sonar, one TB-16 towed-array sonar, and extensive communications and navigation systems **Complement:** 155

USS *Ohio*
The ultimate submarine

Submarines are the ultimate deterrent: stealthy, hard to find, and armed with the most destructive weapons man has ever devised. Their existence is a shield which has protected both East and West from the horrors of nuclear war for half a century. Lurking stealthily beneath the surface of the world's oceans, nuclear-powered ballistic missile submarines carry the threat of ultimate destruction, and it is that threat which has made the prospect of nuclear war too frightening to contemplate.

Early theorists felt that the submarine's main target role would be against the battlefleet, but in practice its greatest successes have been against enemy trade, and in denying the enemy control of the sea. However, in a single lifetime its ability to wage strategic war has increased beyond belief.

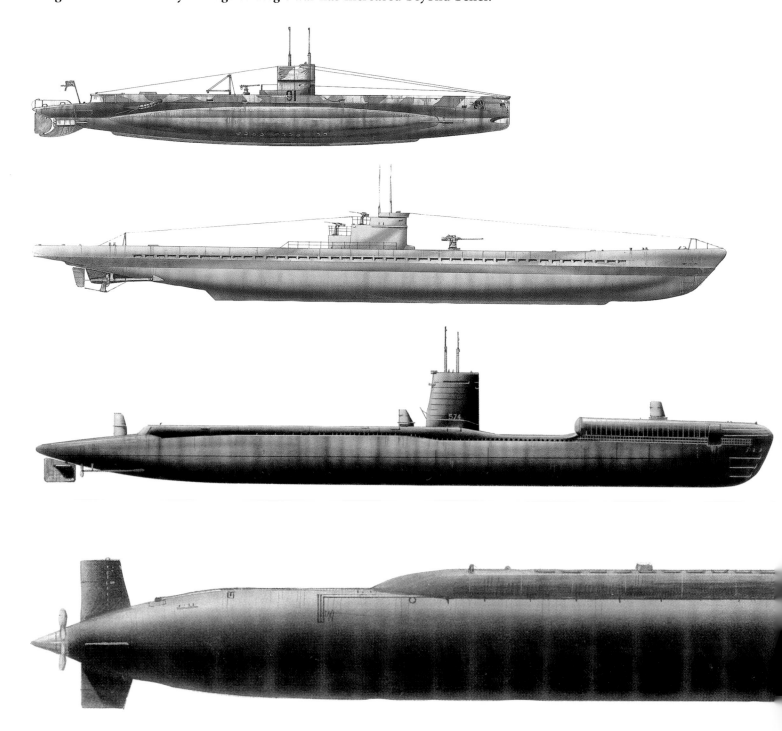

Above: The Trident D-5 is the first submarine-launched intercontinental ballistic missile to be as accurate as its land-based equivalents. Each of its 12 warheads can strike to within 90 m (295 ft 4 in) of a target at ranges in excess of 12000 km (7,456 miles).

E-Class 1914

One of the first truly effective submarines fielded by the British Royal Navy, the 'E'-class boats showed just what the new submersible weapon could do when unleashed against economic targets. Under the command of hard-driving young captains like Max Horton and Martin Naismith, they wrought havoc among German trade along the North Sea Coast, in the Baltic, and with Germany's Turkish allies in the Eastern Mediterranean and the Sea of Marmora.

Type IX 1939

In spite of their small numbers, Admiral Karl Doenitz U-Boats were the only weapons in Adolf Hitler's arsenal which had a truly strategic mission. Their purpose was to cut off Britain's vital Atlantic lifeline, and in 1941 and 1942 their wolfpack tactics accounted for millions of tonnes of allied shipping. Large ocean-going boats like this Type IX were able to extend the war to as far as the Gulf of Mexico, the Caribbean and the South American coasts. However, Allied countermeasures were eventually to prove more effective, and by 1943 the U-Boat threat had been minimised, if not actually defeated.

Grayback 1958

The advent of nuclear weapons changed the face of warfare. In the 1950s, the US Navy envisaged that supersonic cruise missiles would provide its ships with their primary nuclear capability. Submarines like the USS *Grayback* were completed with hangars for firing two Regelus II missiles, each weighing four tons and with a range of over 1600 km (1000 miles). However, boats had to surface to fire, negating the submarine's primary advantage. As long as it is underwater, the submarine is the original stealth machine. Once it surfaces, it becomes a target.

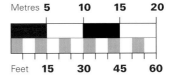

Metres	**5**	**10**	**15**	**20**
Feet	**15**	**30**	**45**	**60**

Ohio 1981

The advent of Polaris changed the face of the world forever. Now a nuclear-powered submarine could remain on patrol for months at a time, with the ability to attack targets from beyond any possible enemy defences. By launching from underwater, the submarine was as near to invulnerable as any weapon system ever built. A continual process of development saw submarines and missiles getting larger and more destructive; by the time the USS *Ohio* set off on its first patrol in 1981, a single submarine could carry more explosive power than had ever been used in combat history.

Inside the Ohio

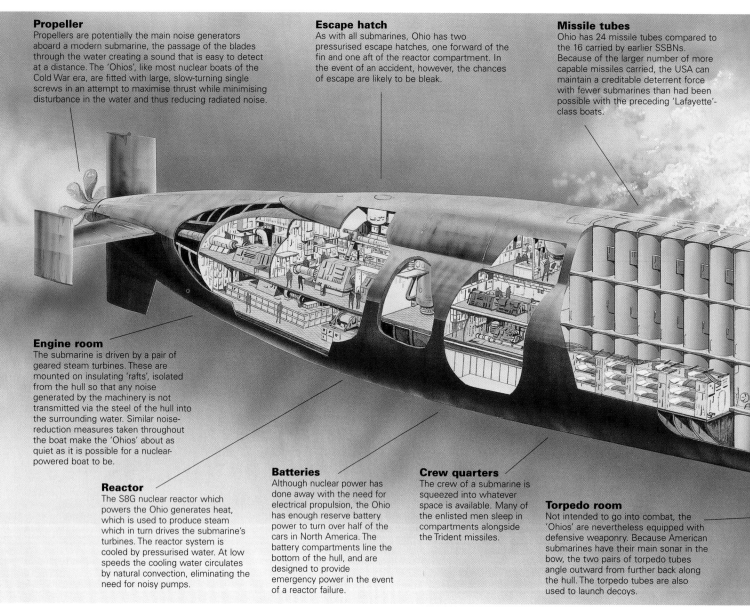

Propeller
Propellers are potentially the main noise generators aboard a modern submarine, the passage of the blades through the water creating a sound that is easy to detect at a distance. The 'Ohios', like most nuclear boats of the Cold War era, are fitted with large, slow-turning single screws in an attempt to maximise thrust while minimising disturbance in the water and thus reducing radiated noise.

Escape hatch
As with all submarines, Ohio has two pressurised escape hatches, one forward of the fin and one aft of the reactor compartment. In the event of an accident, however, the chances of escape are likely to be bleak.

Missile tubes
Ohio has 24 missile tubes compared to the 16 carried by earlier SSBNs. Because of the larger number of more capable missiles carried, the USA can maintain a creditable deterrent force with fewer submarines than had been possible with the preceding 'Lafayette'-class boats.

Engine room
The submarine is driven by a pair of geared steam turbines. These are mounted on insulating 'rafts', isolated from the hull so that any noise generated by the machinery is not transmitted via the steel of the hull into the surrounding water. Similar noise-reduction measures taken throughout the boat make the 'Ohios' about as quiet as it is possible for a nuclear-powered boat to be.

Reactor
The S8G nuclear reactor which powers the Ohio generates heat, which is used to produce steam which in turn drives the submarine's turbines. The reactor system is cooled by pressurised water. At low speeds the cooling water circulates by natural convection, eliminating the need for noisy pumps.

Batteries
Although nuclear power has done away with the need for electrical propulsion, the Ohio has enough reserve battery power to turn over half of the cars in North America. The battery compartments line the bottom of the hull, and are designed to provide emergency power in the event of a reactor failure.

Crew quarters
The crew of a submarine is squeezed into whatever space is available. Many of the enlisted men sleep in compartments alongside the Trident missiles.

Torpedo room
Not intended to go into combat, the 'Ohios' are nevertheless equipped with defensive weaponry. Because American submarines have their main sonar in the bow, the two pairs of torpedo tubes angle outward from further back along the hull. The torpedo tubes are also used to launch decoys.

Although the boats of the 'Ohio'-class are among the largest submarines ever built – only the massive Russian 'Typhoons' are larger – there is no wasted space aboard. The missile compartment, with its 24 launch tubes for the 60-tonne missiles, takes up almost half the available volume. By the time a reactor system and a propulsion system have been fitted, together with a comprehensive sonar suite, an incredible amount of advanced electronics and defensive weaponry, there is not much room for crew and supplies, and they are squeezed in wherever space can be found. Even though the crew is less than half the size of that found on a comparable surface ship, they are still expected to spend 60 days either at work or in a personal space not much bigger than their bunk, with a tiny locker for their personal kit.

Right: The 18 'Ohio'-class Trident missile boats are now the only SSBNs in US Navy service, replacing more than 40 Polaris- and Poseidon-carrying boats.

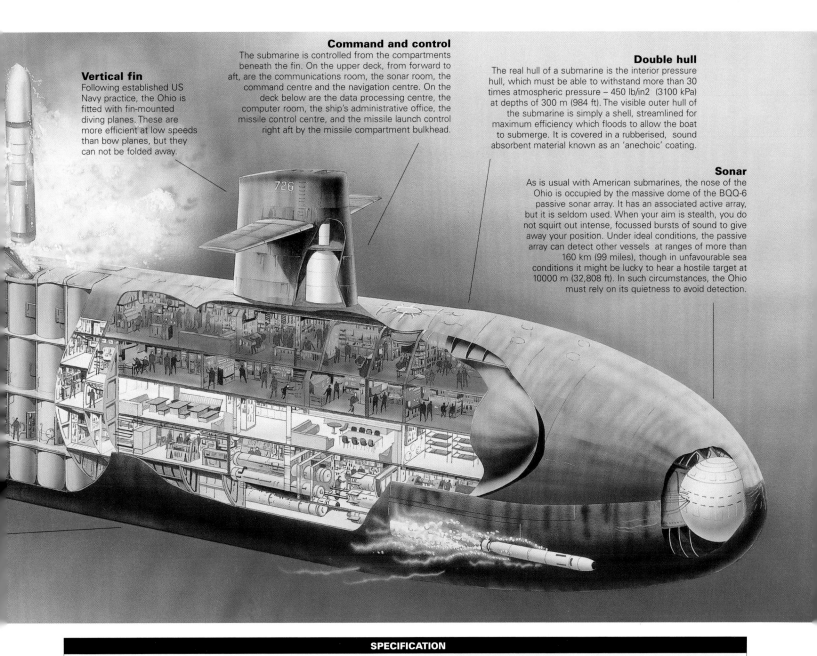

Vertical fin
Following established US Navy practice, the Ohio is fitted with fin-mounted diving planes. These are more efficient at low speeds than bow planes, but they can not be folded away.

Command and control
The submarine is controlled from the compartments beneath the fin. On the upper deck, from forward to aft, are the communications room, the sonar room, the command centre and the navigation centre. On the deck below are the data processing centre, the computer room, the ship's administrative office, the missile control centre, and the missile launch control right aft by the missile compartment bulkhead.

Double hull
The real hull of a submarine is the interior pressure hull, which must be able to withstand more than 30 times atmospheric pressure – 450 lb/in2 (3100 kPa) at depths of 300 m (984 ft). The visible outer hull of the submarine is simply a shell, streamlined for maximum efficiency which floods to allow the boat to submerge. It is covered in a rubberised, sound absorbent material known as an 'anechoic' coating.

Sonar
As is usual with American submarines, the nose of the Ohio is occupied by the massive dome of the BQQ-6 passive sonar array. It has an associated active array, but it is seldom used. When your aim is stealth, you do not squirt out intense, focussed bursts of sound to give away your position. Under ideal conditions, the passive array can detect other vessels at ranges of more than 160 km (99 miles), though in unfavourable sea conditions it might be lucky to hear a hostile target at 10000 m (32,808 ft). In such circumstances, the Ohio must rely on its quietness to avoid detection.

SPECIFICATION

'Ohio'-class SSBN
Builders: General Dynamics Electric Boat Division
Type: nuclear-powered ballistic missile submarine (SSBN)

Dimensions
Length 170.69 m (560 ft); beam 10.06 m (42 ft); draught 11.01 m (36 ft 6 in)

Displacement
16,764 tons surfaced; 18,750 tons submerged

Performance
Speed: 18 kt (33 km/h; 21 mph) surfaced; 20+ kt (37+ km/h; 23 mph) official submerged; actual probably more than 25 kt (46 km/h; 29 mph)
Range: effectively unlimited: primary factor is crew endurance – patrols last up to 90 days, six months supplies carried
Hull: HY-80 steel, outer hull covered in anechoic coating
Operating depth: 'More than 800 feet' admitted to by US Navy; actual depth may be 365.80 m (1,200 ft)

Armament
24 missile tubes for Trident I and II, each missile with up to 12 Mk 4 RVs with 100 kiloton W76 warheads or Mk 5 RVs with variable yield (45-300 kiloton) W88; 4 torpedo tubes to fire Mk 48 or Mk 48 ADCAP torpedoes, MK 57 MOSS torpedo decoy; 8 x launchers for Emerson Mk 2 decoys

Periscopes
One Kollmorgen Type 82, one Kollmorgen Type 152

Electronics
Fire control: CCS Mk 3 combat data system; Mk 98 missile fire control system; Mk 118 digital torpedo fire control system
Radar: BPS-15A surface search/nav
ESM: WLR-8(V)5 intercept; WRL 10 radar warning
Navigation: 2 SINS (Ship's Inertial Navigation System)

Sonar
BQQ-6 bow-mounted passive search with BQS-13 spherical array active search; BQR-15 towed array with BQQ-9 processors BQS-15 high-frequency active/passive BQR-19 high-frequency navigation/under ice

Crew
14/15 officers, 140 enlisted

Units (commissioned)
Ohio (SSBN 726) November 1981; *Michigan* (SSBN 727) September 1982; *Florida* (SSBN 728) June 1983; *Georgia* (SSBN 729) February 1984; *Henry M. Jackson* (SSBN 730) October 1984; *Alabama* (SSBN 731) May 1985; *Alaska* (SSBN 732) January 1986; *Nevada* (SSBN 733) August 1986; *Tennessee* (SSBN 734) December 1988; *Pennsylvania* (SSBN 735) September 1989; *West Virginia* (SSBN 736) October 1990; *Kentucky* (SSBN 737) July 1991; *Maryland* (SSBN 738) June 1992; *Nebraska* (SSBN 739) July 1993; *Rhode Island* (SSBN 740) July 1994; *Maine* (SSBN 741) July 1995; *Wyoming* (SSBN 742) July 1996; *Louisiana* (SSBN-743) September 1997

Left: The lower missile compartment of the USS Ohio stretches into the distance. It could be a chemical works, but it would take a very dull mind to walk through here without a sense of foreboding generated by such awesome destructive potential.

Below: Being a submariner calls for some special characteristics, not least of which is to be not even remotely claustrophobic. It is bad enough to be separated from family and friends for several months at a time, but the cheek-by-jowl living space means that the crewmen of nuclear missile boats have to be able to get on with their fellow crewmen.

Below: Submarines have changed considerably since World War II. Control rooms still have plenty of handwheels, dials and levers, but more and more space is taken up by warning lights, computer displays and keyboards.

*Above: **USS** **O**hio **(SSBN** 726) transits the **H**ood **C**anal as the big boat leaves the Pacific Fleet missile-sub base at **B**angor, **W**ashington State. Large as the boat is, the long whale-back of the missile compartment takes up half of the available space aboard.*

Right: While considerably more luxurious than the galley on a smaller diesel powered boat, the cramped cooking facilities aboard an 'Ohio' would give shore-based chefs nightmares. Yet the galley staff are able to prepare more than 500 nutritious meals per day, every day for two months, in a space smaller than an average family kitchen ashore.

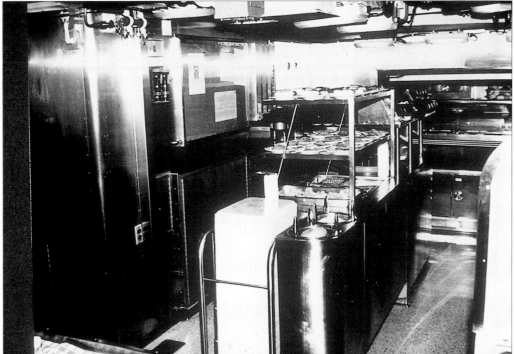

Cold War mission

For four decades, US Navy submariners have been putting to sea on long patrols to deter nuclear attacks on America.

Day 1: USS *Ohio* (SSBN 726) sets off on patrol from Kings Bay, Georgia. Diving to 600 feet, the submarine moves off into the Atlantic at a speed of 15 kt.

Day 4: *Ohio* receives an ELF message. These extremely low frequency radio waves are not stopped by water but they don't carry much information. *Ohio* receives a three-letter pre-arranged code group instructing her to come to periscope depth to receive a satellite message. At 60 ft, the captain orders the needle-thin ESM mast, with its sensitive radar detectors, to be raised. With no radar transmissions in evidence, the captain scans the surface by periscope, then raises the radio antenna. *Ohio* is given orders to proceed with the missile patrol, heading out into the Atlantic and keeping well away from the shipping lanes. Diving to 800 ft, *Ohio* crawls south-east at less than 6 kt (6.89mph; 11.06km/h).

Day 7: After three days, *Ohio* has reached her patrol station. Now it is a task of waiting and listening. Off to the east are the north-south Atlantic shipping lanes, while to the north is the main transatlantic route. *Ohio* has her reactors powered right down and is only making steerage way.

Day 11: The crew has settled down to a normal cruise routine. The main problem they face is boredom. Missile boats are designed to survive by being unobtrusive, so they do nothing to attract attention. There are no high-speed chases, no trailing of enemy submarines, no simulated attacks on huge super-tankers. *Ohio* simply pretends to be a hole in the water, listening for intruders and making virtually no sound at all.

Day 12: Fresh salads run out. From now on the crew will be eating canned and frozen vegetables.

Day 15: Sonar reports an approaching submarine. It is quickly identified as a 'Los Angeles'-class attack boat. *Ohio* slows even further, to little more than a snail's pace. No matter that the hunter-killer is from the same navy; a 'Boomer' survives by not being found, and evading the sophisticated systems of a state-of-the-art American boat is a pretty reliable test of how good at its job the missile submarine is.

Day 16: *Ohio* carries out a missile launch exercise, simulating all of the procedures followed during a nuclear exchange. Unlike the real thing, however, one cannot truly mimic the shudder

*Below: The sheer power of a modern **SSBN** is awesome. Each of the missiles **O**hio carries can deliver more explosive power than 180 Hiroshima bombs – and the big missile boat carries 24 of them.*

Above: High-pressure gas venting from the ominous shape of an 'Ohio'-class boat signals that it is about to dive, not to re-emerge into the daylight for months.

through the boat's hull as compressed air blasts the missile free from its tube. Most of the crew is happy that this is so, and most pray that they will never have to do it for real.

Day 27: The monotony is broken by the passage of an old tramp freighter overhead.

It is the first man-made contact in over a week.

Day 48: A spark of excitement comes on board when the video machine in the enlisted crew's mess breaks down. In the interests of crew morale, and to head off incipient mutiny, the captain has to replace it with the

video from the wardroom. The only other machine is the one from the petty officers' mess, and it would take more than mere rank to make them give it up.

Day 55: USS *Hawaii* left port five days before, and by now will be on station. She is

the *Ohio*'s relief, and once the ELF message comes from Fleet HQ the older boat can go home. Her patrol is over.

Day 60: *Ohio* surfaces off the coast of Georgia at the end of her 60-day patrol. Her crew sees sunlight for the first time in two months.

Below: Although 'Ohio'-class boats make a considerable splash when travelling at speed on the surface, their true environment is under the water. There, they are the quietest, most stealthy submarines ever built.

UGM-96 Trident I and UGM-133 Trident II SLBMs

Above: A Trident II submerged test launch in March 1989 ends in failure. Despite careful design, such complex missile systems can suffer spectacular errors.

SPECIFICATION	
UGM-96A Trident I C4	**UGM-133 Trident II D5**
Weight: 33113 kg (73,000 lb)	**Weight:** 58968 kg (130,000 lb)
Dimensions: length 10.36 m (34 ft); diameter 1.88 m (74 in)	**Dimensions:** length 13.59 m (44 ft 7 in); diameter 2.1 m (82.67 in)
Propulsion: three-stage solid propellant rocket	**Propulsion:** three-stage solid propellant rocket
Guidance system: stellar-inertial	**Guidance system:** stellar-inertial
Range: 6437 km (4,000 miles)	**Range:** 7403 km (4,600 miles)
Warhead: up to eight Multiple Independently-targeted Re-entry Vehicles (MIRVs) with 100-kT thermonuclear warheads	**Warhead:** up to 14 Multiple Independently-targeted Re-entry Vehicles (MIRVs) with 335-kT warheads

The **Trident** programme began on 15 November 1971 with a view to equipping the US Navy's 'Ohio' class of nuclear-powered strategic missile submarines. Based on the UGM-73 Poseidon strategic missile, the Trident was required to nearly double the range of its predecessor. The missile would also need advanced navigation and guidance systems, and re-entry vehicles that could 'porpoise', or manoeuvre to avoid anti-ballistic missile defences.

Development tests

Between 6 March 1974 and 13 November 1975 six prototype flight tests were completed. This led to the development of an entirely new re-entry vehicle, the Mk 4 mounted on the Mk 500 bus and carrying the 100-kT W76 warhead. The maiden flight of the complete **Trident I** system took place on 18 January 1977 with an inert missile launch from Cape Canaveral, Florida.

The first Trident submarine-launched ballistic missile (SLBM) variant, the **UGM-96A Trident I C4**, carries a payload of up to eight MIRVs (Multiple Independently-targeted Re-entry Vehicles). The missile's third stage includes the nuclear warheads and a telescopic 'aerospike' that extends from the missile's nose after launch to cut drag.

On 20 October 1979, the Trident I was deployed for the

Left: Surface launch of a Trident II at Cape Canaveral. It is only after basic capabilities have been proved in this way that the first submarine launches are attempted.

Right: A Trident I missile is launched from the nuclear-powered submarine USS John C. Calhoun off the east coast of Florida during its 1980 shakedown operation.

first time. A flight of 16 missiles was carried aboard the retrofitted USS *Francis Scott Key* on the system's first deterrent patrol.

Improved Trident

Barely two years after the deployment of the Trident I system, plans were afoot for an improved version of the missile to meet an initial operational capability (IOC) deadline of December 1989. The original Trident I system was earmarked to have its stockpile reduced from 969 missiles to 630.

Funding was made available for an entirely new re-entry vehicle and warhead package for the Trident system. The re-entry vehicle, designated Mk 5, would carry the 335-kT W88 warhead and possess an improved ability to penetrate hard targets.

The resulting **UGM-133A Trident II D5** missile is larger than its predecessor and has longer range. Moreover, the missile's electronics and warhead ('physics package') are more advanced.

Service debut

The US Navy introduced the Trident II into service in 1996, first on the USS *Tennessee*. Ten SSBNs in the Atlantic Fleet were equipped to deploy the missile, and eight Pacific Fleet submarines originally fitted for the Trident I were converted to carry the Trident II.

The Trident I is intended to be deployed until 2006. During the 1990s, the British navy purchased the Trident II system to

Right: The USS Tennessee conducts the eighth test launch of a US Navy Trident II missile in January 1990.

carry a warhead designed and produced by the Atomic Weapons Establishment at Aldermaston. Although Trident II was expected to leave US service by 2020, plans now call for it to remain deployed well past this date, until at least 2040.

M4/M45, M5/M51 and S3 series French ballistic missiles

Similar in design to the US Poseidon system, the French **M4** SLBMs were three-stage systems. Following on from the M1 SLBM, deployed in 1971, the M4 was the fourth SLBM to enter service with the French navy's strategic missile submarine fleet.

The M4 was produced in two variants. The **M4A** had a 4000-km

(2,485-mile) range, whereas the later **M4B** variant offered a 5000-km (3,105-mile) range. Each missile carried six MIRVs with the TN-71 warhead thought to have a 150-kT yield.

The first stage of the M4A missile burned for 62 seconds, the second for 71 seconds, and the third for 43 seconds. Each of

the missile's motors had a steerable nozzle for navigation, and the entire system had an inertial guidance system.

The incorporation of a new missile guidance system is thought to have given the M4 an accuracy of 500 m (1,640 ft) CEP from its target. The first test of the M4 took place at the Landes test

range. Between November 1980 (the first flight) and February 1984, some 14 test firings took place. The new system entered service in 1985.

Both the M4A and later upgraded M4B were deployed on five of France's SSBNs, which then comprised the *L'Inflexible, Le Tonnant, L'Indomptable, Le Terrible* and *Le Foudroyant*. It is thought that 16 M4A missiles (one submarine payload) and 48 M4B missiles (three submarine payloads) were operated.

Development of the M4 system culminated in the **M45**. This missile was a considerable improvement on its predecessor in carrying an advanced and electronically hardened re-entry vehicle system with six TN-75 warheads (each with a yield of some 100 kT) and penetration aids. The missile was first test-launched from *Le Triomphant* in February 1995, and has a range of 6000 km (3,730 miles). The M45 entered service in March 1997, when it was deployed on

*Left: Like other major nuclear powers, France has appreciated that maximum survivability and flexibility are provided by the use of ballistic weapons carried in and launched from nuclear-powered submarines. Here, an M4 missile is test-launched from the submarine **Gymnote**, prior to its 1985 service entry with the **L'Inflexible**.*

SPECIFICATION	
M4A	**S3**
Type: submarine-launched ballistic missile	**Type:** intermediate-range ballistic missile
Weight: 35073 kg (77,323 lb)	**Weight:** 25800 kg (56,878 lb)
Dimensions: length 11.05 m (36 ft 3 in); diameter 1.93 m (76 in)	**Dimensions:** length 13.8 m (45 ft 3 in); diameter 1.5 m (59 in)
Propulsion: three-stage rocket including a powered bus for MIRVed warheads	**Propulsion:** two-stage rocket including a re-entry vehicle containing the warhead
Guidance: inertial	**Guidance:** inertial
Range: 4000 km (2,485 miles)	**Range:** 3500 km (2,175 miles)
Warhead: six 150-kT MIRVs	**Warhead:** 1.2 MT

Le Triomphant, the lead unit of a four-boat class, two of which had entered service by 1996.

During the early 1990s the French decided to replace the M4 and M45 systems with a brand new **M5** missile. The M5 was initially thought to have been designed for a range of 11000 km (6,835 miles), but was then redesigned as the **M51** for reduced cost but also reduced capability: for example, the M51 will have a range of 6000 km. The M51 was planned for an IOC in 2008, but this 'in service' date could be brought forward to 2005.

It is thought that the payload of the M51 will be between six and 10 MIRVed 100-kT warheads of a new TN-series type. Some reports have suggested, however, that the missile may carry a payload of advanced TN-76 warheads, which would presumably be an improved version of the TN-75 warheads currently deployed on the M45 missile system.

Land-based missile

During the same year that the M4A was undergoing test flights, the S2 surface-to-surface ballistic missile was being decommissioned. From the early 1970s, the S2 missile system had formed the major part of the French land-based nuclear deterrent, but in 1983 the French government initiated a programme to replace the

system with the **S3** missile, which was deployed in 1980 for service from 1982.

A total of 18 silo-launched S3s (from a total of about) 40 were deployed prior to their retirement in September 1996. The missile was in turn due to be replaced by a land-based M5 derivative, which was itself cancelled in 1993. The S3 inherited the first stage of the S2, with a burn time of 72 seconds; the second stage had a 58-second burn time. A single 1.2-MT TN61 warhead was carried within a radiation-hardened re-entry system.

Above: France's S3 IRBM was designed to be launched from the same heavily protected underground silos as were used by the earlier 150-kT S2.

Right: An S3 IRBM is test launched. The solid-fuel S3 carried a single warhead and it replaced the earlier S2 within silo installations on the Plateau d'Albion.

Modern Soviet SLBMs SS-N-18, SS-N-20, SS-N-23 and SS-N-28

Conceived by the KBM design concern from 1973 on the basis of the R-29 (SS-N-8 'Sawfly') for service on the 'Delta III' class of SSBNs each with 16 missiles, the **R-29R** submarine-launched ballistic missile has the Western reporting designation **SS-N-18 'Stingray'**. The R-29R was the first Soviet SLBM with a post-boost bus able to carry three (**SS-N-18 Mod 1** that entered service in 1979) or seven (**Mod 3** that did not enter service) 200- or 100-kT Multiple Independently targeted Re-entry Vehicles (MIRVs) respectively to a range of 6500 km (4,040 miles) with a claimed CEP of 900 m (985 yards). There was also an **Mod 2** version that entered service in 1977 with a single 450-kT warhead delivered to a range of 8000 km (4,970 miles) with the same accuracy.

Using astro-inertial guidance, the two-stage R-29R has liquid-propellant rocket motors, a launch weight of 35300 kg (77,820 lb), and a length of 14.1 m (46 ft 3 in) with a diameter of 1.8 m (5 ft 11 in).

'Sturgeon' missile
Entering service in 1984 after development from 1973 as another product of KBM, the **R-39** is the SLBM of the 'Typhoon'-class SSBN, and is known in the West as the **SS-N-20 'Sturgeon'**.

The R-39 is a three-stage weapon with solid-propellant rocket motors and a post-boost bus with its own guidance system, a liquid-propellant

propulsion system, decoys and 10 MIRVs. The missile is propelled from its tube by a gas generator, special charges in the first stage creating a gas bubble round the missile, reducing hydrodynamic resistance.

The first missile was launched in 1979, and from 1989 accuracy and warhead coverage were enhanced. Each 'Typhoon' boat can carry 20 R-39 missiles, although missile trials had been conducted with the sole 'Golf V'-class boat.

'Delta IV' service
Another KBM design, again created under the overall supervision of Viktor P. Makeyev, the **R-29RM** is the SLBM associated with the 'Delta IV' class of SSBN, which carries 16 such missiles. Though based closely on the R-29R, the R-29RM is an altogether superior weapon incorporating a number of changes and enhancements, including a 10-cm (3.94-in) increase in diameter (without any need to increase the diameter of the launch tube) and a 70-cm (27.56-in) increase in length to allow the loading of more propellant for an increase in the payload by 1150 kg (2,535 lb) carried over a 300-km (186-mile) greater range.

The R-29RM is known in the West by the reporting designation **SS-N-23 'Skiff'**. The weapon was developed from 1979 for a first test-firing (on land) in May 1983 and a service debut in 1986, and is a three-stage missile with liquid-propellant rocket motors. The post-boost bus can carry either four or 10 100-kT MIRVs,

Above: The Zelenograd *is a 'Delta III'-class (Project 667BDR) SSBN, and therefore carries a primary armament of 16 SS-N-18 'Stingray' (R-29R) SLBMs. A total of 14 'Delta IIIs' were similarly equipped with the R-29R missile. The six remaining boats in service in 2003 operated the three-warhead R-29R model.*

although only the four-MIRV option has been fielded to date.

In 1988 the launch system was updated for improved accuracy and to enable the missiles to be fired on depressed trajectories. Within

the same overall programme the missiles were equipped with improved warheads.

Failed programme
The **R-39M** (or perhaps **R-39UTTH**) submarine-launched

SPECIFICATION	
R-39 (SS-N-20 'Sturgeon')	MIRVs
Length: complete missile 16 m (52 ft 6 in); missile without warhead 8.4 m (27 ft 6¾ in)	**Range:** 8300 km (5,160 miles)
Diameter: 2.4 m (7 ft 10½ in)	**CEP:** approximately 500 m (545 yards) according to Russian sources
Weight: complete missile 90000 kg (198,413 lb); post-boost bus with 10 MIRVs 2550 kg (5,622 lb)	**Launch method:** dry start from submerged tube
Warhead: 10 100-kT thermonuclear	**Guidance:** inertial with full stellar correction

Above: Deployed on the 'Hotel III' and 'Delta I/II' SSBN classes, the single-warhead R-29 (SS-N-8 'Sawfly') was the progenitor of the MIRV-equipped R-29R (SS-N-18 'Stingray'). The R-29 was the first Soviet SLBM with intercontinental range.

Left: The 'Typhoon'-class (Project 941) boats are the world's largest submarines, and in the SSBN role carry 20 SS-N-20 'Sturgeon' (R-39) SLBMs. A total of six 'heavy strategic missile-armed cruisers' of the class were equipped with this weapon after extensive trials had been undertaken with TK-208, the lead ship.

ballistic missile was generally known in the West as the **SS-N-28**. The weapon was designed by the Makeyev Machine-Building organisation, as the KBM concern had been renamed, and was intended for the new 'Borey' class (Project 955) of fourth-generation SSBN and as a retrofit on the earlier 'Typhoon' class. The R-39M was derived from the R-39 with provision for the carriage of up to 10 advanced MIRVs (although considerably fewer were envisaged as the typical load) and their penetration aids for delivery over a range of more than 8000 km (4,970 miles) but with considerably greater accuracy than the R-39. The missile failed in its first three test launches, one being characterised by a catastrophic explosion at an altitude of 200 m (655 ft), and the programme was terminated.

It is believed that the 'Borey' class will be revised to carry the 3M54 Klub (SS-N-27) multi-role cruise missile being developed in five variants at launch weights between 1300 and 2300 kg (2,866 and 5,071 lb). The building of the first 'Borey'-class submarine was slowed after the end of the SS-N-28 programme so that it and its weapons can become operational at about the same time.

Chinese strategic missiles Land- and sea-launched weapons

Above: Now out of service, the single-stage DF-3 (CSS-2) with liquid-fuel rocket power carried a 1/5-MT warhead to 2800 km (1,740 miles).

The research, design, development and production of ballistic missiles for the Chinese forces is overseen by the China Academy of Launch Vehicle Technology (1st Academy) of the China Aerospace Development Corporation. The Chinese nuclear-armed ballistic missiles fall into two primary categories known as Dong Feng (east wind) land-based and Ju Lang (great wave) sea-based weapons, which have Western designations in the CSS and CSS-N series respectively.

By 2003 the oldest land-based weapon still in service is the **DF-4** (**CSS-3**), which is a two-stage weapon carrying a single 1/5-MT warhead to a range of 4750 km (2,950 miles) with a CEP of 3-3.5 km (1.86-2.17 miles). The weapon uses non-storable liquid propellants, and therefore needs up to two hours for fuelling and launch. Greater capabilities are offered by the **DF-5** (**CSS-4**),

Above: An M-9 (export DF-15) surface-to-surface ballistic missile with a 950-kg (2,094-lb) HE warhead is launched at a test site in south-eastern China.

which is a two-stage weapon with storable liquid propellants and therefore capable of launch in a time of between 30 and 60 minutes. The **DF-21** (**CSS-5**), which has a JL-1 (CSS-N-4) SLBM version, is a two-stage weapon with solid propellants and can be launched in a time of less than 15 minutes, carrying a 200/300-kT warhead to 1800 km (1,120 miles) with a CEP of 0.3-0.4 km (0.19-0.25 miles). The **DF-15** (**CSS-6**), for which a nuclear role has yet to be confirmed, is a shorter-range weapon of the single-stage type with solid propellants and a 30-minute launch time. The possible nuclear warhead would have a

yield in the order of 50/350 kT delivered to a range of 600 km (373 miles) with a CEP of 0.3 km (0.19 miles) with the aid of a digitised strap-down inertial platform of the generation replacing the gyro-based inertial platforms of earlier missiles.

Shorter-range ballistic missiles intended mainly for the tactical and/or operational roles are generally equipped with a HE warhead, and include the **DF-11** (**CSS-7**) that can carry a 350-kT nuclear warhead or 800 kg (1,764 lb) of conventional cluster munitions to a range of 300 km (186 miles) and the **M-7/8160** developed for the export market as a variant of the HQ-2 (SA-2

'Guideline') SAM with a 190-kg (419-kg) HE warhead.

Long-range weapons under development by the Chinese are the **DF-31** and **DF-41**, for which no Western designation is known. Both are three-stage weapons with solid-propellant rocket motors weapons and a range of 8000 or 12000 km (4,970 or 7,455 miles) respectively with single 200/300-kT warhead, although an MRV or MIRV capability (with penetration aids) may also have been developed. The DF-31 was created to succeed the DF-4 (CSS-3), has a launch time of 10-15 minutes, and is generally stored underground before be prepared for launch. The DF-41 has a launch time of 3-5 minutes and is a land-mobile system possibly intended as a replacement for the DF-5.

Submarine missiles

The submarine-launched ballistic missiles are the **JL-1** (**CSS-N-3**) and **JL-2** (**CSS-N-4**). The former is basically the DF-21 land-based missile adapted for China's sole 'Xia'-class SSBN, which has 12 launch tubes, and is similar to the DF-31 except for its worse CEP of 1 km (0.62 miles). The latter missile is basically the DF-31, in this case adapted for embarkation on China's sole 'Golf'-class SSN (one tube in the after part of the sail), but intended for use on a new class of SSBNs based on the 'Xia' class but with the hull lengthened for the installation of 16 launch tubes.

The JL-2 has essentially the same performance and capabilities as the DF-31 with the exception of a CEP figure reduced to 1 km (0.62 miles).

SPECIFICATION

DF-5 (CSS-4)
Length: complete missile 32.6 m (106 ft 11½ in)
Diameter: 3.35 m (22 ft)
Weight: complete missile 183000 kg (403,440 lb); re-entry vehicle 3000-3200 kg (6,614-7,055 lb)

Warhead: one 2-MT thermonuclear
Range: 15000 km (9,320 miles)
CEP: 500-3500 m (545-3,825 yards)
Launch method: hot start from a surface site
Guidance: inertial based on a gyroscopic platform and onboard computer

---

Below: Chinese air force officers attend a training session on the latest command centre instruments at a missile-launch training school at Beijing in 1999.

Nuclear Attack Submarines

Cold War hunter-killer operations

During the Cold War, the Soviet nuclear submarine attack force would have been one of the primary elements in any Soviet navy first-strike against NATO naval assets. It was a highly controlled force, with both attack and cruise missile submarines of all capabilities forming the assault units, and was continually being upgraded as new boats and weapons were introduced.

The Soviets operated a wide range of nuclear attack submarines, varying greatly in potential. The 'Echo II' class armed with long-range SS-N-3 or SS-N-12 missiles needed to surface for weapon launch, and, when submerged, was noisy and slow. Torpedo-armed 'Echo' and 'November' classes were useful in 'operational' anti-SLOC roles. The 'Victor' classes and converted 'Yankee' SSNs of various configurations offered high submerged speeds and were suitable for ASW, particularly 'strategic' anti-SSBN missions. They were armed with torpedoes and stand-off ASW missiles. The 'Charlie' classes were slower but had a variety of submerged-launch anti-ship cruise missiles. The most modern Soviet SSGN was the 'Oscar' class with vertical-launched SS-N-19 anti-ship cruise missiles. Never fully understood by the West, the 'Alpha' class was credited with extreme diving depths (up to 1000 m/3,280 ft) and a speed in excess of 40 kts. All the later classes were first-rate craft, capable of working against heavily-defended 'operational' targets such as enemy surface attack groups.

Fleet Admiral Gorshkov testified to the importance of the SSBN and, though not committing himself to reserving them in 'sanctuary' areas, alluded to the problems that this would have caused Western SSNs wishing to attack them.

Above: At the end of the Cold War, the Soviet navy included the 'Akula' class of SSN, similar in capability to the early 'Los Angeles' class and also offering a land-attack capability with the SS-N-21 cruise missile.

Soviet SSNs would, therefore, have been greatly involved in the support of friendly SSBNs and the destruction of those of the enemy. They would not necessarily have worked alone, for Soviet doctrine aimed towards mounting co-ordinated attacks from a variety of platforms, submarine, surface and aerial. The complexity of such attacks demanded

Left: From the early 1980s, protection was increasingly provided by such modern submarines as the 'Victor' class. With advanced electronics, and coated with sound-deadening material, the later 'Victors' were as capable as a large proportion of the US attack force.

centralised control, so much of the initiative demanded of Western SSN skippers in their 'lone ranger' roles was deemed unnecessary.

War of attrition

The Soviets appeared more willing than the West to accept losses. Numerical superiority may have been used to entice a Western boat to betray its presence in order that it could be attacked. This would involve 'coat-trailing' and, if it resulted in attrition at the

COLD WAR SSN SCENARIO: SOVIET SSBN PROTECTION

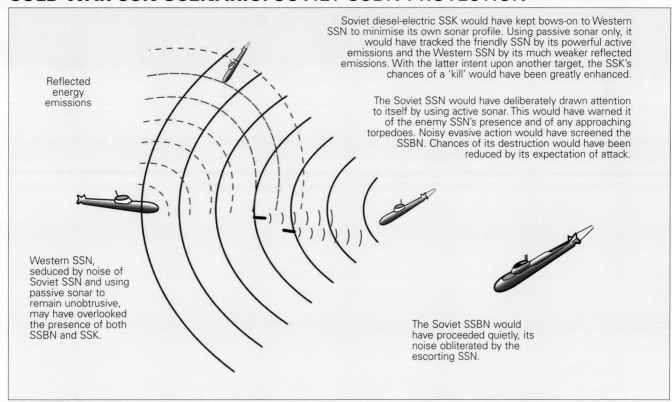

Soviet diesel-electric SSK would have kept bows-on to Western SSN to minimise its own sonar profile. Using passive sonar only, it would have tracked the friendly SSN by its powerful active emissions and the Western SSN by its much weaker reflected emissions. With the latter intent upon another target, the SSK's chances of a 'kill' would have been greatly enhanced.

The Soviet SSN would have deliberately drawn attention to itself by using active sonar. This would have warned it of the enemy SSN's presence and of any approaching torpedoes. Noisy evasive action would have screened the SSBN. Chances of its destruction would have been reduced by its expectation of attack.

Reflected energy emissions

Western SSN, seduced by noise of Soviet SSN and using passive sonar to remain unobtrusive, may have overlooked the presence of both SSBN and SSK.

The Soviet SSBN would have proceeded quietly, its noise obliterated by the escorting SSN.

While within range of friendly air cover, a Soviet navy SSBN may well have proceeded on the surface to minimise mine threat and maximise problems for Western SSNs. To pass through choke points such as the GIUK gap, the SSBN would have been submerged but supported by other submarines,

aircraft or surface group vessels. Unlike the US Navy, the Soviets retained large numbers of diesel-electric patrol submarines in service and these may have had a secondary SSBN escort role.

rate of one-for-one, this may have been considered quite acceptable.

Geography severely circumscribed the Soviet Union. Unless its forces could seize and hold their respective narrow exits, both the Baltic and Black Sea fleets would have been unusable in war. The Mediterranean could not be allowed to become a protected zone for NATO SSBNs, however, so Soviet SSNs would have needed to transit continuously to and from the Northern Fleet, navigating the choke points of the GIUK gap, Gibraltar Strait and perhaps the Sicilian narrows.

Ideally, every available unit would have been at sea before the start of hostilities. Initial targets would have been US Navy carrier attack groups, resupply convoys, Western SSBNs and key shore targets. During passage Soviet SSNs may well have kept in company for mutual support, even on the surface in areas covered by friendly air power, to reduce the threat from mines and ASW weapons. Once on submerged passage, speed would have been selected for minimum noise. An assault on an important ship concentration would have involved allocating specific sectors to the attackers to avoid mutual interference. Range and bearing would have been determined by armament and ability to disengage rapidly after launch, together with the number of submarines taking part. Boats would have needed to be 'held' while the attack force was being built up.

Combined attack

A possible attack programme would have involved several initial probes by aircraft such as the Tu-22M 'Backfire', working on the fringe of the carrier's CAP zone. Supported by EW aircraft, the 'Backfires' would have split up the CAP and then launched their stand-off missiles, virtually simultaneously. A Tu-95RTs 'Bear-D' would have directed aircraft attacks and, if there were any SS-N-3/12 boats on the scene, would have provided missile guidance.

Once the surface group had become committed, these submarines could surface for missile launch. Closer-in would be SS-N-7-armed boats, whose entrance would have been timed to take advantage of the confusion.

Without aerial assistance, attacking submarines would have been much more limited. As it would have been unlikely that central control would have had a plot accurate enough for the setting-in of missile launch data, the boats would have needed to close the target group sufficiently to use active sonar for targeting purposes. Either course would have laid them open to detection and counter-attack. One course of action may have been to use a missile for reconnaissance, sweeping a path either side of the target's suspected bearing. The missile's radar picture would have been sent back to the submarine, which would designate the target when a group of ships had been found.

A problem for the attacker would have been the SSN (or two) that normally accompanied a valuable surface group. This, being quieter, would have had an initial advantage but, once it or they had used active sensors and launched weapons, the Soviets could have broken cover and would have had nothing to lose by fast (noisy) disengagement. As the presence of a Western SSN was to have been expected, active ranging to pinpoint and target it would have been in order once the attack had begun.

Western SSNs would not have been hunted down as a matter of course as this would have been a waste of available assets: far better to tackle those that could be found more easily. Besides those in the company of surface groups, there would have been others attempting to penetrate 'sanctuary' areas. These would have been tackled by advanced boats such as the 'Alpha' and 'Victor' classes, the former being only torpedo-armed (a limitation compensated by an ability to out-run and out-dive an adversary), while the latter also had ballistic ASW weapons. Some of these would have been nuclear-tipped to 'sanitise' a considerable area if the target had been only vaguely located, of high value (such as an SSBN), or looked like escaping.

Below: Soviet ballistic missile submarines such as the 'Delta III' class would have been prime targets for Western attack submarines; one of the main functions of Soviet nuclear attack submarines was the protection of such missile craft from opposing vessels.

Nuclear hunter-killers
The art of underwater ambush

The 'war' waged between nuclear-powered attack submarines was that of cat-and-mouse. Concealment and stealthy approach were vital elements, but so too were quietness of operation, advanced sensors and weapons, and the skills of captains and crews.

Above: Seamen on the casing of a US Navy attack submarine prepare to leave harbour. Nuclear submariners like these from several nations have been waging a shadowy war of nerves beneath the waves for more than four decades. Even with the end of the Cold War, the Hunter-Killers still put to sea.

The nuclear-powered attack submarine (SSN) can undertake 'area defence', tasking the SSN with patrol of a large swath of ocean to safeguard an area against other SSNs and ASW ships, and 'point defence', requiring the SSN to patrol a specific 'point' in the ocean to protect a convoy, task force or ship.

To perform these missions, the SSN 'trails' a target boat (a 'contact') covertly or overtly. The SSN acquires its contact as the target leaves port or passes through a 'chokepoint'. If the contact believes it is being trailed, it can perform a U-turn (a tactic known to Western SSN crews as a 'Crazy Ivan'), tow a detection device to listen for trailers, or launch decoys and countermeasures to confuse the pursuer's sonar. It is important for the trailer to keep contact with the target, and itself remain undetected. This affects how close the trailer can get to its contact, and also its evasive actions to avoid countermeasures.

The second option is 'overt' trailing. This can mean

Above and left: The massive Soviet submarine fleet created during the 1950s was composed of diesel-powered boats like this 'Foxtrot'. The rapid US development of nuclear powered boats like the Pogy, (left), seen here surfaced in the Arctic, meant that the Soviets had to develop their own nuclear boats more quickly.

illuminating the contact with regular sonar bursts. If the trailer stays close to its contact, it can be very difficult for the contact to elude its pursuer. The overtness of the trailing also simplifies the use of countermeasures by the contact, however. Once the contact determines that it is being trailed, it can release large concentrations of bubbles to mask the boat from its pursuer's sonar. The contact can also seek to jam the trailer's sonar with elec-

tronic countermeasures. Finally, the contact can ask friendly submarine and ASW forces to harass its pursuer.

During the Cold War, the US and Soviet navies developed different doctrines for their SSN forces. Soviet SSNs protected their SSBN flotillas and forward-located major surface ships. A Soviet imperative was the destruction of US SSNs before the latter entered the GIUK (Greenland-Iceland-UK) gap, a chokepoint for Soviet ship-

ping between the Barents Sea and the North Atlantic. Once US SSNs were in the Barents Sea they were able to 'mix' with Soviet boats, thereby making their detection and destruction difficult. However, the chokepoints could also work to the Soviets' advantage because any boats beyond the GIUK gap could be regarded as hostile: this provided the Soviet SSNs with a 'stand-off' distance to attack Western boats. The Soviets could also attempt to 'lure' Western SSNs into the launch of a torpedo, giving away their position and facilitating attack by Soviet ASW forces. Some US SSN exercises suggested that there was

only a 50 per cent chance that a single torpedo would destroy an SSN.

Worst-case scenario

For the US, such tactics could have resulted in a 'worst-case' scenario in which their SSNs were drawn into 'dogfights' with Soviet boats. This would have removed the US boats' advantage in being quieter. A dogfight would have revealed the presence of each side's boats to the other, and fortune would not favour the quieter boat but that with the greater firepower, agility, countermeasures and damage resistance.

The priority for the US Navy's SSNs was the protection of carrier battle groups and amphibious forces, as well as seeking out Soviet SSBNs, laying minefields and attacking coastal targets with cruise missiles. To this end, of the 40-45 SSNs that the US Navy might have had available in the Atlantic at any one time during the late part of the Cold War, a dozen might have been detailed with protection of carrier battle groups, nine or ten with patrol of the GIUK chokepoint, and about 20 with the forward area patrol.

The first priority was for the US SSN fleet to deny the Soviets access to the sea from Murmansk and Petropavlovsk on the Atlantic and Pacific coasts respectively. Soviet ASW forces were aware of the US SSN strategy and concentrated their

sensors around the ports, forcing US boats to patrol farther offshore. This widened the gap through which the Soviet SSNs could pass, while hampering the detection efforts of the US submarines. Moreover, the closer the US SSNs got to the Soviet chokepoints, the tighter the concentration of friendly boats. This could cause a commensurate increase in the risk of friendly fire should a shooting war have begun.

Above: The US Navy's 'Seawolf' is the ultimate hunter-killer, with a performance unlikely to be matched for decades. Built to fight the Soviets, it is far too expensive for the post-Cold War world.

Right: In the 1980s, Soviet submarine designs like this 'Akula'-class nuclear-powered attack boat closed a major part of the technological gap between the Soviet Navy and its Western foes.

SSN OF TOMORROW: TWENTY-FIRST CENTURY SUBMARINES

The most advanced nuclear-powered designs currently being built include the US Navy's 'Virginia' class and the British 'Astute'-class boats. The prohibitive unit cost of the 'Seawolf' class and changing strategic requirements led to the US Navy defining a smaller new generation attack submarine. The 'Virginia'-class New Attack Submarine is an advanced, stealthy, multi-mission nuclear-powered vessel designed for deep ocean anti-submarine warfare and for littoral (shallow water) operations. The Royal Navy's 'Astute'-class submarine is a nuclear-powered attack submarine which is to replace the five 'Swiftsure'-class submarines, launched between 1973 and 1977. An evolutionary development of the 'Trafalgar' class, the new design will carry up to 38 tube-launched torpedoes and missiles, increasing fighting power by over 50 per cent.

Above: Since supporting land operations with cruise missile fire has become a key submarine mission, the new 'Virginia' class is designed to operate in shallow coastal waters as well as in the deep ocean and under the ice cap.

Left: A little smaller than the US 'Virginia' class, the 'Astute' class will be armed with a mix of Tomahawk cruise missiles, Harpoon anti-ship missiles and heavyweight wire-guided torpedoes.

'Han' class
Nuclear anti-ship submarine

China began building its submarine force in the 1950s, basing its boats primarily on Soviet designs. However, with the split between Mao Tse Tung and Khrushchev, developments in the 1960s had to be carried out without outside assistance. China lacked the scientific, engineering or technological resources to match the USSR or Western navies, and development of an indigenous nuclear submarine was protracted.

The first of the **'Type 91'** class attack boats, also known as the **'Han' class**, was laid down in 1967. It was commissioned in 1974, but because of continuing problems with the nuclear reactor **Submarine 401** was probably not truly operational for a decade. Four more boats were commissioned through the 1980s. The last three are several metres longer,

and have vertical launch tubes fitted to allow anti-ship missiles to be carried without cutting into the torpedo load.

These boats are rather noisy, even by the standards of the time they were built. Their equipment, based on Soviet designs of the 1950s, was primitive. However, the original Soviet ESM system, as well as the ineffective passive sonar, have been replaced by French equipment, and the last three boats have been given an even more extensive refit.

Anti-ship

The primary function of the Han class appears to be anti-surface-ship: the boats carry a mix of straight-running and homing torpedoes, as well as the C-801 Ying-Ji (Eagle Strike) anti-ship missile. They are too noisy to be effective anti-submarine vessels,

but they have the capability to strike at shipping lanes far beyond China's coastal waters.

The next-generation 'Type 93' SSN is intended to replace the 'Hans'. Being built with Russian help, the design is reportedly based on the Soviet Victor III, which would make it the equivalent of one of the US Navy's 'Sturgeon'-class boats of the 1970s and 1980s. But although the first of the class has been under construction at the

Above: Submarine 404 is a stretched and improved version of the 'Han' class. It serves as part of the North Sea Fleet at Jianggezhuang.

Huludao ship yard since 1994, the programme has been considerably delayed.

As an interim measure, it is believed that the PLA Navy has been looking into the possibility of leasing or buying an 'Akula' class boat from Russia.

SPECIFICATION	
'Han' class	29 mph) dived
Type: Nuclear-powered attack submarine	**Diving depth (estimated):** 200 m (656 ft) normal and 300 m (985 ft) maximum
Displacement: 4,500 tons surfaced and 5,550 tons dived	**Torpedo tubes:** six 533-mm (21-in)
Dimensions: length 98 m (321 ft 6 in); beam 10 m (32 ft 10 in); draught 7.4 m (24 ft 2½ in)	**Basic load:** 18 weapons, usually a mix of homing and straight-running torpedoes, or up to 36 mines
Machinery: one 90-MW pressurized water reactor driving one shaft	**Electronics:** Snoop Tray surface search radar; Trout Cheek medium frequency sonar; DUUX-5 low frequency sonar; Type 921A ESM
Speed: 12 kts (22 km/h; 14 mph) surfaced and 25 kts (46 km/h;	**Complement:** 75

Above: The 'Han' class is a key part of China's expansion plans, which aim to project power out into the Pacific beyond Japan and Taiwan.

'Rubis' class

France's refusal to accept American aid meant that her first nuclear attack boats entered service 20 years after their British equivalents.

In 1964 the French Navy began the design of a 4,000-ton nuclear-powered attack submarine. This was cancelled in 1968, before construction started. A smaller design was then initiated, based on the hull form of the diesel-electric 'Agosta' class and with basically the same fire-control, torpedo-launching and sonar detection systems.

The resulting **'SNA72'** class built at Cherbourg is the smallest SSN type in operational service with any navy, and was made possible by the French development of a small 48-megawatt integrated reactor-heat exchanger system driving two turbo-alternators and a main electric motor. The hull depth was increased compared with the 'Agosta' class,

and has allowed the typical three-deck layout of larger SSNs to be used for the areas forward and immediately aft of the fin. The forward diving planes of the Agostas have been relocated to the fin to improve underwater manoeuvrability.

Left: Although initially a little slower and noisier than contemporary British and American boats, the 'Rubis' class has evolved into a highly effective ASW platform.

Service entry

The first boat, the **Rubis**, was laid down at Cherbourg in 1976, and was commissioned in February 1983. It was followed by three further boats, the **Saphir**, the **Casabianca**, and the **Émeraude**, which were commissioned between 1984 and 1987.

The French Navy had originally planned for two squadrons of these SSNs, one to be based at Brest to cover the SSBN base, and the other at Toulon. In the event, all of the boats are based at Toulon, together with the two boats of the follow-on **'Améthyste'** class. All, however, operate fre-

Above: Currently the world's smallest front-line SSN, the 'Rubis'- class boats are essentially a heavily-modified version of the conventionally-powered 'Agosta'-class boats.

quently in the Atlantic. Originally, the 'Rubis' class were tasked primarily with anti-surface warfare. Endurance, limited primarily by the amount of food which can be carried, is estimated at 45 days.

All of the boats carry versions of the F 17 and L5 torpedoes and, from the middle of the 1980s, have been equipped with the underwater-launched, encapsulated SM.39 Exocet anti-ship missile.

However, in the early 1990s, the 'Rubis'-class submarines were joined by two improved boats, the **Améthyste** and the **Perle**. Built to the same basic design as their predecessors,

SPECIFICATION	
'Rubis' class	**Torpedo tubes:** four 550-mm (21¾-in), all bow
Type: Nuclear-powered attack submarine	**Basic load:** 10 F 17 wire-guided anti-ship and/or L5 mod.3 ASW torpedoes; four SM.39 Exocet missiles; or up to 28 TSM35 10 ground mines
Displacement: 2,385 tons surfaced and 2,670 tons dived	
Dimensions: length 72.1 m (236 ft 6¼ in); beam 7.6 m (24 ft 11 in); draught 6.4 m (21 ft)	**Electronics:** one Kelvin-Hughes surface search radar; one DMUX 20 multi-function sonar and one DSUV 62C passive towed array sonar; ARUR 13/DR 3000U ESM system
Machinery: one 48-MW pressurized water reactor (PWR) powering two turbo-alternators driving one shaft	**Complement:** 66
Speed: 18 kts (33 km/h; 21 mph) surfaced and 25 kts (46 km/h; 29 mph) dived	Boats in class: *Rubis* (S601), *Saphir* (S602), *Casabianca* (S603), *Émeraude* (S604), *Améthyste* (S605) and *Perle* (S606)
Diving depth: 300 m (985 ft) normal and 500 m (1, 640 ft) max	

but stretched by about two metres, the new boats were designed primarily as anti-submarine platforms. They have a more advanced sonar and

electronic fit, and are quieter than the original boats.

Between 1989 and 1995 the early boats underwent the Améthyste modernisation

programme. Standing for AMElioration Tactique HYdrodynamique Silence Transmission Ecoute it brings them up to the standard of

their successors. A new, even larger class of SSN is currently in development, and is expected to enter service some time after 2010.

'November' class Nuclear-powered anti-shipping submarine

The 14-vessel **Project 627** class of submarine was called the **'November'** class by NATO. They were the first operational Soviet nuclear-powered boats, built from 1958 at Severodvinsk.

Contemporary with the American 'Nautilus', 'Seawolf' and 'Skate', they were built primarily for performance rather than stealth.

Armed with nuclear torpedoes, the original task of these boats

was to get close enough to American ports to fire their torpedoes into the harbours. However, the role rapidly changed, the primary function of the 'Novembers' for most of their lives being to attack carrier battle groups in the hope of getting a clear shot at the carrier itself.

Noise makers

By modern standards, the 'Novembers' were very noisy, thanks to their hull form, elderly reactor design and the many free flood holes in the casing. Retractable hydroplanes were carried just aft of the bow sonar systems, and two 406-mm (16-in) anti-escort torpedo tubes were fitted aft. The first of the class was the **Leninskiy Komsomol**, also known as **K3**. Becoming

operational in July 1958, the *Leninskiy Komsomol* was the first Soviet submarine to reach the North Pole, in July 1962. However, it also suffered two major reactor accidents in the 1960s, accidents which would become typical of the class.

The 'Novembers', along with the related 'Echo' and 'Hotel' class missile boats, were a definite radiation hazard to their crews, because of design defects and poor shielding. It is known that several specialist hospitals were set up in the Soviet Union to treat the radiation casualties from these boats, and they acquired the nickname 'widow-makers' amongst Soviet submarine crews.

Four of the submarines were lost to reactor accidents, and there were numerous incidents of machinery breakdown whilst on operational patrol.

Most of the 'Novembers' served with the Northern Fleet, though four of the class were transferred to the Far East in the 1960s. The surviving vessels were decommissioned between 1988 and 1992.

All survivors, except K3, which was preserved as a memorial, remain to this day as radioactive hulks in Russian ports.

SPECIFICATION	
'November' class **Type:** Nuclear-powered attack submarine **Displacement:** 4,200 tons surfaced and 5,000 tons dived **Dimensions:** length 109.7 m (359 ft 11 in); beam 9.1 m (29 ft 10 in); draught 6.7 m (22 ft) **Machinery:** two liquid metal or pressurised water-cooled reactors powering two steam turbines driving two propellers **Speed:** 15 kts (28 km/h; 17 mph) surface; 30 kts (55 km/h; 34 mph) dived **Diving depth:** 214 m (790 ft) operational and 300 m (980 ft)	**Torpedo tubes:** eight 533-mm (21-in) in bow and two 406-mm (16-in) at stern **Basic load:** maximum of 20 533-mm (21-in) torpedoes; normally a mix of 14 533-mm (21-in) anti-ship or anti-submarine and six 533-mm (21-in) anti-ship 15-kiloton nuclear torpedoes, plus two 406-mm (16-in) anti-ship torpedoes **Electronics:** one RLK-101 search radar; one MG-100 Arktika active sonar, one MG-10 Feniks passive sonar, one MG-13 sonar intercept receiver, one Luch mine-detector sonar; VHF/UHF communications and one underwater telephone **Complement:** 24 officers, 86 men

Above: In April 1970, a 'November'-class boat got into difficulty south west of the British Isles. Crewmen are seen here escaping a fire in the reactor room. They were taken off by a Soviet support ship just before the submarine sank.

The 'November' class lacked the efficient 'teardrop' hull standard on later boats. However it was quite fast, and nuclear-tipped torpedoes gave it a big punch.

'Echo' class SSGN/SSN

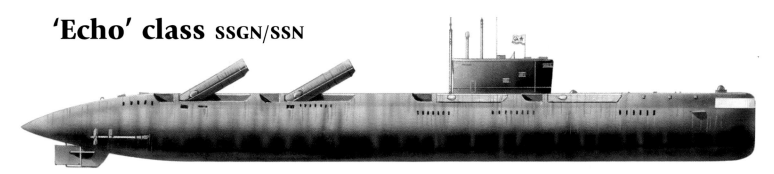

The five **'Echo'-class** SSNs were originally completed at Komsomolsk in the Soviet Far East in 1960-62 as **Project 659** or **'Echo I'-class** SSGNs. Armed with six launchers for the P-5 (SS-N-3c 'Shaddock-B') cruise missile, they had to operate in the strategic rather than ship-attack role as they lacked the fire-control and guidance radars of the later 'Echo II' class. As the

The forward part of the 'Echo II' sail structure rotated through 180 degrees to expose 'Front Piece' and 'Front Door' missile guidance radar antennae before firing. The holes and hull protuberances made the boats very noisy under water.

Soviet SSBN force was built up so the need for these boats diminished, and they were converted to **Project 659T** SSNs between 1969 and 1974. The conversion involved the removal of the 'Shaddock' launchers, the plating over and streamlining of the hull to reduce the underwater noise of the launchers, and modification of the sonar systems to the standard carried by the 'November' class SSNs. All were then deployed with the Pacific Fleet, although **K-45** was badly damaged by fire in 1979 off Okinawa and had to be towed back to its base near Vladivostok for emergency dry-docking. The last two boats were deleted in the early 1990s.

'Echo II' class

The follow-on **Project 675** or **'Echo II' class** was built at Severodvinsk (18 vessels) and Komsomolsk (11 vessels) between 1962 and 1967 as the Soviet Navy's primary anti-carrier missile submarines. They carried eight P-6 (SS-N-3a 'Shaddock-A')

anti-ship cruise missiles mounted in pairs above the pressure hull, and before firing had to surface and elevate the pairs to about 25-30°. The forward section of the sail structure then rotated through 180° to expose the two 'Front' series missile-guidance radars. The paired firing of all eight missiles took some 30 minutes, the submarine then having to remain on the surface until the missile mid-course correction and final target-selection commands had been sent, unless guidance had been passed to a third party such as a Tupolev Tu-95RTs 'Bear-D' fitted with the appropriate system.

From the mid-1970s 14 of the 'Echo II'-class boats were converted during overhauls to carry the more capable Bazalt (SS-N-12 'Sandbox') anti-ship cruise missile. The conversions could be distinguished by the fitting of bulges to each side of the sail and at the forward end of the missile tubes abreast the bridge.

The 'Echo II' boats were divided evenly between the Pacific and Northern Fleets. The boats were obsolete by the mid-1980s, and were deleted in 1989-94.

Left: Some 29 units of the 'Echo II' SSGN entered service with the Soviet navy with the primary armament of SS-N-12 'Sandbox' or SS-N-3a 'Shaddock-A' missiles. The boats' primary failing was that they had to surface to fire and guide their missiles.

SPECIFICATION	
'Echo I' class	tubes (bow) and four 406-mm (16-in)
Displacement: 4,500 tons surfaced; 5,500 tons dived	tubes (stern) for 20 533-mm torpedoes (16 anti-ship or anti-submarine HE and four anti-ship 15-kT nuclear) and two 406-mm anti-ship torpedoes
Dimensions: length 110 m (360 ft 11 in); beam 9.1 m (29 ft 10 in); draught 7.5 m (24 ft 7 in)	
Propulsion: one pressurised water-cooled reactor powering two steam turbines delivering 18640 kW (25,000 shp) to two shafts	**Missiles:** six P-5 (SS-N-3c 'Shaddock-B') with 1000-kg (2,205-lb) HE or 350-kT nuclear warheads
Performance: speed 20 kts surfaced and 28 kts dived	**Electronics:** one 'Snoop Tray' surface search radar, one Hercules sonar, one Feniks sonar, one 'Stop Light' ESM system and one underwater telephone
Diving depth: 300 m (985 ft) operational and 500 m (1,640 ft) maximum	
Torpedo tubes: six 533-mm (21-in)	**Complement:** 75

SPECIFICATION	
'Echo II' class	except only two 406-mm (16-in) stern tubes
Displacement: 5,000 tons surfaced; 6,000 tons dived	**Missiles:** eight P-6 (SS-N-3a 'Shaddock-A'), four with 1000-kg (2,205-lb) HE and four with 350-kT nuclear warheads or, in 14 converted boats, eight Bazalt (SS-N-12 'Sandbox'), same mix as SS-N-3a
Dimensions: length 115 m (377 ft 4 in); beam 9 m (29 ft 6 in); draught 7.5 m (24 ft 7 in)	
Propulsion: one pressurised water-cooled reactor powering two steam turbines delivering 17900 kW (24,010 shp) to two shafts	**Electronics:** 'Snoop Tray' surface search radar, 'Front Door/Front Piece' missile-guidance radars, 'Stop Light' ECM, and Arktika-M, Feniks-M and Herkules sonars
Performance: speed 20 kts surfaced and 25 kts dived	
Diving depth: as for 'Echo' class	
Torpedo tubes: as for 'Echo' class	**Complement:** 90

'Charlie' class SSGN

Above: A 'Charlie I'-class SSGN of the sub-class armed with the SS-N-7 J-band active radar homing anti-ship missile in two banks of four tubes, angled upward on each side of the bow external to the pressure hull.

The first **Project 670 Skat** or 'Charlie I'-class SSGN was launched at the inland shipyard at Gorky in 1967. Over the next five years a further 10 were completed there, with two banks of four missile tubes angled upward on each side of the bow outside the pressure hull. The tubes had large outer doors and were designed to carry the P-120 Malakhit (SS-N-9 'Siren') medium-range anti-ship missile, but delays in the development of this underwater-launched weapon meant that the boats were completed for the short-range P-70 Ametist (SS-N-7 'Starbright') submerged-launch anti-ship missile, a development of the P-15 Termit (SS-N-2 'Styx') surface-launched missile, for pop-up surprise attack on high-value surface targets such as a carrier.

Malakhit missiles

In 1972-79 six units of the improved **Project 670M Skat-M**

or **'Charlie II' class** design were built at Gorkiy with an 8-m (26-ft 3-in) insertion in the hull forward of the fin for the electronics and the launch systems necessary for targeting and firing the longer-range P-120 Malakhit anti-ship missile.

The 'Charlie' classes were conceived for production on a mass-production basis, and it was this that probably prompted the finalisation of the design with a single reactor and five-blade main propeller (supplemented by a pair of two-blade propellers for quiet running) instead of the arrangement of two reactors and two propellers that was preferred by the Soviet navy. One consequence of this cost-cutting measure was that the 'Charlie' boats lacked the speed to operate effectively with high-speed surface battle groups.

It was once thought that there was a 'Charlie III' class to fire a variant of the P-80 Zubr (SS-N-22

'Sunburn') anti-ship missile, but this was not the case. In both the 'Charlie I' and 'Charlie II' classes, once the missiles have been fired the boat had to be reloaded back at port, although the secondary torpedo armament and sonar systems

provided a useful anti-ship and ASW capability. The last boats were retired in 1994. India leased one 'Charlie I' as the **Chakra** between 1988-91, mainly to gain experience in the operation of nuclear-powered submarines.

A total of 17 'Charlie'-class SSGNs were completed in two subclasses between 1967 and about 1981 at the Gorky shipyard. Primarily used for surprise 'pop-up' missile attacks on high-value surface targets such as carriers, the 'Charlies' also had a secondary ASW capability.

'Papa' and 'Oscar' class SSGNs

In 1970 the Soviet shipyard at Severodvinsk launched a single **Project 661 Anchar** unit that became known in NATO circles as the **'Papa' class**. This boat was considerably larger and carried two more missile tubes (for the P-120 Mlakhit/SS-N-9 'Siren' anti-ship missile) than the contemporary 'Charlie'-class SSGNs, and it was for many years a puzzle to Western intelligence services.

The answer appeared in 1980 at the same shipyard, however, with the launch of the even larger **Project 949 Granit** or **'Oscar I' class** SSGN. The 'Papa'-class unit had been con-

ceived from 1958 as the cruise missile-launching predecessor to the titanium-hulled 'Alfa' class high-speed/deep-diving SSN. But because its high underwater noise levels contra-indicated series production, it had then become the prototype for advanced SSGN concepts with a considerably changed power-plant and revised propeller arrangement.

The missile system had been created to test the underwater-launched version of the P-120 for the subsequent 'Charlie II' series of SSGN. The 'Oscar' design introduced more improvements, and these included two 12-round

banks of underwater-launched P-700 Granit (SS-N-19 'Shipwreck') long-range supersonic anti-ship missile tubes outside the main pressure hull on each side of the fin. In common with other Soviet submarines, the 'Oscars' feature a double hull, comprising an inner pressure hull and an outer hydrodynamic hull. The two 'Oscar I' boats paved the way for 11 of a planned 12 **Project 949A Antei** or **'Oscar II'-class** SSGNs with a hull lengthened by some 10 m (32 ft 10 in) and an enlarged fin. Four serve with the Northern and two with the Pacific Fleets with the designation PLARK (*Podvonaya Lodka*

Above: The 'Oscar'-class SSGNs are among the largest submarines in the world, and offer very considerable capabilities at several levels. Kursk, the tenth unit of the 'Oscar II' class, was lost with all hands after an internal weapons explosion in August 2000.

Atomnaya Raketnaya Krylataya, nuclear-powered cruise missile submarine). The two 'Oscar I' boats are laid up, whilst the remaining four 'Oscar IIs' are awaiting disposal. As with preceding classes, the 'Oscars' were primarily intended to attack US aircraft carrier battle groups.

SPECIFICATION
'Papa' class

'Papa' class
Displacement: 5,200 tons surfaced; 7,000 tons dived
Dimensions: length 106.9 m (350 ft 9 in); beam 11.5 m (37 ft 9 in); draught 8 m (26 ft 3 in)
Propulsion: one pressurised water-cooled reactor powering two steam turbines delivering 59650 kW (80,005 shp) to two shafts
Performance: speed 20 kts surfaced and 42 kts dived
Diving depth: 400 m (1,315 ft) operational and 600 m (1,970 ft) maximum
Torpedo tubes: six 533-mm (21-in), tubes (all bow) for a maximum of 12 torpedoes, but normally a mix of eight anti-ship or anti-submarine HE, two anti-ship 15-kT

nuclear torpedoes and two Tsakra (SS-N-15 'Starfish') 15-kT anti-submarine missiles, or a total of 24 AMD-1000 ground mines
Missiles: 10 P-120 Malakhit (SS-N-9 'Siren'), six with 500-kg (1,102-lb HE) and four with 200-kT nuclear warheads
Electronics: one 'Snoop Tray' surface search radar, one Rubin low-frequency bow sonar, one medium-frequency torpedo and missile fire-control sonar, one 'Brick Spit' and one 'Brick Pulp' passive intercept and threat-warning ESM system, VHF/UHF communications, one 'Park Lamp' direction-finding antenna, and one underwater telephone
Complement: 82

SPECIFICATION
'Oscar II' class

'Oscar II' class
Displacement: 13,900 tons surfaced; 18,300 tons dived
Dimensions: length 154 m (505 ft 3 in); beam 18.2 m (59 ft 9 in); draught 9 m (29 ft 6)
Propulsion: two pressurised water-cooled reactors powering two steam turbines delivering 73070 kW (98,000 shp) to two shafts
Performance: speed 15 kts surfaced and 28 kts dived
Diving depth: 500 m (1,640 ft) operational and 830 m (2,725 ft) maximum
Torpedo tubes: four 533-mm (21-in) and two 650-mm (25.6-in) tubes (all bow) for a maximum of 28 533- and 650-mm weapons including Tsakra (SS-N-15 'Starfish') anti-submarine

missiles with 15-kT nuclear warheads and Vodopad/Veder (SS-N-16 'Stallion') anti-submarine missiles with a 200-kT nuclear warhead or Type 40 anti-submarine torpedo, or 32 ground mines
Missiles: 24 P-700 Granit (SS-N-19 'Shipwreck'), with 750-kg (1,655-lb) HE or 500-kT nuclear warheads
Electronics: one 'Snoop Pair' or 'Snoop Half' surface search radar, one 'Punch Bowl' third-party targeting radar, one 'Shark Gill' active/passive hull-mounted search and attack sonar, one 'Shark Rib' passive flank-array sonar, one 'Mouse Roar' active attack hull sonar, one Pelamida passive towed-array sonar, and one 'Rim Hat' ESM system
Complement: 107

'Victor I', 'Victor II' and 'Victor III' class SSNs
Nuclear attack submarines

The **'Victor I' class** was designated by the Soviets as a PLA (podvodaya lodka atomnaya, or nuclear-powered submarine), and together with the contemporary 'Charlie I' SSGN and 'Yankee' SSBN classes formed the second generation of Soviet nuclear submarines. The **Project 671** boats, known to the Soviets as the **'Yersey' class**, were the first Soviet submarines built to the teardrop hull design for high underwater speeds. **K 38**, the first 'Victor,' was completed in 1967 at the Admiralty Shipyard, Leningrad, where the last of 16 units was completed in 1974. The 'Victor Is' were the fastest pressurised-water reactor-powered SSNs afloat, even with the advent of the American 'Los Angeles' class. The enriched uranium-fuelled reactor was of the same type as installed in both the 'Charlie' and 'Yankee' class vessels.

In 1972, the first of the improved **'Victor II' class** was built at the Gorky shipyard, being produced in alternate years to the 'Charlie II' design

there. Four were built there, whilst another three were constructed at the Admiralty Shipyard in 1975

Initially called the **'Uniform' class** by NATO, the 'Victor II' class is marked by a 6.1-m (20-ft) extension inserted into the hull forward of the sail. This was to make room for the new generation of 65-cm (25-in) heavy torpedoes together with the power equipment to handle them.

Silent Victors

In 1976 the first of the **'Victor III'** units was launched at the Admiralty Shipyard. In 1978 the

Above: A Soviet 'Victor I' class SSN in the Malacca Straits during 1974. The personnel seen on the sail structure are sunbathing, a favourite pastime of Soviet sailors in warm climate regions.

Komsomolsk yard joined the production team, building two boats per year after the end of 'Delta I' class production. A total of 26 'Victor III' class boats were built

between 1978 and 1992. Given the Soviet designation of **Schuka**, the 'Victor IIIs' are unofficially known to the US Navy as the 'Walker' class, since many of

SPECIFICATION

'Victor III' class
Displacement: 5,000 tons surfaced and 7,000 tons dived
Dimensions: length 107.2 m (351 ft 6 in); beam 10.8 m (35 ft 4 in); draught 7.4 m (24 ft 2 in)
Machinery: as for 'Victor I' class
Speed: 18 kts surfaced and 30 kts dived
Diving depth: as for 'Victor I' class

Torpedo tubes: as for 'Victor II' class
Basic load: as for 'Victor II' class
Missiles: as for 'Viktor II' plus two Granat (SS-N-21 'Sampson') cruise missiles or two Vodopei (SS-N-16 'Stallion') rocket torpedoes
Electronics: as for 'Victor II' class plus one Pithon towed sonar
Complement: 115

SPECIFICATION

'Victor I' class
Displacement: 4,100 tons surfaced and 6,085 tons dived
Dimensions: length 92.5 m (303 ft 5 in); beam 11.7 m (38 ft 5 in); draught 7.3 m (23 ft 11 in)
Machinery: two VM-4T PW reactors powering one OK-300 steam turbine delivering 22.7 MW 31,000 shp one five-blade propeller. Two two-blade 'creep' props also fitted
Speed: 12 kts surfaced and 32 kts dived
Diving depth: 320 m (1,050 ft) operational and 396 m (1,300 ft) maximum
Torpedo tubes: six 533-mm (21-in), two with 406-mm (16-in) liners, all bow
Basic load: maximum of 18 533-mm (21-in) torpedoes, but

normally a mixture of eight 533-mm (21-in) anti-ship or anti-submarine, 10 406-mm (16-in) anti-submarine and two 533-mm (21-in) anti-ship 15-kiloton nuclear torpedoes, or a total of 36 AMD-1000 ground mines
Missiles: two Tsakra (SS-N-15 'Starfish') nuclear anti-submarine 15-kiloton missiles
Electronics: one MRK-50 Topol surface-search radar, one low-frequency MGK-300 Rubin active/passive bow sonar, one MG-24 Luch mine-detection sonar, one Zhaliv-P passive intercept and threat-warning ESM system, one MG-14 sonar intercept receiver, VHF/UHF communications, and one MG-29 Khost underwater telephone
Complement: 100

A Soviet 'Victor III' class vessel. The pod on the top of the upper rudder is for a towed sonar array, which was the first such installation on a Soviet submarine. To match the sonar's long range, the class can carry both SS-N-15 and SS-N-16 ASW missiles.

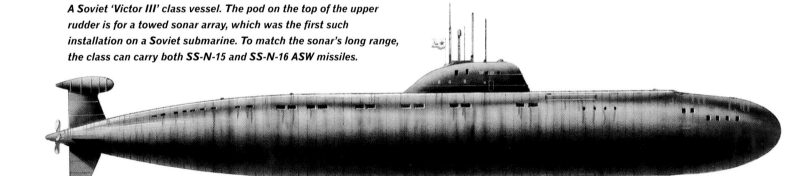

Left: A windfall for Western naval intelligence, this Soviet 'Victor III' class SSN got into difficulties off the North Carolina coast in November 1983. The vessel had to be towed to Cuba for repairs after becoming the most photographed submarine in the Soviet navy.

the improvements in quieting the boats and in providing them with more effective sensors were the product of the activities of the Walker spy ring during the 1970s and 1980s.

The 'Victor III's have a 3-m (9-ft 10-in) hull extension forward of the fin and a pod mounted atop the upper rudder which deployed a brand new towed sonar array. The extension provided the extra volume for the additional electronic equipment required to process the data from the towed array and two new flank arrays.

'Clusterguard' anechoic coatings helped to decrease radiated noise levels as the design was improved, the 'Victor III' class being described officially in US Navy circles as the equivalent to the USS 'Sturgeon' class SSN in quietness. They also have bow hydroplanes that retract into the hull at high underwater speeds or when a boat is on the surface. Like all boats after the 'Hotel' SSBN, 'Echo' SSGN and 'November' SSN classes, the 'Victor' class submarines had two of their 533-mm (21-in)

SPECIFICATION	
'Victor II' class	**Basic load:** as for 'Victor I' class plus six 650-mm weapons
Displacement: 4,700 tons surfaced and 7,190 tons dived	**Missiles:** as for 'Victor I' class
Dimensions: length 101.8 m (334 ft); beam 10.8 m (35 ft 4 in); draught 7.3 m (23 ft 11 in)	**Electronics:** one low-frequency MGK-400 Rubikon active/passive bow sonar; rest as for 'Victor I' class plus one Paravan towed VLF communications buoy and one floating ELF communications antenna for Molniya-671 communication system
Machinery: as for 'Victor I' class	
Speed: 12 kts surfaced and 31.7 kts dived	
Diving depth: as for 'Victor I' class	
Torpedo tubes: as for 'Victor I' plus two 650-mm (25.6-in) bow	**Complement:** 110

tubes fitted with 406-mm (16-in) ASW torpedo liners for self-defence use. Two of these weapons are carried in the place of every 533-mm (21-in)

reload offloaded. Surviving Victor I and II boats had been decommissioned by 1996, together with about a dozen of the first Victor IIIs.

'Akula' class Nuclear-powered attack submarine

Above: The 'Akula' class of nuclear-powered attack submarines was designed to provide the Soviet navy with much enhanced attack submarine capability. Officially designated Shuka-B (pike) by the Russians, it is commonly known in service as the Bars (snow leopard).

The steel-hulled submarines of the **Project 971 Shuka-B** or **'Akula' class** were easier and cheaper to build than the

'Sierras', and are essentially successors to the prolific 'Victor' class. Today, they make up about half of Russia's dwindling

SPECIFICATION

'Akula' class (Project 971)
Displacement: 7,500 tons surfaced and 9,100 tons submerged
Dimensions: length 111.7 m (366 ft 5 ½ in); beam 13.5 m (44 ft 3½ in); draught 9.6 m (31 ft 6 in)
Propulsion: one OK-650B pressurised water reactor powering a steam turbine delivering 32060 kW (43,000 shp) to one shaft
Speed: 20 kts surfaced and 35 kts submerged
Diving depth: 450 m (1,475 ft) maximum
Torpedo tubes: four 650-mm (25.6-in) and four 533-mm (21-in) tubes
Armament: 3M10 (SS-N-21 'Sampson') SLCMs, RPK-6/7 (SS-N-16 'Stallion') rocket-delivered nuclear depth charges/torpedoes,

VA-111 Shkval underwater rockets, 533-mm SET-72, TEST-71M and USET-80 torpedoes, 650-mm Type 65-76 torpedoes, or 42 mines
Electronics: (Russian designations) Chiblis surface search radar, Medvyedista-945 navigation system, Molniya-M satcom; Tsunami, Kiparis, Anis, Sintez and Kora communications, Paravan towed VLF receiver, Vspletsk combat direction system, MGK-503 Skat-3 active/passive sonar, Akula flank-array sonar, Pelamida towed-array sonar, MG-70 mine-detection sonar, Bukhta integrated ESM/ECM system, two MG-74 Korund decoys, MT-70 sonar intercept receiver, and Nikhrom-M IFF
Complement: 62 (25 officers and 26 enlisted)

fleet of nuclear-powered attack submarines. The first seven boats (designated in the West as the **'Akula I' class**) were constructed between 1982-90, and are the **Puma**, **Del'fin**, **Kashalot**, **Bars**, **Kit**, **Pantera** and **Narval**. Five more (the **Volk**, **Morzh**, **Leopard**, **Tigr** and **Drakon** built between 1986-95) are classified as the **Project 971U** or **'Improved Akula' class**, while a 13th boat, the **Vepr** of the **Project 971M** or

'Akula II' class, was launched in 1995 but is still incomplete at the end of 2002. Three additional boats, the **Belgograd**, **Kuguar** and **Nerpa** launched between 1998-2000 as 'Akula II' boats, are also incomplete. At least two more were projected but were not built.

Evolutionary design

The design was approved in the early 1970s but modified in 1978-80 to carry the Granat (SS-N-21 'Sampson') land attack cruise missile. The 'Akula' marked a significant improvement in Soviet submarine design as it is far quieter than the 'Victor' and earlier SSNs. The use of commercially available Western technology to reduce noise levels played an important role in this, eroding a long-held NATO advantage in the underwater Cold War. Sensors were also much

improved, the use of digital technology enabling them to detect targets at three times the range possible in a 'Victor'.

The 'Akulas' sport a massive tear-drop shaped pod on the after fin: this houses the Skat-3 VLF passive towed array. There is an escape pod built into the fin. The 'Improved Akula' and 'Akula II' boats are fitted with six additional 533-mm (21-in) external torpedo tubes: as these cannot be reloaded from within the pressure hull, it is considered likely they are fitted with the Tsakra (SS-N-15 'Starfish') anti-submarine missile. Additionally, the 'Akula II' boats are credited with an increased operational diving depth.

Four 'Akula I' boats were paid off in the late 1990s and are unlikely to return, and the surviving boats are divided between the Northern and Pacific Fleets.

Left: A notable feature of the 'Akula' class design is its highly streamlined shaping, a fact that reduces underwater noise and enhances speed.

Below: The large fairing atop the upper fin of the 'Akula' class submarine carries the sensor array and cable for the Skat-3 'Shark Gill' active/passive towed sonar system.

'Valiant' and 'Churchill' classes
Nuclear-powered attack submarines

Essentially an enlarged 'Dreadnought' design with all-British reactor plant and systems, **HMS** *Valiant* was ordered in August 1960 as the lead boat of the **'Valiant' class** and completed in July 1966, a year later than planned because of the priority accorded to the British Polaris programme. A sister ship, **HMS** *Warspite*, was followed by three others built to a modified and quieter-running **'Churchill' class** design as **HMS** *Churchill*, **HMS** *Conqueror* and **HMS** *Courageous*.

All of the submarines were fitted with the Type 2001 long-range active/passive LF sonar mounted in the optimum 'chin' position, although from the late 1970s the five submarines were retrofitted with the Type 2020 set as a replacement during overhauls. The five boats were also retrofitted with the clip-on Type 2026 towed-array LF sonar. Other sonars identified with the submarines were the Type 2007 long-range passive set and the joint Anglo-Dutch-French Type 2019 PARIS (Passive/Active Range and Intercept Sonar). A Type 197 passive ranging sonar for detecting sonar transmissions was also carried. When completed, the submarines each carried a

Right: Essentially an enlarged version of the 'Dreadnought' class design, HMS Valiant was built at the same time as the Polaris boats with an all-British reactor plant and associated control systems.

main armament of Mk 8 anti-ship torpedoes dating from the period before World War II, the 1950s technology wire-guided Mk 23 ASW torpedo, and World War II Mk 5 ground and Mk 6 moored mines. The armament was later modernised to include, in addition to the Mk 8 anti-ship torpedo, the Mk 24 Tigerfish wire-guided dual-role torpedo, the Sub-Harpoon anti-ship missile, and the new Stonefish and Sea Urchin ground mines. It was the *Churchill* that tested the Sub-Harpoon for the Royal Navy. During the 1982 Falklands War the *Conqueror*, *Courageous* and *Valiant* were deployed to the Maritime Exclusion Zone, the first sinking the Argentine cruiser *General Belgrano* on 2 May 1982. All five submarines

Remaining in service until the mid-1990s, the five 'Valiant'- and 'Churchill'-class vessels were committed to modernisation refits as they came in for overhauls during the 1980s.

were gradually switched to the anti-surface ship role as quieter boats entered anti-submarine service. The *Valiant*, *Warspite*, *Churchill*, *Conqueror* and *Courageous* were decommissioned in 1997, 1993, 1990, 1990 and 1992 respectively.

SPECIFICATION	
'Valiant' and 'Churchill' classes	**Basic load:** 32 Mk 8 and Mk 24
Displacement: 4,400 tons surfaced and 4,900 tons submerged	Tigerfish torpedoes or 64 Mk 5 and Mk 6 mines, later changed to 26
Dimensions: length 86.9 m (285 ft); beam 10.1 m (33 ft 3 in); draught 8.2 m (27 ft)	torpedoes and six UGM-84B Sub-Harpoon anti-ship missiles, or Stonefish and Sea Urchin mines
Propulsion: one Rolls-Royce pressurised water-cooled reactor powering two steam turbines driving one shaft	**Missiles:** see above
	Electronics: one Type 1006 surface search radar, one Type 2001 sonar,
Speed: 20 kts surfaced and 29 kts dived	one Type 2026 towed sonar, one Type 2007 sonar, one Type 2019
Diving depth: 300 m (985 ft) operational and 500 m (1,640 ft) maximum	sonar, one Type 197 sonar, one direction-finding antenna, one ESM system, one DCB torpedo fire-control system, and one
Torpedo tubes: six 21-in (533-mm) bow	underwater telephone
	Complement: 103

'Swiftsure' class
Nuclear-powered attack submarine

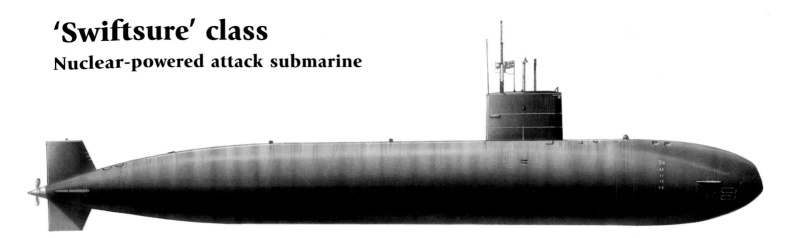

In 1971 the first of the UK's **'Swiftsure' class** of second-generation SSNs was launched at the Vickers shipyard at Barrow-in-Furness. This **HMS Swiftsure** introduced a hull form shorter and fuller than that of the 'Valiant' class in order to provide greater volume and create a stronger pressure hull for operation at greater depths and speeds than the previous class. The fin is smaller and the retractable diving planes are located below the water line. The *Swiftsure* was followed by

Quieter than their predecessors, the 'Swiftsure'-class submarines proved to be excellent anti-submarine platforms, especially after the original sonar equipment had been upgraded and the Mk 24 Tigerfish heavyweight torpedo added to the armament. Refits have also added upgraded tactical weapons systems, Spearfish torpedoes, improved decoys, and Tomahawk missiles. Spartan can be fitted with a dry deck hangar.

five sister ships, **HMS Sovereign**, **HMS Superb**, **HMS Sceptre**, **HMS Spartan** and **HMS Splendid**. The submarines are currently used both in the ASW screening role for task forces, and in the independent anti-ship and ASW roles because of the quieter machinery used. Their sonar fit is basically the same as that of the 'Valiant' class, and all had the Type 2020 fitted as the Type 2001 replacement during normal refits. The armament is reduced by one tube and seven torpedoes, but this reduction is balanced by the fact that it takes only 15 seconds to reload individual tubes. Emergency power is provided by the same 112-cell electric battery and associated diesel generator

and electric motor as fitted in the 'Valiant' and 'Churchill' classes.

In 1976 the *Sovereign* demonstrated the Royal Navy's ability to conduct ASW operations under the ice pack when it undertook a trip to the North Pole, the operational aspects being combined with a successful scientific voyage.

The *Spartan* and *Splendid* were both involved in the Falklands War. At the end of 2002 four of the submarines were still in service with the Royal Navy, the *Swiftsure* having been decommissioned in 1992 after cracks were found in its reactor during a refit. Since 1998 two boats have been armed with Tomahawk cruise missiles.

SPECIFICATION

'Swiftsure' class
Displacement: 4,200 tons surfaced and 4,900 tons submerged
Dimensions: length 82.9 m (272 ft); beam 9.8 m (32 ft 4 in); draught 8.2 m (27 ft)
Propulsion: one pressurised water-cooled reactor powering two steam turbines driving one shaft
Speed: 20 kts surfaced and 30 kts submerged
Diving depth: 400 m (1,315 ft) operational and 600 m (1,970 ft) maximum
Torpedo tubes: five 21-in (533-mm) bow

Basic load: 20 Mk 8 or Mk 24 Tigerfish torpedoes plus five UGM-84B Sub-Harpoon AShMs, or 50 Stonefish and Sea Urchin mines; Tomahawk Block III SLCM since 1998 (*Spartan* and *Splendid* only)
Missiles: see above
Electronics: one Type 1006 surface search radar, one Type 2001 sonar, one Type 2026 towed sonar, one Type 2007 sonar, one Type 2019 sonar, one Type 197 sonar, one ESM system, one DCB torpedo and missile fire-control system, and one underwater telephone
Complement: 97

'Trafalgar' class Nuclear-powered attack submarine

Essentially an improved 'Swiftsure'-class design, the **'Trafalgar' class** constitutes the third generation of British SSNs built at the Vickers shipyard in Barrow-in-Furness. The lead boat, **HMS Trafalgar**, was launched in 1981 and commissioned into the Royal Navy in March 1983, serving with the 'Swiftsure'-class boats at the Devonport naval base. The class total of seven boats also includes **HMS Talent**, **HMS Tireless**, **HMS Torbay**, **HMS Trenchant**, **HMS Triumph** and **HMS Turbulent**.

The major improvements over the 'Swiftsure' class include several features to reduce the underwater radiated noise. These comprise a new reactor system, a pumpjet propulsion system rather than a conventional propeller, and the covering of the pressure hull and outer surfaces with anechoic tiles to give the same type of protection as afforded by the Soviet 'Clusterguard' coating in reducing noise. The *Trafalgar* was the first boat to be fitted with the Type 2020 sonar, and was used as the development test platform for the system. According to other reports there has also been a rearrangement of the internal compartments to allow a rationalisation and centralisation of the operations, sound and ESM/radar rooms. The remaining systems, the armament and the sonars are the same as fitted to the 'Swiftsure'-class boats, although a thermal imaging periscope is now carried as part of the search

Right: Similar in many respects to the 'Swiftsure' class, HMS Trafalgar was the first Royal Navy submarine to be covered with anechoic tiles reducing underwater radiated noise.

Above: With the aircraft carrier HMS Illustrious in the background, HMS Trafalgar enters Devonport naval base to tie up at the 2nd Submarine Squadron berth.

and attack periscope fit, and Type 197 sonar is no longer carried. The fin, like those of the earlier British SSNs, houses an SHF DF antenna, communications antennae, and snort induction, radar and ESM masts. Underwater communications are believed to be conducted via a towed buoy and/or a floating antenna.

The primary mission of the 'Trafalgar'-class submarines, all of which remain in service with the Royal Navy, is anti-submarine warfare, with anti-surface ship warfare as a secondary role. The boats can launch the Tomahawk Block IIIC cruise missile.

SPECIFICATION	
'Trafalgar' class	**Torpedo tubes:** five 21-in (533-mm) bow
Displacement: 4,800 tons surfaced and 5,300 tons submerged	**Basic load:** 20 Spearfish and Mk 24 Tigerfish torpedoes and five UGM-84B Sub-Harpoon anti-ship missiles, or 50 Stonefish and Sea Urchin mines; Tomahawk SLCM carried from 1999
Dimensions: length 85.4 m (280 ft 3 in); beam 9.8 m (32 ft 4 in); draught 8.2 m (27 ft)	
Propulsion: one Rolls-Royce pressurised water-cooled reactor powering two steam turbines driving one shaft with pumpjet propulsion	**Missiles:** see above
	Electronics: one Type 1007 surface search radar, one Type 2020 sonar, one Type 2026 towed sonar, one Type 2007 sonar, one Type 2019 sonar, one ESM system, and one DCB torpedo and missile fire-control system
Speed: 20 kts surfaced and 29 kts submerged	
Diving depth: 400 m (1,315 ft) operational and 600 m (1,970 ft) maximum	**Complement:** 97

USS *Nautilus*, USS *Seawolf* and 'Skate' class Early SSNs

Left: Seen on initial sea trials, USS Nautilus was the world's first nuclear-powered warship. The S2W reactor delivered 11185 kW (15,000 shp) for a submerged speed of 25 kts. Six bow torpedo tubes were fitted.

The **USS *Nautilus*** was the world's first nuclear-powered submarine. Launched in January 1954, the boat was commissioned only eight months later. In January 1955, *Nautilus* cast off and made the historic signal 'Under way on nuclear power'. Establishing a succession of speed and endurance records, the boat made the first underwater passage to the North Pole in August 1958, travelling 2945 km (1,830 miles) beneath the ice and establishing the Pole as a new region of strategic importance. Overhauled in 1959, *Nautilus* was assigned to the US 6th Fleet in the Mediterranean, steaming 321850 km (200,000 miles) during the next six years. *Nautilus* continued to serve alongside subsequent classes of SSN until being decommissioned in 1980.

Launched in 1955 and commissioned two years later, the second nuclear-powered submarine, the **USS *Seawolf*** was generally similar to the *Nautilus* in terms of overall design, but was fitted with a liquid sodium reactor but this did not prove satisfactory,

steam leaks occurring shortly after it first went critical in 1956. It was replaced by a pressurised water-cooled reactor during an overhaul of 1958-60. With the 6th Fleet in the early 1960s, *Seawolf* formed part of the first all-nuclear task force, a carrier group built around the CVN USS *Enterprise* and two nuclear-powered cruisers. The boat was transferred to the Atlantic Fleet and then to the Pacific Fleet in 1970. The *Seawolf* was decommissioned in 1987.

'Skate' class

These two 'one-off' designs were followed by the **'Skate' class** of four SSNs (**USS *Skate*, USS *Swordfish*, USS *Sargo*** and **USS *Seadragon***) launched in 1957-58 and commissioned in 1957-59. These were the first series production SSNs for the US Navy, and utilised certain technologies tested by the *Nautilus* and *Seawolf*. Three of them took part in further exploration missions to the Arctic. The *Skate* sailed for the Pole in March 1959, testing the practicality of operations there during the winter when the

ice is at its thickest. The boat travelled nearly 6440 km (4,000 miles) under the ice, surfacing through it 10 times. The *Sargo* made another voyage to these frigid waters 12 months later, carrying new scientific instruments for a sustained exploration of the Arctic basin. *Sargo* covered 17700 km (11,000 miles), 9661 km (6,003 miles) of them below the ice, and gathered vital information for subsequent operations, including

the discovery of very deep water at the western end of the northwest passage. In July 1962 the *Skate* returned to the Pole for a rendezvous with *Seadragon*: the two boats operated in company under the ice and surfaced together at the Pole on 2 August. The 'Skate' class was decommissioned in 1984-89 and all were scrapped in 1995.

Right: A stern view of the USS Sargo, the third of four 'Skate'-class SSNs. The first six US Navy SSNs all retained the long, thin hull and twin propellers of the German Type XII of World War II.

Below: The USS Seawolf was the prototype used for evaluation of the S2G reactor cooled by liquid sodium. The installation was unsuccessful and replaced by an S2Wa pressurised water-cooled reactor (PWR) powering two steam turbines.

SPECIFICATION	
'Skate' class **Ships in class (launched):** *Skate* (1957), *Swordfish* (1957), *Sargo* (1957) and *Seadragon* (1958) **Displacement:** 2,550 tons surfaced; 2,848 tons dived **Dimensions:** length 102.72 m (337 ft); beam 8.23 m (27 ft); draught 8.53 m (28 ft) **Propulsion:** one S5W pressurised water-cooled reactor powering one	turbine delivering 11185 kW (15,000 shp) to two shafts **Speed:** 15.5 kts surfaced; 18 kts dived **Diving depth:** 244 m (800 ft) **Torpedo tubes:** six 21-in (533-mm) Mk 59 torpedo tubes (six forward, two aft) **Electronics:** one Mk 88 missile and torpedo fire-control system, one WLR-1 countermeasures system **Complement:** 101 (normal)

'Skipjack' class SSN

Although built in the late 1950s, the five-strong **'Skipjack' class** of SSNs had a long operational career and, until the advent of the 'Los Angeles' class, were the fastest submarines available to the US Navy. A sixth boat, the **USS Scorpion**, whose original hull was used in the construction of the first American SSBN, the USS *George Washington*, was lost in May 1968 south-west of the Azores while en route from the Mediterranean to Norfolk, Virginia, with all 99 men aboard. The class was notable for being the first to use the S5W reactor design, which was subsequently used in all US nuclear submarine classes up to the 'Glenard P. Lipscomb' class. The 'Skipjack' class also introduced the classic teardrop hull shape, and as such acted as the model for the British 'Dreadnought' and 'Valiant'/'Churchill' classes, the long rearward taper of the hull forcing the designers to dispense with stern torpedo tubes and adopt a single-shaft propulsion arrangement. The diving planes were also relocated to the fin to increase underwater manoeuvrability, a feature which the British did not copy. All the engine room fittings except the reactor and steam turbines were duplicated to minimise total breakdown possibilities. In the later parts of their careers, four boats (**USS Skipjack**, **USS Scamp**, **USS Sculpin** and **USS Shark**) served in the Atlantic Fleet and one (**USS Snook**) in

Above: The USS Shark is seen at its maximum surfaced speed of 18 kts. With an underwater speed of 30 kts, the 'Skipjack'-class submarines were long considered to be effective front-line boats.

the Pacific Fleet. By the mid-1980s, age was catching up with the boats, however, and after the *Snook* had been decommissioned in 1986 following severe damage in a rescue operation, the other boats were decommissioned in 1990-91.

SPECIFICATION	
'Skipjack' class **Ships in class (launched):** *Skate* (1958), *Scamp* (1960), *Scorpion* (1959), *Sculpin* (1960), *Shark* (1960) and *Snook* (1960) **Displacement:** 3,075 tons surfaced; 3,515 tons dived **Dimensions:** length 76.7 m (251 ft 9 in); beam 9.6 m (31 ft 6 in); draught 8.5 m (27 ft 10 in) **Propulsion:** one Westinghouse S5W pressurised water-cooled reactor powering two steam turbines delivering 11185 kW (15,000 shp) to one shaft	**Speed:** 18 kts surfaced; 30 kts dived **Diving depth:** 300 m (985 ft) operational and 500 m (1,640 ft) maximum **Torpedo tubes:** six 21-in (533-mm) tubes (all bow) for 24 Mk 48 dual-purpose torpedoes or 48 Mk 57 moored mines **Electronics:** one surface search radar, one modified BQS-4 sonar suite, one Mk 101 torpedo fire-control system, and one underwater telephone **Complement:** 114

Compared with subsequent US nuclear-powered attack submarines, the boats of the 'Skipjack' class were limited in their armament and sonar, having only Mk 48 torpedoes and a modified BQS-4 sonar system. No ASROC ASW missiles or towed sonar array were carried as the expense of retrofitting them was considered too great.

USS *Triton*, USS *Halibut* and USS *Tullibee*
Radar picket/SSN, SSGN/SSN and experimental SSN

Laid down in 1958, **USS *Triton*** made the first underwater circumnavigation of the earth on its shakedown cruise in 1960, taking 60 days and 21 hours to do so. (The *Triton*'s sail did break the surface once – to transfer a sick sailor to a surface ship off Uruguay.) The achievement and the speed were both significant, demonstrating the global reach of nuclear submarines. The *Triton* was conceived as a radar picket, a short-lived concept developed from experience in World War II. With two reactors for an unprecedented speed (achieving over 30 kts on trials), the *Triton* was to operate on the surface, using radar and ESM to detect enemy air and surface forces well ahead of a US task force. It was even envisaged that the boat could control interceptions by carrierborne fighters. Its role as a command platform complete, *Triton* would then submerge and operate as a conventional submarine. The rapid pace of Soviet submarine construction made ASW the overriding priority, however, and the radar picket concept was abandoned. The *Triton* was reconfigured as an attack submarine in 1962 with four 21-in (533-mm) torpedo tubes. The vessel was the flagship of the Atlantic Fleet's submarine force in 1964-67, but was one of 50 boats to be decommissioned at the end of the 1960s instead of being overhauled.

Halibut SSGN

The 'one-off' **USS *Halibut*** was the first nuclear-powered submarine designed to launch guided missiles (SSGN) and was launched in 1959. The boat's odd shape was determined by the need to keep the main deck as dry as possible once it had surfaced to fire its five RGM-6 Regulus I cruise missiles. *Halibut* undertook its first test-firing in March 1960 but emerging technology ages quickly and the system was phased out in 1964. The *Halibut* was converted to an attack submarine in 1965-67 and served in the ASW role in the Pacific Fleet until decommissioned in 1976.

Laid down in 1958, the diminutive **USS *Tullibee*** was commissioned in 1960 intended specifically for the ASW role, and served as an experimental platform for sonar systems and other ASW equipment and tactics. The boat was the first with turbo-electric nuclear power, and was the world's quietest SSN until the arrival of the 'Glenard P. Lipscomb' class, and the first with bow sonar. As a result of the latter, the four 21-in (533-mm) torpedo tubes were moved back. Extensively overhauled in 1965-68, *Tullibee* served with the 6th Fleet then returned to the US in 1971 for further evaluation of SSN tactics, and tested PUFFS sonar equipment in a 'shark fin' installation. Highly automated, it was deigned to operate with a small crew of around 50. The boat alternated between the Mediterranean and the Atlantic for the remainder of its service life before being decommissioned in 1988.

SPECIFICATION	
USS *Halibut*	(15,000 shp) to two shafts
Displacement: 3,655 tons surfaced; 5,002 tons dived	**Performance:** speed 15 kts surfaced; 28 kts dived
Dimensions: length 106.7 m (350 ft); beam 9 m (29 ft 6 in); draught 6.3 m (20 ft 9 in)	**Armament:** five Regulus I SSMs, and six 21-in (533-mm) Mk 59 torpedo tubes (four bow, two stern)
Propulsion: one S3W pressurised water-cooled reactor powering two steam turbines delivering 11185 kW	**Diving depth:** 214 m (700 ft)
	Complement: nine officers and 108 enlisted men

Left: The first nuclear submarine designed specifically for the ASW mission, the USS Tullibee had vertical dorsal-like fins fore and aft containing sonar gear.

'Permit' class SSN

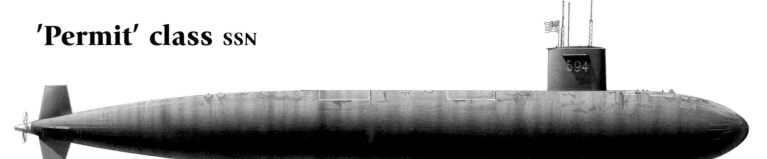

*The 'Permit' class (**USS** Permit is seen here) received new sonars and weapon-control systems so that they could operate as first-line units into the 1990s to pave the way for the 'Los Angeles' class.*

The first of the SSNs in the US Navy with a deep-diving capability, advanced sonars mounted in the optimum bow position, midships angled torpedo tubes with the SUBROC ASW missile, and a high degree of machinery quieting, the **'Thresher' class** remained an important part of US attack capability until the early 1990s. The lead boat of this class, the **USS Thresher**, was lost with all 129 crew on board during diving trials off the coast of New England on 10 April 1963, midway through the period between 1960 and 1966 in which the 14 boats of the class were being built by five yards (three each by Portsmouth Navy Yard, New York Shipbuilding, Electric Boat and Ingalls, and two by Mare Island Navy Yard).

The class was then renamed as the **'Permit' class** after the second boat. As a result of the lessons learned from the enquiry following the *Thresher*'s loss, the last three of the class were modified during construction with improved safety features as part of the 'Sub-safe' programme, heavier machinery, the hull lengthened from 84.89 m (278 ft 6 in) to 89.08 m (292 ft 3 in) to allow the incorporation of the BQQ-5 bow sonar in place of the BQQ-2 system that had been fitted in the earlier boats, and the sail increased in height to 6.1 m (20 ft) from the figures of 4.22 or 4.57 m (13 ft 10 in or 15 ft) that had been typical of the earlier boats. As such, these three boats were the prototypes for the follow-on 'Sturgeon' class.

Altered design

In addition, the **USS Jack** was built to a slightly different design with two propellers on one shaft and a contra-rotating turbine without reduction gear to test a new method of reducing machinery operating noises. This system was unsuccessful, however, and the vessel was refitted with standard machinery. During the boats' normal refit programme, the original Mk 113 torpedo fire-control system and the BQQ-2 sonar suite were replaced by the all-digital Mk 117 FCS and the BQQ-5 sonar suite with clip-on towed sonar array facilities. All the submarines were also later fitted to carry and fire the tube-launched version of the Harpoon anti-ship missile, but no provision was made for the carriage of Tomahawk cruise missiles.

SUBROC was to be replaced by a new stand-off ASW missile in the late 1980s, with the choice of either a nuclear depth bomb or an

Below: USS Barb executes a high-speed turn on the surface. Underwater, the submarine would be 'flown' throught the water using controls similar to those found aboard aircraft, exploiting its maximum manoeuvrability and speed.

SPECIFICATION

'Permit' class
Displacement: 3,750 tons surfaced; 4,311 tons dived, except *Jack* 3,800 tons surfaced; 4,470 tons dived, and *Flasher*, *Greenling* and *Gato* 3,800 tons surfaced; 4,642 tons dived
Dimensions: length 84.89 m (278 ft 6 in) except *Jack* 85.9 m (297 ft 5 in) and *Flasher*, *Greenling* and *Gato* 89.08 m (292 ft 3 in); beam 9.6 m (31 ft 8 in); draught 8.8 m (28 ft 10 in)
Propulsion: one Westinghouse S5W pressurised-water reactor powering two steam turbines delivering 11185 kW (15,000 shp) to one shaft
Performance: speed 18 kts surfaced and 27 kts dived, except *Jack*, *Flasher*, *Greenling* and *Gato* 18 kts surfaced and 26 kts dived
Diving depth: 400 m (1,315 ft) operational and 600 m (1,970 ft)

maximum
Torpedo tubes: four 21-in (533-mm) Mk 63 amidships with a load initially comprising 17 Mk 48 wire-guided active/passive-homing torpedoes and six UUM-44A SUBROC ASW missiles but later modified to 15 Mk 48 torpedoes, four SUBROC missiles and four UGM-84A/C Harpoon anti-ship missiles; an alternative load was 46 Mk 57 deep water mines, Mk 60 Captor mines or Mk 67 mines
Missiles: initially none, but see above
Electronics: one BPS-11 surface search radar, one BQQ-2 or BQQ-5 sonar suite (the latter with towed array), one Mk 113 or Mk 117 torpedo fire-control system, one WSC-3 satellite communications system, one ESM system, and one underwater telephone
Complement: 122-134

Above: The first US Navy SSN class with a deep-diving capability, advanced sonars, midships torpedo tubes and machinery-quietening systems, the 'Permit' class is epitomised by the USS Plunger off the coast of Hawaii during its first fleet deployment in 1963.

ASW torpedo as the payload, but this project was cancelled. Eight boats in the 'Permit' Class (**Permit**, **Plunger**, **Barb**, **Pollack**, **Haddo**, **Guardfish**, **Flasher** and **Haddock**) served with the Pacific Fleet and five (**Jack**, **Tinosa**, **Dace**, **Green-ling** and **Gato**) served with the Atlantic Fleet. The last of these boats, the *Gato*, was finally withdrawn from US Navy service in 1996.

'Narwhal' class SSN

SPECIFICATION

'Narwhal' class
Displacement: 4,450 tons surfaced; 5,350 tons dived
Dimensions: length 95.9 m (314 ft 8 in); beam 11.6 m (38 ft); draught 7.9 m (25 ft 11 in)
Propulsion: one General Electric S5G pressurised-water reactor powering two steam turbines delivering about 12675 kW (17,000 shp) to one shaft
Performance: speed 18 kts surfaced and 26 kts dived
Diving depth: 400 m (1,315 ft)

operational and 600 m (1,970 ft) maximum
Torpedo tubes: four 21-in (533-mm) Mk 63 amidships for 17 Mk 48 wire-guided active/passive-homing torpedoes and six SUBROC ASW missiles (later modified to 15 Mk 48 torpedoes, four SUBROC and four Harpoon anti-ship missiles), or 46 Mk 57, Mk 60 or Mk 67 mines; by the late 1980s the load comprised 11 Mk 48 torpedoes, four Harpoon missiles and eight Tomahawk

(TASM) anti-ship cruise missiles
Missiles: initially none, but see above
Electronics: one BPS-11 surface search radar, one BQQ-2 or BQQ-5 sonar suite (the latter with towed array), one Mk 113 or Mk 117 torpedo fire-control system, one WSC-3 satellite communications system, one ESM system, and one underwater telephone
Complement: 120

The **'Narwhal' class** was one of two single-boat classes built as testbeds for major new submarine technology. The **USS Narwhal** was constructed in 1966-67 to evaluate the natural-circulation S5G nuclear reactor plant. This used natural convection rather than several circulator pumps, with their associated electrical and control equipment, for heat transfer operations via the reactor coolant to the steam generators, thus effectively reducing at slow speeds one of the major sources of self-generated radiated machinery noise within

Left: The USS Narwhal was the testbed for the natural-circulation S5G nuclear reactor, which used natural convection rather than circulator pumps for heat transfer to the steam turbines in order to reduce the self-generated noise levels at low speeds. The boat was claimed to be the quietest submarine when introduced.

ordinary nuclear-powered submarines. In all other respects the boat was similar to the units of the 'Sturgeon' class, and was retrofitted with new electronic equipment and missiles (including Tomahawk cruise and Harpoon anti-ship missiles) in the course of a regular refit. The *Narwhal* operated with the Atlantic Fleet as a operational unit up to 1999.

'Glenard P. Lipscomb' class SSN

In contrast to the USS *Narwhal*, the **USS *Glenard P. Lipscomb*** was laid down in June 1971 and launched in August 1973, again by the Electric Boat Division of the General Dynamics Corporation at Groton in Connecticut, as a considerably larger submarine. The type was the later of the two single-boat SSN types designed and built as testbeds, in this instance for the evaluation under operational conditions of a turbine-electric drive propulsion plant as first pioneered, more than a decade earlier, by the USS *Tullibee*.

This propulsion arrangement eliminated the noisy reduction gear of the steam turbine plant that was otherwise standard in the US Navy's nuclear-powered submarine fleet, and introduced a number of new and quieter machinery systems into the boat. It was confirmed in trials, however, that the inevitable penalty which had to be paid for the system's greater weight and volume (and thus the hull's greater size) was a significant reduction in underwater speed by comparison with that of other US Navy SSN classes of the time.

Ongoing project

The *Glenard P. Lipscomb* was used in an ongoing project designed to allow a realistic at-sea evaluation of noise-reduction techniques as a counter to current and possible anti-submarine measures. Some of the concepts were seen to offer very real advantages, and some of the quietening techniques that caused no degradation of underwater speed were accordingly worked into the design of the 'Los Angeles' class.

The *Glenard P. Lipscomb* served with the Atlantic Fleet as a fully operational unit until retirement in 1989.

SPECIFICATION	
'Glenard P. Lipscomb' class **Displacement:** 5,800 tons surfaced; 6,840 tons dived **Dimensions:** length 111.3 m (365 ft); beam 9.7 m (31 ft 9 in); draught 9.5 m (31 ft) **Machinery:** one Westinghouse S5Wa pressurised-water reactor powering two steam turbines delivering power to one shaft **Performance:** speed 18 kts surfaced	and 24 kts dived **Diving depth:** 400 m (1,315 ft) operational and 600 m (1,970 ft) maximum **Torpedo tubes:** four 21-in (533-mm) Mk 63 amidships for the same basic load as the *Narwhal* **Missiles:** initially none, but later fitted for Harpoon and Tomahawk **Electronics:** as for *Narwhal* **Complement:** 120

Right: Though quiet at low speeds, the **Glenard P. Lipscomb** *had a special propulsion arrangement that demanded the use of an enlarged hull. This meant that underwater speed was adversely affected.*

'Sturgeon' class SSN

Essentially an enlarged and improved 'Thresher'/'Permit' design with additional quieting features and electronic systems, the **'Sturgeon' class** of SSNs built between 1965 and 1974 were the largest class of nuclear-powered warships built anywhere until the advent of the

boats of the 'Los Angeles' class. Like the previous class they were intended primarily for ASW, and employed the standard American SSN amidships torpedo battery aft of the fin, with two tubes firing diagonally outwards from the hull on each side. This allows a larger torpedo

handling room than in bow-battery boats, and facilitates fast access, weapon choice and reloading of the tubes. The last nine of the class were length-

Above: USS Queenfish (SSN-651) surfaces in the Arctic ice pack at a region of thin ice known as a polynya. Such ASW patrols beneath the ice-cap were vital to search out Soviet nuclear-armed SSBNs.

ened to accommodate more electronic equipment. What is not widely known, however, is that these were the boats used in one of the most closely guarded and classified naval intelligence programmes of the Cold War. Codenamed 'Holy Stone', the programme was initiated in the late 1960s and involved the use of these submarines in highly specialised intelligence-gathering missions close to the coasts of nations unfriendly towards the US. The additional intelligence-gathering

Left: USS Queenfish at its maximum surface speed of 18 kts. During a patrol an SSN rarely surfaces or comes to periscope depth, preferring to remain deep.

USS Sturgeon (SSN-637). The clean external lines have no unnecessary protuberances that could radiate noise. The 'Sturgeons' were armed with the 10-kT yield SUBROC ASW missiles and any orders to fire this weapon had to be cleared by the President of the United States, as it was considered to be a theatre tactical nuclear weapon.

equipment was located in special compartments and was operated by National Security Agency personnel specifically carried for the task. During these operations several collisions with other underwater and surface craft occurred, resulting sometimes in damage to the US boats involved; and on one occasion at least a 'Holy Stone' submarine was accidentally grounded for several hours during a mission within the territorial waters of the Soviet Far East. As in the case of the 'Thresher'/ 'Permit' class, the boats were retrofitted with the Mk 117 FCS and BQQ-5 sonar suite, and both the SubHarpoon and Tomahawk. A total of 22 (including five 'Holy Stone') vessels served in the Atlantic and 15 (including the remaining four 'Holy Stone' vessels) in the Pacific. The **USS Hawkbill**, **USS Pintado** and several others were also converted to carry a DSRV (deep submergence rescue vehicle) aft for launch and recovery underwater during SUBSMASH rescue operations.

Of the 22 'Sturgeon'-class SSNs that were operational with the Atlantic Fleet, it is thought

Right: US attack submarines, like USS Pogy (SSN-647) were increasingly seen in British waters as they took mid-patrol rest between voyages at selected ports during their extensive patrol periods.

that the 'standard' boats were the **USS Sturgeon**, **USS Whale**, **USS Grayling**, **USS Sunfish**, **USS Pargo**, **USS Ray**, **USS Lapon**, **USS Hammerhead** **USS Sea Devil**, **USS Bergall**, **USS Spadefish**, **USS Seahorse**, **USS Finback**, **USS Flying Fish**, **USS Trepang**, **USS Bluefish** and **USS Billfish**, while the 'Holy Stone' boats were probably the **USS Archerfish**, **USS Silversides**, **USS Batfish**, **USS L. Mendel Rivers** and **USS Richard B. Russell**. The Pacific Fleet's 15 'Sturgeons' were the 'standard' **USS Tautog**, **USS Pogy**, **USS Aspro**, **USS Queenfish**, **USS Puffer**, **USS Sand Lance**, **USS Gurnard**, **USS Guitarro**, USS *Hawkbill*, USS *Pintado* and **USS Drum**, and the 'Holy Stone' **USS William H. Bates**, **USS Tunny**, **USS Parche** and **USS Cavalla**.

Nuclear power can regenerate onboard air for considerable periods and, with a hull optimised for submerged performance, the 'Sturgeon' did not need to surface for the duration of its patrol. The endurance was really that of the 107-strong crew. At 26 kts, the submerged speed of a 'Sturgeon' was high because, unlike conventionally-powered boats, it was driven by steam

turbines. Steam for these was raised by a boiler heated, via a heat exchanger, from the reactor. The water operated in a closed circuit to minimise loss.

Hull profile

In contrast with the sharply-tapered 'high speed' hulls of earlier classes, the 'Sturgeons' had a long, low freeboard over a parallel midbody that offered

---

SPECIFICATION

'Sturgeon' class

Displacement: 4,266 tons surfaced and 4,777 tons dived

Dimensions: length 89 m (292 ft 3 in) except *Archerfish*, *Silversides*, *William H. Bates*, *Batfish*, *Tunny*, *Parche*, *Cavalla*, *L. Mendel Rivers* and *Richard B. Russell* 92.1 m (302 ft 2 in); beam 9.65 m (31 ft 8 in); draught 8.9 m (29 ft 3 in)

Machinery: one Westinghouse S5W pressurised-water reactor powering two steam turbines driving one shaft

Speed: 18 kts surfaced and 26 kts dived

Diving depth: 400 m (1,315 ft) operational and 600 m (1,970 ft) maximum

Armament: four 21-in (533-mm) Mk 63 torpedo tubes amidships; basic load 17 Mk 48 21-in torpedoes and six SUBROC anti-submarine missiles (later modified to 15 Mk 48 torpedoes, four SUBROC missiles and four Sub-Harpoon anti-ship missiles), or 46 Mk 57, Mk 60 or Mk 67 mines; in the late 1980s a typical load comprised 15 Mk 48 torpedoes, four Sub-Harpoon missiles, and four Tomahawk cruise missiles. SUBROC was phased out in 1990

Electronics: one BPS-15 surface search radar, one BQQ-2 or BQQ-5 sonar suite (the latter with towed array), one Mk 113 or Mk 117 torpedo fire-control system, one ESM suite, one WSC-3 satellite communication system, one underwater telephone

Complement: 121-134

Above: **USS** Ray (SSN-653) carried a **BQR-7** passive bow conformal sonar array (effective at 30-100 nm against a snorkling submarine, and 10-50 nm against a cavitating target), and a **BQS-6** active spherical bow array that could operate in bottom-bounce and convergence-zone modes near to the coasts of **Cold War** rivals for intelligence gathering operations.

more internal volume. The external hull was smooth and featureless, with no unnecessary protuberances that could cavitate and cause noise. The single, large-diameter propeller turned on a centreline shaft abaft the cruciform rudder and after hydroplane assembly. The boats' great speed was used sparingly, for to be fast is to be noisy.

For the greater part of a patrol, a 'Sturgeon' would progress at 'loiter' speeds, not only to reduce the chances of detection but also to decrease the interference to its own sensors caused by water and hull noise. These can be passive, active or dual function. Active sets were not used indiscriminately, being

equivalent to a beacon that advertises a boat's presence and so invites a homing weapon.

American designers take the view that the sonars are important enough to occupy prime siting. For this reason, the torpedo tubes of the 'Sturgeon' were not right forward but amidships, releasing the bow position for the enormous AN/BQS-6 sonar, an active set with the many individual transducers built into a 4.5-m (15-ft) diameter sphere. For surveillance purposes, an AN/BQR-7 passive sonar was used.

The 'teeth' of the 'Sturgeon' were the weapons launched from the four amidships tubes. Dependent upon target, these could be full-sized Mk 48 torpedoes with wire guidance, homing and considerable intelligence for use against submarine or surface targets out to a claimed 50 km (31 miles), encapsulated Harpoon missiles for 'pop-up' tactics against surface targets, nuclear-tipped SUBROC missiles for countering high-value submerged targets at long range or mines.

USS Sturgeon		
1 Propeller	**13** Under-ice navigation sonar	**21** Reactor room, lower level
2 Navigation light	**14** Aft hatch	**22** Boiler
3 Upper rudder	**15** Auxiliary machinery upper level no. 1	**23** Bulkheads
4 Starboard diving plane	**16** Auxiliary machinery lower level no. 2	**24** Nuclear reactor
5 Lower rudder		**25** Stores
6 Shaft	**17** Auxiliary machinery lower level no. 3 (generators etc)	**26** Air-conditioning plant
7 Turbine		**27** Radio room
8 Steam pipe	**18** Tunnel through reactor area	**28** Hatch
9 Condenser	**19** Reactor room, upper level	**29** Sonar operating room
10 Upper engine room	**20** Reactor deck	**30** Control room and attack centre
11 Lower engine room		**31** Access to sail (conning tower)
12 Engine control area		**32** Frozen food store

33 Galley	**46** Ballast tanks	**51** Diesel generating room
34 Mess room	**47** Inner hull easing	**52** Sonar sphere
35 Leisure room	**48** Fore escape/access hatch	**53** Sail (conning tower)
36 Sonar equipment	**49** Machine room	**54** Sail plane
37 Crew quarters	**50** Escape capsule	**55** Sail decks
38 Wardroom		**56** Bridge
39 Auxiliary machine room (generators etc)		**57** BPS-15 search radar
40 Passage		**58** Periscopes
41 Laundry		**59** Snorkel
42 Torpedo room		**60** ECM mast
43 Torpedo control area		**61** WSC-3 satellite receive
44 Pump room		**62** Radio aerial
45 Battery compartment		

'Los Angeles' class SSN

Comprising the largest number of nuclear-powered vessels built to one design, the **'Los Angeles' class** couples the speed advantage of the elderly 'Skipjack' class with the sonar and weapons capability of the 'Permit' and 'Sturgeon' classes. The significant increase in size is mainly the result of doubling the installed power available by the fitting of a new reactor design, the S6G pressurised-water reactor based on the D2G reactor fitted in the nuclear-powered cruisers of the 'Bainbridge' and 'Truxtun' classes. Reactor refuelling takes place every 10 years. The boats originally carried the BQQ-5 passive/active search and attack sonar system. From the **USS San Juan (SSN-751)** onward, the BSY-1 system was fitted. The **USS Augusta** and the **USS Cheyenne** were both fitted with a BQG-5D wide-aperture flank array. All boats have the BQS-15 active close-range high-frequency sonar for ice detection. Other sensors include a MIDAS (Mine and Ice Detection Avoidance System) first fitted in the San Juan, and

all the boats from this onward were fitted with sound-reducing tiles and hydroplanes relocated from the fin to the forward part of the hull.

Soviet 'Victor'?

Thanks to its electronic systems, the class has proved to be an exceptionally good ASW platform although, on one occasion on the first out-of-area 'Alpha I' deployment, the Soviet boat was easily able to outrun a trailing 'Los Angeles'-class boat off Iceland just by using its superior underwater speed. Against more conventional Soviet-designed nuclear-powered boats the success rate of detection and tracking is quite high. The advanced BQQ-5 system on one occasion acquired and held contact with two Soviet 'Victor'-class SSNs for an extended time.

The class features a very potent weapons array including the Tomahawk Tactical Land Attack Missile (TLAM) with a range between 900 and 1700 km (559 and 1,056 miles). Current versions of the missile

Above: Full steam ahead on the USS City of Corpus Christi as it heads towards the Colombian city of Cartagena. The boat's commander is seen on the right and is flanked by a navigator and an observer.

are the TLAM-C version, which can carry a single 454-kg (1,000-lb) warhead, and the TLAM-D which carries a submunition payload to 900 km. The standard unitary HE warhead can also be replaced by a 318-kg (692-lb) shaped-charge warhead. In order to overcome the prob-

lem of limited weapons stowage, all boats from the **USS Providence (SSN-719)** onward are fitted with a vertical launch system in which the launch tubes for the TLAMs are placed outside the pressure hull behind the sonar array. Although the Tomahawk is nuclear-

Below: The USS Birmingham (SSN-695) shows off an emergency surfacing drill during its sea trials. Note the large volumes of water pouring from the fin and the early fin-mounted diving planes. A normal surfacing is achieved gradually by selective blowing of ballast tanks. This boat was withdrawn in 1999.

With a total of 51 boats still in service out of a total of 62 hulls completed, the 'Los Angeles' design is the most numerous nuclear-powered warship class, as well as being the second most expensive SSN type after the new 'Seawolf' class.

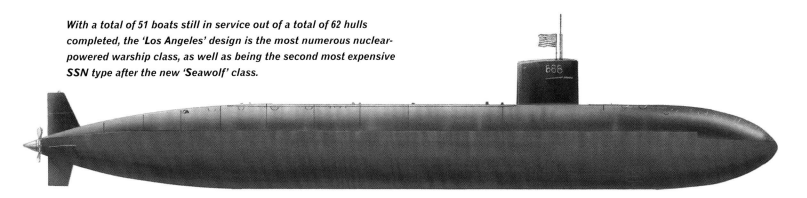

SPECIFICATION

'Los Angeles' class
Displacement: 6,082 tons surfaced; 6,927 tons dived
Dimensions: length 110.34 m (362 ft); beam 10.06 m (33 ft); draught 9.75 m (32 ft)
Propulsion: one S6G pressurised water-cooled reactor powering two steam turbines delivering 26095 kW (35,000 shp) to one shaft
Speed: 18 kts surfaced; 32 kts dived
Diving depth: 450 m (1,475 ft) operational and 750 m (2,460 ft)

maximum
Torpedo tubes: four 21-in (533-mm) tubes amidships for 26 weapons including Mk 48 torpedoes, Sub-Harpoon and Tomahawk missiles, plus (from SSN-719) 12 external tubes for Tomahawk SLCMs (TLAM-C and TLAM-D now carried)
Electronics: one BPS-15 surface search radar, one BQQ-5 or BSY-1 passive/active search and attack low-frequency sonar, BDY-1/BQS-15 sonar array, TB-18 passive towed array and MIDAS
Complement: 133

capable, such weapons are not now deployed on a routine basis.

Furthermore, the boats can also carry the 21-in (533-m) Mk 48 active/passive homing torpedo with a wire-guidance option. This guidance is suitable for ranges up to 50 km (31 miles) or 38 km (23 miles) in the active or passive modes respectively. The torpedo has a 267-kg (588-lb) warhead, and 26 Mk 48 weapons can be carried by a 'Los Angeles'-class boat

though another load is 14 torpedoes and 12 tube-launched TLAMs. These are fired out of four tubes placed amidships in the vessel. The 'Los Angeles' class has already participated in operations in Iraq, Kosovo and Afghanistan. Furthermore, the boats have also continued their under-ice operations, and in mid-2001, the **USS Scranton** (**SSN-756**) surfaced through the Arctic ice cap. Eleven of the class have been retired.

'Seawolf' class SSN

The boats of the **'Seawolf' class** are the most advanced but also the most expensive hunter-killer submarines in the world. The first completely new American submarine design for some 30 years, the **USS Seawolf** was laid down in 1989 as the lead boat in a class of 12. The cost of the 'Seawolf' class in 1991 was estimated at $33.6 billion (25 per cent of the naval construction budget), making it the most expensive naval building programme ever. At that time the US Navy planned an additional 17 boats. Then the 'peace dividend' resulting from the collapse of the USSR and the end of the Cold War caused US politicians to question the need for more ultra-quiet boats, and the class was capped at three units and the replacement

for the 51 current 'Los Angeles'-class boats will be a much cheaper design.

The 'Seawolf' class was intended to restore the technological edge which the US Navy had enjoyed over the Soviets from 1945 until the mid-1980s, when espionage and the cynical trading practices of some US allies somewhat eroded it. The new boats were designed to operate at greater depths than existing US submarines and to operate under the polar ice cap. New welding materials have been used to join the hull subsections and the 'Seawolf' class are the first attack submarines to use HY-100 steel rather than the HY-80 used for previous boats. (HY-100 was used in experimental deep-diving submarines during the 1960s.) The

Left: The US Navy's 'Seawolf' class is the most expensive submarine design: the research costs for the pressurised water reactor alone are thought to have cost in excess of $1 billion. Retractable bow planes improve surfacing capabilities through thick polar ice.

most important advantage of the 'Seawolf' class design is its exceptional quietness even at high tactical speeds. Whereas most submarines need to keep their speed down to as little as 5 kts to avoid detection by passive sonar arrays, the 'Seawolf' class are credited with being able to cruise at 20 kts and still be impossible to locate.

Sound of silence

The US Navy describes the 'Seawolf' as 10 times as quiet as an improved 'Los Angeles' and 70 times as quiet as the original 'Los Angeles' boat: a 'Seawolf' at 25 kts makes less noise than a 'Los Angeles' tied

up alongside the pier! However, during their construction and subsequent trials, several problems were experienced on the *Seawolf* after acoustic panels kept falling off the boat.

With eight torpedo tubes in a double-decked torpedo room, the 'Seawolf' class are capable of dealing with multiple targets simultaneously. Now that the originally intended targets are rusting at anchor in Murmansk and Vladivostok, it is the 'Seawolf's ability to make a stealthy approach to enemy coasts that makes it so valuable. The third and last unit, the **USS Jimmy Carter**, which was commissioned in December 2001,

incorporates a dry deck shelter, for which its hull was lengthened by 30.5 m (100 ft). The dry deck hangar is an air transportable device that can be fitted piggy-back style to carry swimmer delivery vehicles and combat swimmers. There is a combat swimmer silo too, an internal lock-out chamber that can fit up to eight swimmers and their equipment. The irony of such a submarine being named after the president who bungled the Iran hostage rescue mission is not lost on older US Navy personnel!

Armament

The class is completed by its second unit, the **USS Connecticut**, and all three of the boats can carry Tomahawk TLAM cruise missiles. The boats also have eight 26-in (660-mm) torpedo tubes. A total complement of 50 torpedoes and missiles can be carried by the boats of the 'Seawolf' class, but an alternative is up to 100 marine mines in place of either the torpedoes or the cruise missiles. It is thought that in the future the vessels

Above: The USS Seawolf, the first boat in the class, conducts 'Bravo' trials in September 1996. The 'Seawolf' class is arguably the quietest design of submarine constructed.

may also be fitted for the carriage, deployment and recovery of Uninhabited Underwater Vehicles (UUVs). The state of the art electronic system on the boats features a BSY-2 sonar suite with an active or passive sonar array and a wide-aperture passive flank array; TB-16 and TB-29 surveillance and tactical towed arrays are also fitted. The class features a BPS-16 navigation radar and a Raytheon Mk 2 weapons control system. A countermeasures suite includes the WLY-1 advanced torpedo decoy system.

The boats have great manoeuvrability, and additional space was built into the class for improvements in weapons development. Despite their potent weapons load, their ultra-quietness, and their robust electronics fit, the 'Seawolf' class are yet to be deployed in combat.

SPECIFICATION	
'Seawolf' class	**Diving depth:** 487 m (1,600 ft)
Displacement: 8,080 tons surfaced; 9,142 tons dived	**Armament:** eight 26-in (660-mm) torpedo tubes with up to 50 Tomahawk cruise missiles; Mk 48 ADCAP torpedoes or 100 mines
Dimensions: length 107.6 m (353 ft); beam 12.9 m (42 ft 4 in); draught 10.7 m (35 ft)	**Electronics:** one BPS-16 navigation radar, one BQQ-5D sonar suite with bow spherical active/passive array, TB-16 and TB-29 surveillance and tactical towed sonar arrays, and BQS-24 active close-range detection sonar
Propulsion: one S6W pressurised water-cooled reactor powering steam turbines delivering 38770 kW (52,000 shp) to one pumpjet propulsor	
Speed: 18 kts surfaced; 35 kts dived	**Complement:** 134

'Los Angeles' class SSN

A 'Los Angeles'-class SSN is larger than a light cruiser of World War II, and faster than almost anything else in the fleet. Each vessel accommodates a crew of 130 and the living space and supplies needed to sustain them for months at a time. Added to this is a nuclear powerplant and a vast array of electronics and computers in addition to weapons and sensors. The boats of the 'Los Angeles' class form the backbone of the US submarine attack force, with some 51 examples from the original total of 62 hulls still in service.

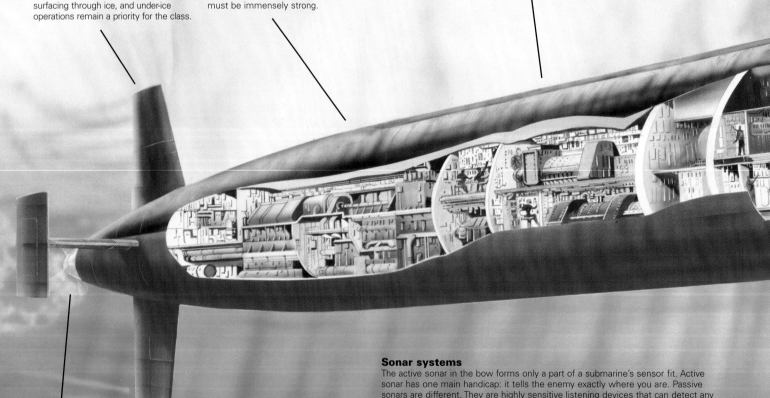

Pressure hull
Modern submarines have a two-layer hull. The external casing is smooth and featureless; the more streamlined the hull, the less noise it makes going through the water. The space between the hulls fills with water when the boat submerges. As there is water on both sides of the outer casing, it does not have to bear any great pressure. The inner, pressure hull is very different. Inside, the crew works at normal atmospheric pressure. When the submarine dives, however, the external pressure rises dramatically. At its maximum operating depth of 450 m (1,475 ft), the water pressure on a 'Los Angeles'-class boat is more than 40 times normal, so the pressure hull must be immensely strong.

Tailfins
Modern submarines manoeuvre using their cruciform tailfins. The vertical surfaces act as stabilisers and rudders, while the horizontal fins work in the same way as elevators on an aircraft. In fact, the boats are 'flown' through the water by one helmsman operating an aircraft-style control column. From SSN-751 onwards, the vessels of the 'Los Angeles' class have forward hydroplanes fitted forward instead of on the fin. These planes are retractable for surfacing through ice, and under-ice operations remain a priority for the class.

Turbines
Steam that has been generated by the nuclear reactor is pumped through a system of turbines. These huge fans rotate under the pressure of the steam, and this rotation is used to power the drive shaft, which turns the propeller and pushes the boat through the water. The submarine's turbines rotate many thousands of times per minute, while at its fastest the propeller is unlikely to revolve at more than 120 turns per minute. A reduction gear is used in order to reduce the speed of rotation from to the other. With 26099.5 kW (35,000 shp) available, the submarine's reduction gear takes up a fair proportion of the engine space.

Sonar systems
The active sonar in the bow forms only a part of a submarine's sensor fit. Active sonar has one main handicap: it tells the enemy exactly where you are. Passive sonars are different. They are highly sensitive listening devices that can detect any and every noise in the water around, filtering out natural sounds and identifying man-made noises. The two main systems are at the bow, which can be used passively, and at the stern where a highly sensitive towed array trails at the end of a cable several hundred metres long. In addition, the submarines are equipped with a lateral array, which is a series of hydrophones mounted behind square panels down the side of the boat. The towed sonar array is stowed in a blister on the side of the casing.

Propeller
Noise is perhaps the submarine's greatest enemy, and fast-moving propellers make a lot of noise. Submarines use large, slow-turning, multi-bladed propellers to provide maximum thrust while disturbing the water as little as possible. At slow speeds, they are almost noiseless. From SSN-751 onwards, the 'Los Angeles' class has been fitted with acoustic tile cladding in order to augment the standard 'mammalian' outer casing coating.

Left: The USS **Salt Lake City** *transits the mouth of Apra Harbour for a visit to Guam. The boat is ported in San Diego, California. From the 29th vessel onwards, the 'Los Angeles' class has been fitted with acoustic tile cladding in order to augment the standard 'mammalian' outer casing coating.*

Nuclear powerplant

The GE PWR S6G nuclear reactor is very heavy, which is why it is located behind extra-thick bulkheads at the submarine's centre of mass. The function of the reactor is to use the heat generated by controlled nuclear fission to turn water into steam, which is then used to drive steam turbines. The reactor must not be allowed to overheat while it is operating, which means the coolant must be in continuous flow around the reactor. While some Soviet submarines used exotic cooling systems, utilising liquid metals, most Western types use pressurised water (but not the same water that drives the turbines). In older boats the coolant pumps made a considerable amount of noise, but the water in the 'Los Angeles' class circulates by natural convection, making the boats quieter.

Control deck

This is the heart of the submarine in action. From the control room the ship's speed, direction and depth are regulated, with helmsmen manning the controls. The sonarmen have millions of dollars' worth of sensors at their command, with powerful computers to help them filter and analyse incoming signals. The boat is fought and weapons are controlled from the attack centre beneath the sail, or conning tower.

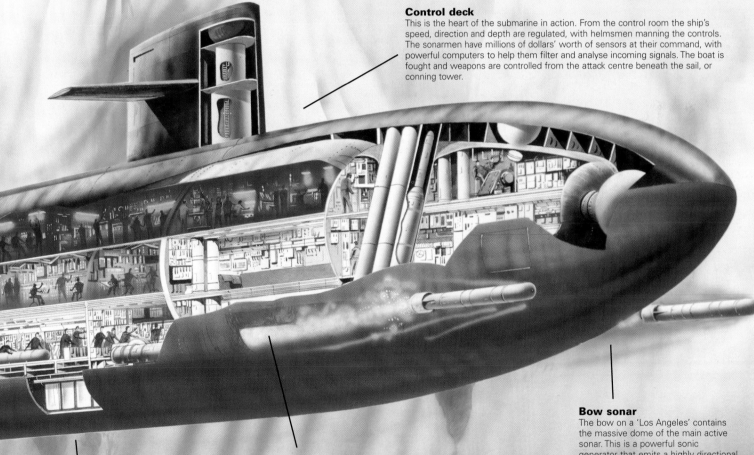

Bow sonar

The bow on a 'Los Angeles' contains the massive dome of the main active sonar. This is a powerful sonic generator that emits a highly directional pulse of sound. A target will reflect some of that sound back to the submarine's highly sensitive listening devices and analysis of the sound will identify the target's range and direction.

Torpedo and missile tubes

The torpedo tubes on US submarines angle outwards from amidships, because the bow space is taken up by the captive sonar. With modern guided weapons it is no longer necessary for a submarine to be pointing at a target to fire at it. Unfortunately, the position is not ideal for handling weapons, because in that position the tubes take up more room inside the boat. Submarine weapons are large and take up a lot of space. Big though it is, a 'Los Angeles'-class boat has room for only 26 tube-launched weapons internally, and if you carry missiles you cut down on your torpedo load. A typical load may comprise 12 Tomahawk and 14 torpedoes. From SSN-719 onwards, however, the 'Los Angeles' class has been fitted with 12 vertical launch tubes for Tomahawk missiles in the space between the pressure hull and the outer casing. This allows a significant offensive missile load to be carried without reducing the numbers of the boat's primary ASW weapon, its torpedoes. A normal internal load of 12 UGM-109C conventioanl land attack (TLAM-C) missiles is carried, in addition to the external tubes carried by the later boats. Nuclear warheads are now not normally carried. The conventional version has a range of around 900 km (560 miles) and a CEP of 10 m (33 ft). The UGM-109D (TLAM-D) version replaces the 454-kg (1,000-lb) HE warhead with submunitions.

Batteries

Auxiliary power aboard a nuclear submarine is provided by diesel and electric generators, together with a battery compartment that can provide emergency power when necessary. Unlike conventional boats, however, the batteries cannot drive the submarine under water for any length of time.

High-tech hunter-killers

Entering service in 1976 and remaining in production until 1995, the 'Los Angeles'-class SSNs had a triple tasking during the Cold War: the tracking and destruction of hostile SSBNs, the protection of Carrier Battle Groups against cruise-missile submarines, and lastly acting in the intelligence-gathering role as covert surveillance platforms.

The main Cold War mission of the 'Los Angeles' class was to prevent Soviet SSBNs from leaving their home ports of Murmansk and Vladivostok. Units of the 'Los Angeles' class patrolled near these bases, and around the heavily-defended Soviet SSBN 'bastions' and natural 'choke-points' in order to track the Soviet fleet. In addition, they would also act as the ears of the Carrier Battle Group, listening out for Soviet hunter-killer boats, patrolling hundreds of miles ahead to 'clear a path' for the fleet. The 'Los Angeles' boats also had a secondary role of targeting and sinking Soviet surface shipping. The boats had a final and more covert surveillance mission, which was to collect signals intelligence (SIGINT) and electronic intelligence (ELINT).

The boats carried a potent array of weapons. These included Mk 48 ADCAP torpedoes, UGM-84 Sub-Harpoon anti-shipping missiles and UGM-109B Tomahawk anti-ship cruise missiles. However, Sub-Harpoon is no longer carried, and anti-ship SLCMs were replaced by Tomahawk land-attack missiles (TLAM) from 1983 onwards. These weapons were initially carried internally, for launching from the boat's torpedo tubes. However, from USS *Providence* (SGN-719) onwards, the boats were adapted to fire Tomahawk missiles from 12 vertical tubes which were located outside the boat's pressure hull, but within its overall casing. This allowed the original complement of 26 torpedoes to be retained. Later boats also carry an integrated command system and new silencing methods. The submarine's ability to carry the UUM-44A Subroc nuclear ASW missile was phased out in 1990. Furthermore, it is possible that in the future either Predator or Sea Ferret UAVs might be launched from the torpedo tubes via Harpoon missile canisters. Two boats in the class performed trials to this effect during 1996-97.

The boat's ability to carry the Tomahawk land attack missile has proved to be especially useful in the post-Cold War environment. During October 2001, USS *Providence* fired its Tomahawk missiles against Taliban and al-Qaeda targets in Afghanistan.

Above: When acting autonomously, the submerged hunter-killer is completely blind, but its sense of hearing is acute. Here sonar operators scan for the slightest sound pattern emanating from an enemy vessel. The 'Los Angeles' boats have been steadily improved to incorporate digital fire-control and sonar systems.

Below: As much or even more than the highly visible Carrier Battle Group, 'Los Angeles'-class nuclear-powered hunter-killer submarines like the USS Houston are at the heart of US naval power. During the Cold War, the Soviet navy made little secret of its intention to destroy the US aircraft Carrier Battle Groups at the beginning of any 'hot' war, and one role of the 'Los Angeles' class was the protection of the task group against Soviet SSNs.

'Los Angeles' class
In action

Perhaps the most advanced nuclear hunter-killer submarine, the 'Los Angeles'-class SSN has shown an unparalleled versatility. Originally conceived to protect US carrier fleets and hunt Soviet SSBNs, it is now a potent cruise missile carrier, able to strike a devastating blow against the enemy at the start of a conflict.

Above: The 'Los Angeles'-class attack submarine USS Pogy surfaces through the Arctic ice flow at sunrise. In this instance, the boat embarked a team of scientific researchers and for the purpose of the voyage a portion of the ship's torpedo room was converted into laboratory space. Nevertheless, the Pogy was at no time removed from its status as a front-line warship.

DSRV: DEEP SEA ESCAPE CAPSULE

Submarine accidents are rare, but when they do happen they are very serious. Modern boats have escape capsules – air locks through which the crew can escape from a disabled submarine. In shallow water the crew float to the surface using simple breathing apparatus, but in deep water it requires a DSRV, or Deep Submergence Recovery Vehicle (above right), to lock on to the hatch and to ferry the crew back to safety. The 'Los Angeles'-class boat USS *La Jolla* was seen with a DSRV embarked, alongside the JMSDF command and control ship *Bungo* (above left), during a joint rescue training exercise in the Pacific Ocean during 2002. The DSRV was developed at immense cost by Lockheed in the wake of the USS *Thresher* accident. The attack submarine *Thresher* sunk during a test to dive to 396 m (1,300 ft) on 10 April 1963, and marked the US Navy's first loss of a nuclear submarine; the accident claimed 129 lives. The DSRV-1 (unofficially named

Mystic) is a quick-reaction, all-weather rescue vehicle, which is transportable by the C-141 or C-5 airlifters of the USAF, as well as specially-modified mother ships. The carrying submarine can launch and recover the DSRV while submerged, or even under ice. Although six vehicles were planned, only two were completed; one of these has since been decommissioned. The hull of the DSRV comprises three interconnected steel spheres: the forward sphere accommodates the pilot and co-pilot, while the centre and aft spheres can house 24 passengers in addition to two life-support technicians. Beneath the centre sphere is a hemispherical 'skirt' which seals the hatch of the disabled submarine and forms an airlock to allow the transfer of personnel. The DSRV's operating depth is 1525 m (5,000 ft) while the rescue depth is limited to 610 m (2,000 ft). The DSRV is due to be replaced by the Submarine Rescue, Diving and Recompression System (SRDRS) in 2005.

Above left: The USS Key West conducts surface operations in the Pacific as part of the carrier USS Constellation's battlegroup, which was en route to the Arabian Gulf to enforce the no-fly zones over Iraq and monitor shipping in the region. Note the original sail-mounted foreplane position of this boat.

Above right: The USS Chicago completes a training manoeuvre off the coast of Malaysia. Despite a primary armament of torpedoes and Tomahawk missiles, the 'Los Angeles' class retains a significant minelaying capability, and is capable of laying Mk 67 Mobile and Mk 60 Captor mines.

Left: Aircrew assigned to the ASW unit HS-5 'Nightdippers', embarked aboard the carrier USS John F. Kennedy for Operation Enduring Freedom, lower a package on a rescue hoist from their SH-60F to the sail of the USS Boise.

*Above: Crewmen aboard the **USS** Baltimore stand by atop the sail with a grappling hook to snag a mail shipment as it is lowered by a **US** Navy SH-60 Seahawk helicopter.*

'Los Angeles' class SSN

Below: The 'Los Angeles'-class attack submarine USS Baltimore pulls alongside the US Navy's guided missile frigate USS Samuel B. Roberts (centre) and the nuclear-powered aircraft carrier USS George Washington during a battle group formation exercise. The battlegroup was returning to port in 1996 after a six-month Mediterranean deployment, which included sustained operations in support of the NATO-lead peacekeeping in Bosnia and UN sanctions against Iraq in the Persian Gulf.

Above: The primary weapons of any submarine are its torpedoes. In the case of the 'Los Angeles' class, these are Mk 48 ADCAP Mod 5/6 (ADvanced CAPability) weapons with a maximum speed of 55 kts and a range of 38 km (24 miles). The weapon is wire-guided by the submarine's fire-control system until it is within 4000 m (4,374 yards) of the target. Then the Mk 48's own sonar takes over, and the weapon homes in automatically. The 267-kg (588-lb) warhead has a shaped charge originally designed to deal with the very tough hulls of Soviet submarines.

Below: The USS Columbus conducts a dramatic emergency surface training exercise 56 km (35 miles) off the coast of Oahu, Hawaii. The boat is home-ported at Pearl Harbor. Various staged design improvements to the 'Los Angeles' class have added some 220 tons to the original displacement of between 668 and 773 tons.

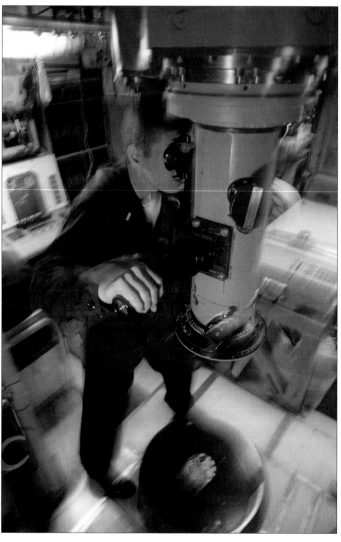

Right: A US Navy ensign aboard the USS Tuscon uses the periscope to search for surface ships in the Persian Gulf. The 'Los Angeles'-class boat was operating in support of Operation Southern Watch. The land-attack mission has been a notable feature of operations in Iraq, Kosovo and Afghanistan. The key weapon used by the 'Los Angeles' class for the land attack role is the conventionally-armed Tomahawk cruise missile.

'Astute' class Nuclear-powered attack submarine

Ordered by the Ministry of Defence for service with the Royal Navy, the **'Astute'-class** boat is an SSN (nuclear-powered attack submarine). It is of the type designed to replace the service's five 'Swiftsure'-class nuclear-powered attack submarines laid down in 1970-77 and commissioned in 1974-81, and therefore nearing the end of their operational lives. The Ministry of Defence issued invitations to tender in July 1994 for the construction of an initial three submarines with an option on a further two, and in December 1995 GEC-Marconi (now BAE Systems Marine) was selected as the prime contractor. The initial order was for a first tranche of three submarines, as fixed in the original invitation to tender, but the Ministry of Defence later announced that it was planning a follow-on order for another three rather than just

two submarines. The contract decision for the second tranche was expected in 2002, but is now likely to be placed in 2004 for the commissioning of the resulting submarines in 2012-14.

The performance specification for the 'Astute'-class submarines is essentially a development of that which characterises the 'Trafalgar Batch 1'-class boats operated by the 2nd Submarine Squadron from the Royal Navy's base at Devonport. The design requirements included a 50 per cent increase in weapons load and a significant reduction in radiated noise levels. The design matured into what was in effect a development of the fully modernised 'Trafalgar'-class submarine with a longer fin and two Thales (originally Pilkington) Optronics CM010 optronic periscopes whose masts do not penetrate the hull.

As prime contractor respond-

Above: The 'Astute'-class SSN is designed to replace the 'Swiftsure'-class submarines, and is notable for its quiet operation, large weapons load and use of a life-long reactor core.

ing to the initial order placed in March 1997, BAE Systems Marine is building the 'Astute Batch 1'-class submarines at its facility in Barrow-in-Furness, the first metal being cut late in 1999, and the manufacture of prefabricated components allowing the formal laying down of the first submarine in January 2001. The schedule envisages the launch of this unit in January 2005 some three years later.

Initial batch of three

The 'Astute Batch 1'-class submarines are to be named HMS **Astute**, **Ambush** and **Artful**, and are scheduled to enter service in 2008, 2009 and 2010 respectively. The electronic core of the submarines' capabilities is the ACMS (Astute Combat Management System) developed by Alenia Marconi Systems as an improved version of the SMCS (Submarine Command System) in service with all current classes of British submarines. The ACMS receives data from the sonars and other sensors and, employing advanced algorithms and data handling, displays real-time images on the command consoles. Factory acceptance of the operational software was received in July 2002. Tied into

the ACMS is the WHLS (Weapon Handling and Launch System) created by Strachan and Henshaw.

The 'Astute'-class submarines' major long-range weapon systems, each carrying a high explosive rather than nuclear warhead, are the Raytheon (originally General Dynamics) Tomahawk Block III land-attack cruise missile and the Boeing (originally McDonnell Douglas) Sub-Harpoon anti-ship missile, each launched from the 21-in (533-mm) torpedo tubes. The Tomahawk uses an inertial navigation system with TERCOM (Terrain Contour Mapping) update for accurate long-range navigation, the Block III missile having improvements such as upgraded propulsion, enhanced terminal guidance, and improved navigation through the installation of a GPS receiver. The Sub-Harpoon is a sea-skimming missile with high subsonic cruising speed, a range of more than 80 miles (129 km) and active radar terminal guidance.

Sensor equipment

For the launch of these missiles and also the torpedoes that constitute their primary shorter-range weapons system, the 'Astute'-class submarines have

---

SPECIFICATION	
'Astute' class	**Armament:** six 21-in (533-mm) tubes (all bow) for 36 Spearfish wire-guided torpedoes, Harpoon anti-ship missiles, Tomahawk land-attack cruise missiles, and mines in proportions dependent on the tactical requirement
Displacement: 6,500 tons surfaced; 7,200 tons dived	
Dimensions: length 97 m (318 ft 3 in); beam 10.7 m (35 ft 1 in); draught 10 m (32 ft 10 in)	
Propulsion: one Rolls-Royce PWR 2 nuclear reactor supplying steam to two Alsthom steam turbines delivering not available power to one shaft driving one pump jet propulsor	**Electronics:** one surface search and navigation radar, one ACMS combat data system, one UAP 4 ESM system, and one Type 2076 integrated sonar suite with reelable towed array
	Aircraft: none
Performance: speed 29 kts dived; endurance limited only by consumables	**Crew:** 98 plus 12 spare

six 21-in (533-mm) torpedo tubes, and will be equipped with Spearfish torpedoes with mines as an alternative. There is capacity for a total of 36 torpedoes and missiles. The Spearfish torpedo from BAE Systems is a wire-guided weapon with active/passive homing and a range of 65 km (40.4 miles) at 60 kts while carrying an advanced directed-energy warhead.

The submarines' suite of countermeasures equipment includes the Racal UAP 4 ESM system and decoys, the former using non-penetrating Thales Optronics and McTaggart Scott masts. The Ministry of Defence also has a requirement for a new CESM (Communications-band Electronic Support Measures) system for the 'Astute'-class submarines and also for the 'Trafalgar'-and 'Swiftsure'-class submarines. The system

is designed to ensure that all of the submarines possess a suitably advanced means of intercepting, recognising, localising and in general monitoring a wide range of communications signals.

The 'Astute'-class submarines are fitted with I-band navigation radars, but of considerably greater operational importance is the Thales Underwater Systems (formerly Thomson Marconi Sonar) Type 2076 integrated active/passive search and attack sonar suite with bow, intercept, flank and reelable towed arrays. This sonar suite is also being retrofitted on four of the 'Trafalgar'-class submarines. Atlas Hydrographic is providing the DESO 25 high-precision echo sounder, which is able to provide depth measurements down to 10000 m (32,810 ft). The two Thales CM010 optronic masts, with much of the hard-

ware developed by McTaggart Scott, carry thermal imaging, low-light-level TV and colour CCD (charge-coupled device) TV sensors. Raytheon Systems is providing the submarines' SIFF (Successor Identification, Friend or Foe) transponder system.

Advanced powerplant

The considerable quantities of power needed by these large submarines is provided by the Rolls-Royce PWR 2 nuclear reactor, and propulsion is entrusted to a pair of two Alsthom (originally GEC) turbines driving a single shaft powering a Rolls-Royce pump jet propulsor unit. This last comprises rotor blades turning in a fixed duct to provide 'jet' propulsion. There are also two diesel alternators as well as a single emergency drive motor powering a retractable auxiliary propeller. The digital integrated controls and the associated

instrumentation system for steering, diving, depth control and overall platform management are provided by CAE Electronics.

The PWR 2 is a second-generation pressurised water-cooled nuclear reactor initially developed for the 'Vanguard' class of Trident SLBM submarines. While most current PWRs provide a range equivalent to some 20 circumnavigations of the world, the PWR 2 with Core H offers about twice that capability, in effect meaning that the submarines so fitted will not have to be refuelled during their operational lives. The key sub-elements of the PWR 2 are the reactor pressure vessels from Babcock Energy, the main coolant pumps from GEC and Weir, and the protection and control instrumentation elements from Siemens Plessey and Thorn Automation.

'Virginia' class Nuclear-powered attack submarine

The US Navy's **'Virginia'-class** nuclear-powered attack submarine, which is also called the **New Attack Submarine**, was conceived as an advanced 'stealthy' type with multi-mission capability for the

completion of deep-ocean service in the anti-submarine role and also for shallow-water service in a whole range of littoral tasks. The design of this new class so soon after that of the 'Seawolf' class, created as the

successor to the 'Los Angeles' class and whose first unit was commissioned in July 1997, may seem a little strange. However,

the 'Seawolf' class soon showed itself to be too costly and insufficiently versatile at a time after the dissolution of the USSR into

Below: In the oceanic role, the primary weapon of the 'Virginia'-class submarine is the Mk 48 torpedo, of which 26 can be carried.

Left: In the littoral role the 'Virginia'-class boat can be used for the delivery of special forces troopers, of whom 40 (with all their gear) can be embarked in place of the torpedoes.

the CIS had removed the grand strategic threat of the Soviet forces and ushered in a new world order demanding cheaper solutions to a whole range of lower-threat operational tasks. The US Navy therefore wanted a new generation of SSNs smaller than the 'Seawolf' class.

The Electric Boat Division of the General Dynamics Corporation is the lead design authority for the new submarine after it was contracted by the US Department of Defense for the first and third units, namely the USS *Virginia* and USS *Hawaii* to be laid down in 1999 and 2001 for commissioning in 2006 and 2008 respectively. Northrop Grumman Newport News are contracted for the second and fourth units which

are the USS *Texas* and USS *North Carolina*. They are to be laid down in 2000 and 2002 for commissioning in 2007 and 2009 respectively. The building programme is in fact collaborative, with Electric Boat making the cylindrical central section of the hull, and Newport News the bow and stern sections as well as three modules to be inserted in the central hull; each of the companies makes the reactor plant module for the submarines it completes.

The hull contains structurally integrated enclosures carrying equipment of two standard widths to facilitate the installation, maintenance, repair and upgrade of major systems. The design also includes modular isolated deck structures:

the command centre, for example, is fitted as a unit resting on cushioned mounting points. Control is based on computer touch screens, and the steering and diving are controlled by means of a two-axis 'joystick' fitted with four buttons.

The requirement for the 'Virginia' class demanded an acoustic signature no greater than that of the notably quiet 'Seawolf' class, so the 'Virginia' class uses new types of anechoic coatings, isolated deck structures, and a new design of pump jet propulsor.

Command and control

The C^3I (Command, Control, Communication and Intelligence) system is the responsibility of a team under the leadership of Lockheed Martin Naval Electronics & Surveillance Systems – Undersea Systems and, based on open system architecture, this integrates the entirety of the submarine's tactical systems (the sensors, countermeasures, navigation and weapons control). Weapons control is the responsibility of a variant of the Raytheon CCS Mk 2 combat system. The launch of weapons is allocated to 12 vertical-launch tubes for Tomahawk submarine-launched cruise missiles and to four 21-in (533-mm) torpedo tubes. The latter are used to fire up to 26 Mk 48 ADCAP Mod 6 wire-guided heavyweight torpedoes and UGM-84 Sub-Harpoon anti-ship missiles. Additionally, Mk 60 CAPTOR mines can also be delivered from the torpedo tubes.

The submarines each carry the Northrop Grumman WLY-1 acoustic countermeasures system, which provides range and bearing data to the fire-control

system, and the Lockheed Martin BLQ-10 mast-mounted ESM system.

For littoral operations, an inbuilt lock-out/lock-in chamber provides a special operations capability. This chamber can also support a mini-submarine such as the Northrop Grumman ASDS (Advanced SEAL Delivery System) for the insertion of special forces teams.

Multi-faceted sonar

The primary sensor for the underwater warfare role is the sonar suite, which includes a version of the BQQ-10 acoustic data processing system and an active/passive bow array, two passive wide-aperture flank array, active high- frequency keel and fin arrays, a TB-16 towed array and a TB-29A thin-line towed array. Surface navigation is enhanced by the provision of a BPS-16 radar. Each of the submarines has a pair of BVS-1 Universal Modular Mast 'photonic' masts, which do not penetrate the hull, rather than traditional optical periscopes. Sensors mounted on the 'photonic' masts include low-light-level TV and thermal imaging cameras as well as a laser rangefinder. The UMM was created by Kollmorgen and Calzoni, an Italian subsidiary.

Developed by Boeing, the LMRS (Long-term Mine Reconnaissance System) comprises two autonomous unmanned underwater vehicles each 6 m (19 ft 8 in) long, one robotic recovery arm at 18 m (59 ft) long, and the relevant support electronics.

The core of the boat's propulsion system is the General Electric S9G pressurised water reactor with a core designed to last as long as the submarine and thereby remove the need for refuelling. Steam from the reactor drives a pair of turbines geared to a single shaft powering the pump jet propulsor unit.

SPECIFICATION	
'Virginia' class **Displacement:** 7,800 tons dived **Dimensions:** length 114.9 m (377 ft); beam 10.4 m (34 ft); draught 9.3 m (30 ft 6 in) **Propulsion:** one General Electric S9G nuclear reactor supplying steam to two steam turbines delivering 29825 kW (40,000 shp) to one shaft driving a pump jet propulsor **Performance:** speed 34 kts dived; endurance limited only by consumables **Armament:** four 21-in (533-mm) tubes for 26 Mk 48 ADVCAP Mod 6 wire-guided torpedoes and/or Harpoon anti-ship missiles, or	Mk 67 Mobile and/or Mk 60 CAPTOR mines, and 12 vertical-launch system tubes for 12 Tomahawk land-attack missiles **Electronics:** one BPS-16 navigation radar, one CCSM combat data system, one WLQ-4(V) ESM system, one WLY-1 acoustic countermeasures system, 14 external and one internal countermeasures launchers, and an advanced sonar suite including an active/passive bow array, two passive wide-aperture flank arrays, active keel and fin arrays, and TB-16 and TB-19 towed arrays **Aircraft:** none **Crew:** 134

Diesel Attack Submarines
Cold War diesel submarine patrol

Britain is one of the few nations with a significant nuclear submarine capability, but like the other nuclear navies (with the notable exception of the United States) until the 1990s it also maintained a large conventional submarine force. The 'Oberon' class provided the backbone of that force for over 20 years.

In the 1980s the Royal Navy's conventional submarine force comprised 13 'Oberon'- and two 'Porpoise'-class vessels. Of these 15 boats, nine served with the 1st Submarine Squadron based at HMS *Dolphin*, Portsmouth, and two with the nuclear attack submarine 3rd Submarine Squadron at HMS *Neptune*, Faslane. The remaining four were either undergoing refit or engaged in specialist trials. Because of the general enthusiasm for nuclear-powered submarines, the demise of the diesel boat had been discussed by factions within the Ministry of Defence, but it rapidly became apparent that these larger and much more expensive craft could not undertake certain roles that an SSK could attempt either with the same safety factor or with reasonable chance of success. Thus the conventional submarine laid superior claim to the conduct of operations within the shallow waters of the continental shelf region, or as the main platform for conducting clan-

Right: The limited space on the hull of a surfaced submarine is underlined in this photograph of a crewman being winched aboard a Sea King helicopter. Practice in such manoeuvres is essential, as sickbay facilities aboard a crowded sub are not geared to serious cases.

destine operations with special forces, or for missions of a surveillance or reconnaissance nature. The use of the 'Oberon'-class boat HMS *Onyx* with Special Boat Service units aboard and for various beach surveys in the Falkland Islands during the 1982 war is a case in point.

'Oberon' roles

Royal Navy conventional submarines were also employed in the more standard tasks of countering hostile surface shipping (for both sea denial and economic warfare reasons), search and rescue of downed airmen, the laying of small offensive minefields in restricted shipping routes (to block or hinder the passage of high-value surface units or convoys), and as listening posts at natural 'choke points'. This last allowed SSKs to monitor and report the movements of hostile subsurface craft (especially SSNs) so that friendly SSNs could be vectored on to them to trail or, in wartime, sink them. The latter task also

opened up the possibility of the conventional boat being able to 'ambush' the hostile craft with its own weapon systems, although this would alert the enemy to its presence. The other major task which also took up a

considerable amount of the British units' time was to act as training vessels for both subsurface and surface ASW units. They did this by acting as 'targets' during exercises and by providing experience for personnel in

Above: HMS Orpheus *is seen leaving Malta in the days when it was an important Royal Navy base. The boats at Malta were inheritors of a fighting tradition second to none, dating from the bitter struggle for control of the Mediterranean in World War II.*

'OBERON' CONTROL ROOM: OPERATIONS CENTRE

Space is at a premium in diesel-electric boats, unlike their larger nuclear-powered counterparts. A World War II submariner would have felt at home in the 'Oberon' control room, red-lit for night operations. The control room contained the sensor, fire-control, propulsion and diving controls, and the action information systems required to control and fight the submarine in a submerged state. Sonar, communication and radar/ECM systems had their own 'shacks' within the control room area, while the rest shared the remaining space available.

the running and operating of a submarine at sea.

On patrol the heart of the 'Oberon' was the control room, which was the area directly beneath the sail structure. Because of the difference in speed between the submerged 'Oberon' and any potential target, the skipper had to use his search and attack periscopes more than would his counterpart in a nuclear submarine. This helped him to anticipate what the target was about to do so that he could place his boat in the best available position to engage it. Although he had a torpedo fire-control system with computer to aid him, the skipper still had to obtain the course and speed of the target ship through finding its bearing and range via the periscopes.

Target acquisition

The bearing is simply the angle from the submarine at which the target was seen, and was read off a 360° scale when the periscope was pointed precisely at the ship. Taking the range was more complicated and required a split-image device on the periscope to raise a second image of the target above the true image. When the waterline of the raised image was located at the top of the real image's masts the resulting angle in minutes of arc was read off a scale; an imaginary right-angle triangle was then drawn from which the third unknown angle was deduced, and using the height of the target's masts (which would be known from intelligence data if it was an enemy warship) the length of the

triangle's base (the range) in yards could be calculated. By taking precise timings as the ranges were obtained, an accurate measure of the target's speed could be determined. All the data from the sensors and periscope observations were used to prepare a target plot from which the relevant information was fed into the torpedo fire-control computer to work out the firing solution (i.e. the point at which the torpedo launch has the greatest chance of success with the conditions given).

To attack the target the skipper had a choice of two torpedo types. For the simple beam attack and in areas where wire-guided or acoustic-homing torpedoes would be relatively useless, he had the trusty and well proven Mk 8, which began its life back in 1927 and served throughout World War II. Unfortunately, to make a

really effective attack with this model the skipper had to close to a point well within its maximum range. The Mk 8 could be fired at offset gyro angles if required, and had two speed settings (44.5 kts or 40 kts) for ranges of 4.54 km (2.82 miles) and 6.36 km (3.95 miles) respectively. After 1981 the skipper also had available the Mk 24 Mod 1 Tigerfish dual-role wire-guided torpedo. With a top speed of 35 kts for attack and a slower search speed, the maximum range was around 22 km (13.67 miles).

Now retired, the 'Oberons' were to be succeeded by the 'Upholder' class, effectively nuclear submarines in weapons fit and capability but powered by diesel engines. However, in the 1990s the Royal Navy decided to dispense with diesel power altogether and sold the 'Upholder'-class boats to Canada.

Below: The 1st Submarine Squadron berth at Gosport. The 'Oberons' and the two remaining 'Porpoise'-class boats were briefly replaced by the newly developed 'Upholder' class in the 1990s.

Special operations

Since their earliest days, submarines have been used to conduct clandestine operations in enemy waters. Missions have included providing a base for sabotage teams, intelligence-gathering and landing and taking off secret agents. Diesel submarines are smaller and quieter than nuclear-powered submarines, which makes them ideal for the purpose. However, the US Navy and Royal Navy no longer operate diesel submarines, so they have been forced to rely on nuclear vessels. To reduce their vulnerability, special operations subs are equipped to operate swimmer delivery vehicles – miniature submarines which can carry special forces into the beach from several miles offshore.

*Above: Members of the **US** Navy's **SEAL (Sea Air Land) Team** Two conduct **SEAL Delivery Vehicle (SDV)** training in the warm waters of the Caribbean.*

*Left: Diesel-powered boats like the Royal Navy's 'Oberon' class were ideal for special operations. Here, members of the **SBS** practise 'float-off' drills in the 1970s.*

*Below: Submarines equipped with lock-out chambers allow special forces teams like these **SBS** divers to operate without the need to come to the surface.*

Above: The commander of a US Navy SSN scans the surface around the boat before surfacing at the end of a patrol. SSNs can remain submerged for months at a time.

Diesel vs Nukes
Power and stealth

Above: The US Navy continues to operate the conventionally-powered USS Dolphin for research purposes. Here the boat is seen in difficulty in the Pacific in May 2002 after a fire and flooding onboard.

The development of effective nuclear powerplants in the 1950s revolutionised underwater warfare. Until that time, submarines were more properly described as submersibles – torpedo boats which could submerge temporarily, but which were nevertheless tied to the surface. Nuclear boats were true creatures of the deep, able to remain underwater indefinitely. That ability came at a considerable price, however: the SSN is massively expensive, and the cheaper diesel-electric boat still has an important role to play.

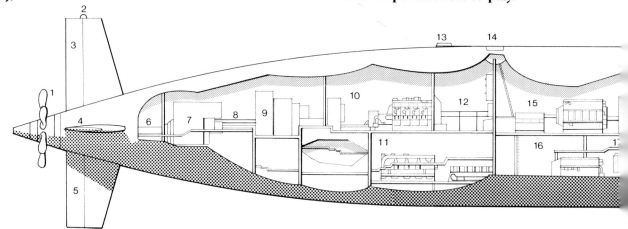

SPECIFICATION	
'Sturgeon' class	**Powerplant**
Displacement	One pressurised water reactor; two steam turbines delivering 11190 kW (15,000 shp)
4,777 tons (dived)	
Dimensions	**Performance**
Length: 89 m (291 ft 11 in) **Beam:** 9.65 m (31 ft 7 in) **Draught:** 8.9 m (29 ft 2 in)	**Speed:** 30 kts (55 km/h; 34 mph) dived **Diving depth:** 400 m (1,312 ft)

SPECIFICATION	
'Sjöormen' class	**Powerplant**
Displacement	Four diesels delivering 1641 kW (2,200 shp), one ASEA electric motor
1210 tons (dived)	
Dimensions	**Performance**
Length: 41 m (134 ft 6 in); **Beam:** 6.1 m (20 ft); **Draught:** 5.8 m (19 ft)	**Speed:** 20 kts (37 km/h; 23 mph) dived **Diving depth:** 150 m (492 ft)

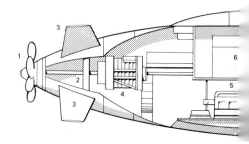

Left: The compact nature of a diesel-electric boat is apparent as the Danish navy's **HDMS S**aelen is lifted aboard a contract vessel for transport from Bahrain to Denmark. Such transport operations are possible with a boat of limited dimensions.

Below: The US Navy 'Los Angeles' attack submarine **USS** La Jolla **(SSN-701)**, with the deep submergence rescue vehicle **Mystic (DSRV-1)** attached. **Mystic** was specifically designed to rescue the crews of sunken submarines.

USS Sturgeon

Cutaway drawing key
1 Propeller
2 Navigation light
3 Upper rudder
4 Starboard diving plane
5 Lower rudder
6 Shaft
7 Turbine
8 Steam pipe
9 Condenser
10 Upper engine room
11 Lower engine room
12 Engine control area
13 Under-ice navigation sonar
14 Aft hatch
15 Auxiliary machinery upper level no. 1
16 Auxiliary machinery lower level no. 2
17 Auxiliary machinery lower level no. 3 (generators etc.)
18 Tunnel through reactor area
19 Reactor room, upper level
20 Reactor deck
21 Reactor room, lower level
22 Boiler
23 Bulkheads
24 Nuclear reactor
25 Stores
26 Air-conditioning plant
27 Radio room
28 Hatch
29 Sonar operating room
30 Control room and attack centre
31 Access to sail (conning tower or fin)
32 Frozen food store
33 Galley
34 Mess room
35 Leisure room
36 Sonar equipment
37 Crew quarters
38 Wardroom
39 Auxiliary machine room (generators etc.)
40 Passage
41 Laundry
42 Torpedo room
43 Torpedo control area
44 Pump room
45 Battery compartment
46 Ballast tanks
47 Inner hull casing
48 Fore escape/access hatch
49 Machine room
50 Escape capsule
51 Diesel generating room
52 Sonar sphere
53 Sail (conning tower)
54 Sail plane
55 Sail decks
56 Bridge
57 BPS-14 search radar
58 Periscopes
59 Snorkel
60 ECM mast (electronic counter-measures)
61 WSC-3 satellite receiver
62 Radio aerial

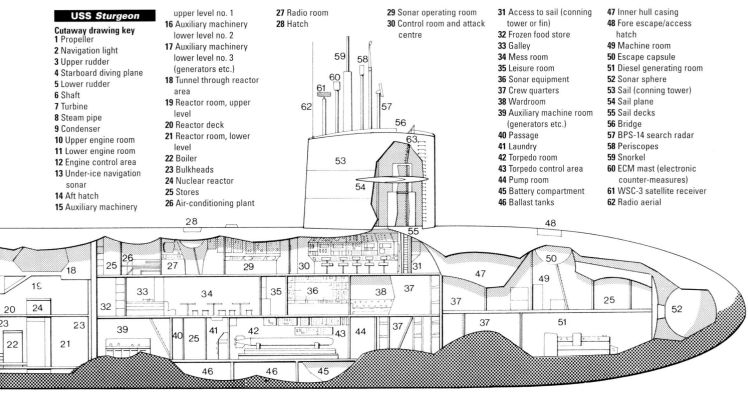

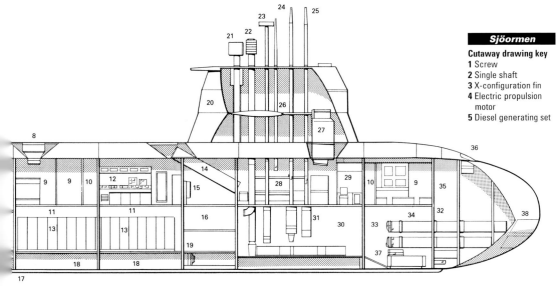

Sjöormen

Cutaway drawing key
1 Screw
2 Single shaft
3 X-configuration fin
4 Electric propulsion motor
5 Diesel generating set
6 Central monitoring station
7 Outer casing
8 Aft escape hatch with coupling for rescue craft
9 Crew quarters
10 Washroom
11 Battery room
12 Control room
13 Batteries
14 Torpedo loading hatch
15 Watertight communication hatch
16 Fuel tank
17 Keel
18 Ballast tank
19 Pump
20 Conning tower
21 Snorkel
22 Omnidirectional antenna
23 Directional antenna
24 Observation periscope
25 Attack periscope
26 Bridge fin with hoisting equipment
27 Access trunk
28 CIC
29 Radio room
30 Torpedo store
31 Periscope wells
32 Watertight bulkheads
33 Torpedo room
34 Torpedo tubes
35 Trim tank
36 Forward escape/access hatch
37 Compressed air store
38 Bow tube covers

HUNTER-KILLERS: CLOSING THE GAP

During the Cold War, the primary mission for fleet submarines would have been hunting down and killing enemy submarines, particularly ballistic missile boats. Both nuclear submarines and diesel boats are currently tasked with that mission, and development of new sensors and electronic systems mean that the current generation of SSKs are hardly less capable in most kinds of combat than nuclear boats. However, nuclear submarines are considerably faster than diesel boats – typically maximum dived speed is 30 knots (55 km/h; 34 mph) sustainable indefinitely, compared with a 20 knot (37 km/h; 23 mph) dash speed which can be sustained for only a few hours. Since nuclear-powered boats are generally larger, there is more room aboard for weapons systems, sonar sensors, electronic warfare systems and electronic counter-measures. Nevertheless, small coastal submarines, operating defensively in local waters, can be extremely effective. They do not need the high transit speeds and long endurance typical of US Navy boats, which are expected to deploy operationally all over the world.

*Above: At sea aboard the attack submarine **USS Seawolf**, a fire technician stands the battle station watch. The boat's missile control console incorporates modern touch screen technology.*

Left: The British 'Upholder' class (now in service with Canada as the 'Victoria' class) are typical of recent diesel submarine designs, having similar weapons and sensor fits to nuclear boats.

THE DIESEL OPTION: SILENT RUNNING

Proponents of nuclear power might consider the diesel-electric submarine to be an old-fashioned, second-rate weapon system operated by navies unable or unwilling to pay the cost of nuclear power. However, while the economic argument has a certain amount of truth – diesel boats certainly are cheaper to build and to run – that is far from the whole story. In the right place, the diesel submarine is at least as effective as an SSN, and may sometimes be the preferred option.

Diesel-electric boats are inherently quieter than SSNs. They are smaller and handier in enclosed or shallow waters, and in certain waters they are much harder to detect. ASW techniques

Above: The Republic of Korea submarine Nadaeyung (SS-069) *surfaces while taking part in Exercise RIMPAC 2002. Based on a German coastal submarine design, the 'Chang Bogo'-class boats are able to carry out short open-ocean patrols.*

developed to track nuclear boats in the deep ocean are of little use in trying to pinpoint a small, quiet boat in the waters of the continental shelf. This was graphically demonstrated at the end of the Cold War, when the Swedish navy had great difficulty in intercepting or even identifying Soviet submarine incursions into Sweden's territorial waters. The Soviets were using old 'Whiskey'-class boats for the missions: modern diesel boats are far more sophisticated and would present an even greater challenge.

Below: U-28, *a Type 206A submarine of the Bundesmarine, is typical of the advanced small coastal boats delivered by Germany's shipbuilding industry to navies all over the world. Built from non-magnetic steel, it displaces less than 500 tons and can be operated by a crew of 22. Delivered in the 1970s, the Type 206 boats have all received extensive upgrades.*

ARCTIC PATROLS: UNDER THE ICE

One area in which nuclear submarines have an overwhelming advantage over conventional boats is in under-ice operations. The advantage of nuclear-power is that it makes the submarine a fully self-contained system. Diesel engines need air to run, which means that the boat must surface or use a snorkel. The Americans were the first to realise that nuclear boats could operate under the Arctic ice cap, but it was the Soviets who realised that the ice could also protect ballistic missile submarines. Most Soviet boats were designed with strengthened fins to allow them to break through the ice. If the US Navy and Royal Navy wanted to keep a close watch on Soviet missile boats, they would have to follow them under the ice. From the 1970s onwards, British and American hunter-killers regularly operated beneath the ice cap, occasionally surfacing through areas of thin ice known as polnyas.

Above: In May 1986, the US Navy sent three submarines to conduct joint operations under the ice. At the end of the exercise, the 'Sturgeon'-class boats USS Ray, Archerfish *and* Hawkbill *surfaced together at the North Pole.*

Below: Although the Cold War is over, US Navy boats continue to operate in the Arctic. The USS Pogy (SSN-647) *is seen on one of five scientific missions carried out in the year 2000.*

ESCORT MISSION: CARRIER BATTLE GROUP

The most visible symbol of American power on the oceans of the world is the carrier battle group. On the face of it, the submarine has no place in such a force. Submarines are the ultimate stealth weapon, designed to remain unseen and to strike without warning. The carrier, by contrast, is all about power projection. It is an overt threat to anybody thinking of harming American interests, and the more visible the power, the more effective is its projection.

In recent years, however, the US Navy has regularly attached a 'Los Angeles'-class attack submarine to battle groups steaming into hostile waters. In part, this is because the '688' boats are fast enough to keep up with the battle group at flank speed. They are also an answer to the changing nature of the threat. In the post-Cold War era, the US Navy has become an expeditionary force, operating in littoral waters in support of American operations on land. One of the biggest threats in coastal waters is the small diesel-powered submarine, and the best weapon for dealing with submarines is another submarine. In addition, most American boats can launch Tomahawk missiles, adding to the battle group's firepower.

Left: An SH-60F Ocean Hawk from the USS George Washington hovers in front of the 'Sturgeon'-class attack submarine USS Grayling during an operation in the western Mediterranean. On this occasion, the US navy carrier battle group was undertaking joint operations with the French carrier Charles de Gaulle.

Below: A rigid hull inflatable boat (RIB) crew from the USS Nimitz approach the attack submarine USS Pasadena (SSN-752) to pick up an emergency medical patient. The carrier's strike force was deployed in support of Iraqi Freedom. Nuclear-powered attack submarines regularly provide cover for carrier battle groups during such operations.

'Upholder' and 'Victoria' classes Patrol submarines

To meet the requirement for a diesel-electric submarine type to succeed the 'Oberons' in Royal Navy service, Vickers Shipbuilding and Engineering Ltd developed the **Type 2400** or **'Upholder' class**. As in most new submarine classes, the emphasis was placed on standardisation and automation to reduce manning requirements. The first of the class was ordered in 1983 and completed in June 1990, and there followed another three boats ordered in 1986 and completed in 1991-93. It had at first been planned to order 12 such boats, but this scheme was trimmed first to 10 and then nine before being curtailed at just four as part of the 'peace dividend' at the end of the Cold War in the early 1990s.

Also included in the design were advanced noise-attenuation features to reduce the radiated noise levels below those of the already very quiet 'Oberon' class. There was also a reduction in the short time required to recharge the batteries to ensure a minimum exposure time of any part of the masts above the water. The armament fit includes a new positive discharge and fully automated weapon-handling system to avoid the stability problems at torpedo launch and the limita-

Above: The 'Upholder' class had only a very short British career, being deemed surplus to requirements in the early 1990s and laid up before Canadian purchase.

tions that are sometimes made on the platform's speed and manoeuvrability.

HMS **Upholder**, HMS **Unseen**, HMS **Ursula** and HMS **Unicorn** were laid up in 1994, and in 1998 were bought by Canada for service from 2000 as the **'Victoria' class**. These are named HMCS **Chicoutimi**, HMCS **Victoria**, HMCS **Cornerbrook** and HMCS **Windsor** respectively.

SPECIFICATION	
'Victoria' class	**Torpedo tubes:** six 21-in (533-mm) tubes (all bow) for 18 Mk 48 Mod 4 wire-guided active/passive-homing dual-role torpedoes; provision for mines and Sub-Harpoon anti-ship missiles has been removed. Anti-aircraft capability may be added.
Displacement: 2,168 tons surfaced; 2,455 tons dived	
Dimensions: length 70.3 m (230 ft 7 in); beam 7.6 m (25 ft); draught 5.5 m (17 ft 8 in)	
Propulsion: two Paxman Valenta 16SZ diesels delivering 2700 kW (3,620 shp) and one GEC electric motor delivering 4025 kW (5,400 shp) to one shaft	**Electronics:** one Type 1007 navigation radar, one Type 2040 passive bow sonar, one Type 2007 passive flank-array sonar, one MUSL passive towed-array sonar, one Librascope fire-control system, one AR 900 ESM system, and two SSE decoy launchers
Performance: speed 12 kts surfaced and 20 kts dived; range 14805 km (9,200 miles) at 8 kts snorting	
Diving depth: 300 m (985 ft) operational and 500 m (1,640 ft) maximum	**Complement:** up to 53

The single-hulled 'Upholder'-class submarines were trimmed to just four in number, and entered British service from 1990 with provision for advanced weapons such as the Spearfish torpedo and UGM-84B Sub-Harpoon anti-ship missile.

'Shishumar' class Patrol submarine

In December 1981 the Indian government reached an agreement with Howaldtswerke-Deutsche Werft, a German organisation based in Kiel, for a four-section contract covering four conventional submarines of the Type 1500 variant of the very successful boats of the Type 209 class. The four-part contract covered the construction in Germany of an initial pair of submarines of the **'Shishumar' class**, packages of equipment and components for the building of another two boats by the Mazagon Dock Ltd. of Mumbai (Bombay), the training of specialised design and construction personnel employed by

28 km (17.4 miles) at 23 kts and 12 km (7.5 miles) at 35 kts. The fifth and sixth boats were to have been completed with provision for the carriage and firing of anti-ship missiles, but the existing boats lack this facility. They do have, however, provision for the addition of external 'strap-on' carriers.

The *Shishumar* started a mid-life refit in 1999, with the other boats in the 'Shishumar'-class following in order of completion, and improvements that may be retrofitted are French Eledone sonar and an Indian action data system.

Mazagon, and the provision of logistical support and consultation services during the manufacture and early service of the boats. In 1984 it was announced that another two boats would be built at Mazagon, giving the Indian navy a total of six 'Shishumar'-class submarines, but this scheme was overtaken in the later part of the decade by changes in the thinking of the Indian navy, and in 1988 it was revealed that the arrangement with Howaldtswerke would end with the completion of the fourth boat.

The decision was reviewed 1992 and 1997, and in 1999 the Indian navy decided to move ahead with its Project 75 for the Indian construction of three submarines of the French 'Scorpène' class design.

The four 'Shishumar' boats are the **Shishumar, Shankush, Shalki** and **Shankul**. Built in Germany, the first two boats were laid down in May and September 1982 for launching in December and May 1984 and completion in September and November 1986, while the last two boats, built in India, were laid down in June 1984

and September 1989 for launching in September 1989 and March 1992 and completion in February 1992 and May 1994.

The submarines are basically conventional with a single central bulkhead, their most notable operational features being the provision of an IKL-designed escape system. This latter comprises an integrated escape sphere able to accommodate the entire 40-man crew. This sphere can withstand the same pressure as the hull, has its own eight-hour air supply, and is outfitted for short term survival and communications.

Bow tubes

The eight torpedo tubes are all grouped in the bows, and provision is made for the embarkation of six reload torpedoes. The standard weapon for these tubes is a German torpedo, the AEG SUT, which is a wire-guided weapon with active/passive onboard terminal

Right: The 'Shishumar'-class boats have given the Indian navy effective operational capability and also invaluable experience in modern submarine thinking.

guidance. The weapon carries a 250-kg (551-lb) HE warhead, and its two primary capabilities in terms of range and speed are

SPECIFICATION
'Shishumar' class

Displacement: 1,660 tons surfaced; 1,850 tons dived
Dimensions: length 64.4 m (211 ft 2 in); beam 6.5 m (21 ft 4 in); draught 6 m (19 ft 8 in)
Propulsion: four MTU 12V 493 AZ80 diesels delivering 1800 kW (2,415 shp) and one Siemens electric motor delivering 3430 kW (4600 shp) to one shaft
Performance: speed 11 kts surfaced and 22 kts dived; range 14825 km (9,210 miles) at 8 kts snorting
Diving depth: 260 m (855 ft) operational
Torpedo tubes: eight 533-mm (21-in) tubes (all bow) for 14 torpedoes; provision for mines
Electronics: one Calypso surface search radar, one CSU 83 active/passive hull sonar, one DUUX 5 passive ranging sonar, Librascope Mk 1 fire-control system, AR 700 or Sea Sentry ESM, and C 303 acoustic decoys
Complement: 40

'Collins' class Patrol submarine

Needing a successor to its obsolescent 'Oberon' class diesel-electric submarines, the Royal Australian Navy decided in the first part of the 1980s to consider the full range of foreign-designed submarines that would meet the RAN's operational requirement and also be suitable for construction in an Australian yard. The decision eventually went to a Swedish design, the Type 471 designed by Kockums, and in June 1987 the Australian Submarine Corporation contracted with Kockums for six such submarines, to be built in Adelaide, South Australia, and known in Australian service as the **'Collins'-class**. The contract included an option for another two boats, but this option was not exercised.

Fabrication of the boats' initial assemblies began in June 1989, and the bows and midships sec-

tions of the first submarines were produced in Sweden and shipped to Adelaide to be mated with locally built sections. The

boats were laid down between February 1990 and May 1995, launched between August 1993 and November 2001, and completed between July 1996 and a time in 2003, and are named **HMAS Collins**, **HMAS Farncomb**, **HMAS Waller**, **HMAS Dechaineux**, **HMAS Sheean** and **HMAS Rankin**.

The armament and fire-control/combat system, the latter proving very troublesome during development and initial service, are along American lines, while the sonar is basically of French and Australian origins. As noted above, the Boeing/Rockwell combat system has been plagued by problems, and only after the Raytheon CCS Mk 2 system has been installed will the boats be regarded as fully operational from about 2007. All but the Collins, which was retrofitted, were built with anechoic tiles on their outer surfaces, and the periscopes are British, in the form of the Pilkington (now

Above: The 'Collins'-class submarines are based at the Royal Australian Navy's Fleet Base West (HMAS Stirling) in Western Australia, with pairs of boats making regular deployments to the east coast.

Thales) Optronics CK43 search and CH93 attack units. The tubes are all located in the bows, and are designed to fire either the Mk 48 Mod 4 heavyweight torpedo or the UGM-84B Sub-Harpoon underwater-launched anti-ship missile, of which a combined total of 22 can be shipped. An alternative is 44 mines. The Mk 48 Mod 4 is a wire-guided dual-role weapon with active/passive homing, and can carry its 267-kg (590-lb) warhead to a range of 38 km (23.6 miles) at 55 kts or 50 km (31.1 miles) at 40 kts. The tube-launched weapons are discharged by an air turbine pump arrangement.

Great development effort has improved the boats' reliability and quietness. The revision of the boats with a Stirling air-independent propulsion system in a lengthened hull is being considered, and a test rig has been bought from Sweden.

SPECIFICATION	
'Collins' class	**Diving depth:** 300 m (985 ft) operational
Displacement: 3,051 tons surfaced; 3,353 tons dived	**Torpedo tubes:** six 533-mm (21-in) tubes (all bow) for 22 torpedoes or missiles, or 44 mines
Dimensions: length 77.8 m (255 ft 3 in); beam 7.8 m (25 ft 5 in); draught 7 m (23 ft)	**Electronics:** one Type 1007 navigation radar, one Scylla sonar with active/passive bow and passive flank arrays; one Kariwara, Narama or TB 23 passive towed-array sonar; Boeing/Rockwell data system, AR740 ESM, and two SSE decoys
Propulsion: three Hedemora V18B/14 diesels delivering 4500 kW (6,035 shp) and one Jeumont Schneider electric motor delivering 5475 kW (7,345 shp) to one shaft	
	Complement: 42
Performance: speed 10 kts surfaced and 20 kts dived; range 21,325 km (13,250 miles) at 10 kts surfaced	

Left: The RAN's six-strong class of 'Collins' boats are typical of modern submarine design, and may be retrofitted with an air-independent propulsion system (AIPS).

'Dolphin' class Patrol submarine

Left: The three 'Dolphin'-class submarines provide Israel with a capable cruise missile deterrent, interdiction, surveillance and also a swimmer delivery capability.

swimmers can leave and re-enter the boat. It is also likely that the boats are fitted with the Triten anti-helicopter SAM system.

Weapons fit

Primary anti-ship and anti-submarine armament is the STN Atlas DM2A4 Seehecht wire-guided torpedo carrying a 260-kg (573-lb) warhead to a range of 13000 m (14,215 yards) in active mode at 35 kts, or to 28000 m (30,620 yards) in passive mode at 23 kts. Pending the delivery of the complete DM2A4 package from Germany, a number of NT 37E torpedoes are included in the torpedo fit. Tube-laid mines are an alternative to the 16 torpedoes, and other weapons that can also be launched are up to five UGM-84C Sub-Harpoon underwater-launched AShMs, or conventionally armed cruise missiles of Israeli design and manufacture. In addition to the six 533-mm (21-in) conventional tubes, the boats also have four 650-mm (25.6-in) tubes optimised for the launch of swimmer delivery vehicles (SDVs) but with provision for the carriage of liners so that they can also be used as conventional torpedo tubes.

The boats are painted in blue and green for reduced visibility in the shallow water of the East Mediterranean.

SPECIFICATION	
'Dolphin' class **Displacement:** 1,640 tons surfaced; 1,900 tons dived **Dimensions:** length 57.3 m (188 ft); beam 6.8 m (22 ft 4 in); draught 6.2 m (20 ft 4 in) **Propulsion:** three MTU 16V 396 SE 84 diesels delivering 3165 kW (4,245 shp) and one Siemens electric motor delivering 2890 kW (3,875 shp) to one shaft **Performance:** speed 11 kts snorting and 20 kts dived; range 14825 km (9,210 miles) at 8 kts surfaced and	780 km (485 miles) at 8 kts dived **Diving depth:** 350 m (1,150 ft) operational **Torpedo tubes:** six 533-mm (21-in) and four 650-mm (25.6-in) tubes (all bow); for weapons see text **Electronics:** Elta surface search radar, CSU 90 active/passive hull sonar, PRS-3 passive ranging sonar, FAS-3 passive flank-array sonar, ISUS 90-1 torpedo fire-control system, and Tinmex 4CH(V) 2 ESM **Complement:** 30

To replace three elderly Type 206 coastal submarines deleted in 1999-2000, the Israeli navy decided in 1988 to purchase two boats of the the **'Dolphin'** or **Type 800 class** as variants of the German Type 212 class design by IKL. On the basis of promised American FMS (Foreign Military Sales) funding, Israel contracted with the Ingalls Shipbuilding Division of the Litton Corporation as prime contractor for the boats, to be built in Germany by Howaldtswerke of Kiel with participation by Thyssen Nordseewerke of Emden. Funding was made available in July 1989 and the contract became effective in January 1990, but in November it was cancelled because of funding pressures in the period leading up to the 1991 Gulf War. The programme was revived with German funding in April 1991, and then in July 1994 Israel exercised its option for a third boat of the same class.

The first steel for the three boats was cut in April 1992, and the boats were laid down in October 1994, April 1995 and December 1996 for completion in July 1999, November 1999 and July 2000 as the **Dolphin**, **Leviathan** and **Tekuma**.

The three boats are similar to the Type 212 class except for internal revisions to permit the incorporation of a 'wet and dry' compartment so that underwater

'Västergötland' class Patrol submarine

In the late 1970s the Swedish navy began to consider building a class of patrol submarines to replace the 'Draken'-class boats built in the late 1950s and early 1960s, and to supplement the 'Sjöormen' classes built in the second half of the 1960s, which were eventually sold to Singapore as training boats in the second half of the 1990s. The result was the **'Västergötland' class** of diesel patrol submarines.

The design of this class was contracted to Kockums of Malmö during April 1978. The type was conceived with a single hull, X-type after control surfaces combining rudder and hydroplane functions, and a Pilkington Optronics CK 38 optronic search periscope enhanced with night vision capability. Four boats in the class were commissioned in the period 1987-90. They were constructed by Kockums on the basis of its own central section and bow and stern sections by Karlskrona varvet.

Operations in the acoustically tricky shallow waters of the Baltic demanded special consideration

SPECIFICATION

'Västergötland' class
Displacement: 1,070 tons surfaced; 1,143 tons dived
Dimensions: length 48.5 m (159 ft 1 in); beam 6.06 m (19 ft 11 in); draught 5.6 m (18 ft 4 in)
Propulsion: two Hedemora V12A/15-Ub diesels delivering 1640 kW (2,200 shp) and one Jeumont Schneider electric motor delivering 1350 kW (1,810 shp) to one shaft
Performance: speed 10 kts surfaced and 20 kts dived
Diving depth: 300 m (985 ft)

operational
Torpedo tubes: six 533-mm (21-in) and three 400-mm (15.75-in) tubes (all bow) for 12 and six torpedoes respectively; 48 mines can be carried in an external girdle
Electronics: Terma surface search and navigation radar, CSU 83 active/passive hull sonar, passive flank-array sonar, IPS-17 (Sesub 900A) torpedo fire-control system, and Argo AR-700-S5 or Condor CS 3071 ESM
Complement: 28

Above: Commissioned in January 1990, Östergötland was the last 'Västergötland' completed, and is being modernised. The first pair may be leased to Denmark.

Above: There are four boats in the 'Västergötland' class: **Västergötland, Hälsingland, Södermanland and Östergötland.**

of quietening features, and the boats are also coated with an anechoic layer to reduce their reflection of active sonar pulses. The torpedo tubes are all located in the bow, and comprise six 533-mm (21-in) tubes over three 400-mm (15.75-in) tubes. All the tubes are used for wire-guided torpedoes, the larger-diameter tubes firing swim-out FFV Type 613 passive-homing anti-ship weapons carrying a 240-kg (529-lb) warhead to a range of 20 km (12.4 miles) at 45 kts, and the smaller-diameter tubes firing

FFV Type 431/451 active/passive-homing anti-submarine weapons carrying a 45-kg (99-lb) shaped-charge warhead to a range of 20 km at 25 kts.

The last two boats are being lengthened by 10 m (32 ft 10 in) to allow the incorporation of a Stirling-cycle AIPS (Air-Independent Propulsion System) providing a submerged endurance of some 14 days.

The first two boats may be passed to Denmark, which already has one 'Näcken'- class submarine from Sweden.

'Kilo' class Patrol submarine

The **Project 877** or **Vashavyanka** diesel-electric submarine, better known in the West as the **'Kilo' class**, was designed in the early 1970s for the anti-submarine and anti-ship defence of Soviet naval bases, coastal installations and sea lanes, and also for the patrol and surveillance tasks. First delivered from the shipyard at Komsomolsk in eastern Siberia, but then built in the western USSR at Nizhny Novgorod and the Admiralty Yard in Leningrad

Built at Komsomolsk and two other yards, the 'Kilo' diesel-electric submarines were derived from the longer-range 'Tango' class, and despite problems with its batteries in hotter conditions has achieved respectable export sales to countries of North Africa, the Middle East and the Far East.

Above: Poland received a single 'Project 877E' class submarine, the letter suffix indicating export, in June 1986. Based at Gdynia, the submarine is named **Orzel.**

Above: Between 1986 and 2000 India received 10 'Kilos'. Known as the 'Sindhughosh' class, after the name of the first boat delivered, the submarines are allocated to the 11th Submarine Squadron (four boats at Vishakapatnam) and the 10th Submarine Squadron (six boats based at Mumbai). Five boats are armed with 3M54 Alfa (SS-N-27) active radar homing SLCMs with a supersonic attack phase and a range of 180 km (112 miles).

SPECIFICATION	
'Kilo' (Project 4B) class **Displacement:** 2,325 tons surfaced; 3,076 tons dived **Dimensions:** length 73.8 m (242 ft 2 in); beam 9.9 m (32 ft 6 in); draught 6.6 m (21 ft 8 in) **Propulsion:** two diesels delivering 2720 kW (3,650 shp) and one electric motor delivering 4400 kW (5,900 shp) to one shaft **Performance:** 10 kts surfaced and 17 kts dived; range 11125 km (6,915 miles) at 8 kts snorting and 740 km (460 miles) at 3 kts dived	**Diving depth:** 240 m (790 ft) operational **Torpedo tubes:** six 533-mm (21-in) tubes (all bow) for 18 torpedoes or 24 mines, and provision for one short-range SAM launcher **Electronics:** one 'Snoop Tray' radar, one 'Shark Teeth'/'Shark Fin' active/passive hull sonar, one 'Mouse Roar' active attack hull sonar, MVU-110EM or MVU-119EM torpedo fire-control system, and 'Squid Head' or 'Brick Pulp' ESM **Complement:** 52

(now St Petersburg), the boat is of the medium-endurance type and the first example of this boat was launched in 1979 for completion in 1982.

Soviet deletions

Some 24 'Kilos' were built for the Soviet navy, and by the first part of the 21st century the Russian navy had deleted 15 of these, leaving it with nine boats with the Northern and Pacific Fleets (three and four respectively), and single

boats with the Baltic and Black Sea Fleets, the latter's boat having been modified with pump-jet propulsion.

In design the 'Kilo' class is a development of the 'Tango' class with an improved hull form. Even so, the boat can be considered only basic by comparison with contemporary Western submarines. The Soviets procured the submarine in four variants: the Project 877 baseline model, **Project 877K** with improved fire-control, **Project 877M** with provision for wire-guided torpedoes from two tubes, and the slightly longer **Project 4B** with uprated diesels, an electric motor turning more slowly for less noise, and an automated data system to provide fire-control data for two simultaneous interceptions. Boats have been exported to Algeria (two), China (four), India (10), Iran (three), Poland (one) and Romania (one). Some of these boats are **Type 636** submarines with improved propulsion and fire-control systems.

Left: With the retirement of its more maintenance-intensive vessels, the earlier 'Kilo'-class submarines have disappeared from the Russian navy's active submarine list.

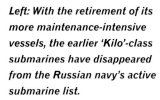

'Tupi' class Patrol submarine

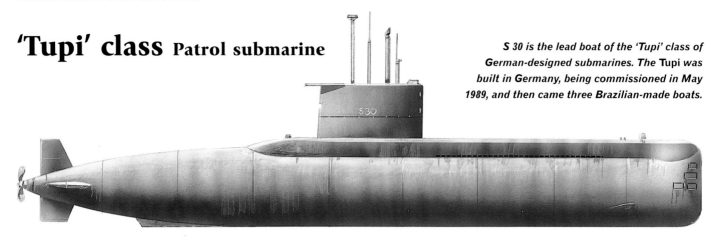

S 30 is the lead boat of the 'Tupi' class of German-designed submarines. The Tupi was built in Germany, being commissioned in May 1989, and then came three Brazilian-made boats.

In 1984 Brazil contracted with Howaldtswerke-Deutsche Werft for six **'Tupi' class** submarines to the 'Type 1400' subvariant of the 'Type 209' model, the first built in Kiel and the other five in Rio de Janeiro. Financial constraints trimmed the Brazilian-built quantity to three, while the pair of **'Tikuna'-class** boats, to an improved 'Tupi' class standard, are far behind schedule: the *Tikuna*'s commissioning date is delayed from 2000 to 2005 and work on the *Tapuia* has been suspended.

Brazil established an uranium-enrichment plant in 1988 with the announced intention of building an SSN, but this project has not proceeded beyond the design stage. The 'Tikuna'-class boats were described as intermediate between the older SSKs and an SSN.

Brazilian torpedoes

The 'Tupi' class boats operate from Moncangue island's Base Almirante Castro e Silva across the bay from Rio. These are well armed small boats, carrying a combination of British Mk 24 Tigerfish torpedoes and an anti-submarine torpedo developed by the IPqM (Instituto de Pesquisas da Marinha, or naval research institute). Eight torpedoes are carried in the tubes and there are eight reloads. The Tigerfish is a wire-guided torpedo capable of active homing at 35 kts

Below: The Tamoio was built in Brazil as the second unit of the 'Tupi' class, and was completed in December 1994 at the end of a construction effort lasting somewhat more than eight years.

SPECIFICATION	
'Tupi' class **Boats in class:** *Tupi, Tamoio, Timbira* and *Tapajo* **Displacement:** 1,400 tons surfaced; 1,550 tons dived **Dimensions:** length 61.2 m (200 ft 9 in); beam 6.2 m (20 ft 4 in); draught 5.5 m (18 ft) **Propulsion:** four MTU 12V 493 AZ80 diesels delivering 1800 kW (2,414 shp) and one Siemens electric motor delivering 3425 kW (4,595 shp to one shaft **Performance:** speed 11 kts	surfaced/snorting and 21.5 kts dived; range 15000 km (9,320 miles) at 8 kts surfaced and 740 km (460 miles) at 4 kts dived **Diving depth:** 250 m (820 ft) **Armament:** eight 533-mm (21-in) tubes with up to 16 Mk 24 Mod 1 or 2 Tigerfish torpedoes or IPqM anti-submarine torpedoes **Electronics:** Calypso navigation radar; DR-4000 ESM, CSU 83/1 hull-mounted passive search/attack sonar **Complement:** 30

Right: The Brazilian 'Tupi'-class submarines offer generally good capabilities, and it is planned that their torpedo armament should be upgraded in the future with the advanced Bofors 2000 torpedo.

to a range of 13 km (8 miles) or passive homing at 24 kts to 29.6 km (18.4 miles). The IPqM torpedo has a swim-out launch system and travels up to 18.5 km (11.5 miles) at 45 kts.

The 'Tikuna'-class boats are larger, at 2,425 tons dived, and have a crew of 39. Designed for an endur-ance of 60 days, they are designed to carry MCF-01/100 acoustic-magnetic mines (produced by IPqM) instead of some torpedoes.

'Type 212A' Patrol submarine

Above: The U 31 under way just off the yard in which its final assembly was undertaken. The 'Type 212A'-class boats are notable for their AIPS and their streamlined exterior lines.

Below: The AIPS, created and manufactured by Siemens and HDW, offer extended underwater endurance. The attack periscopes are by Zeiss.

Since the 1980s there has been a steadily rising level of interest among the world's navies in the advantages offered by the intro-duction of an air-independent propulsion system to create true 'submarines' out of what are otherwise conventionally powered 'submersibles'.

Germany trialled such a sys-tem in a 'Type-205' boat adapted with an AIPS in 1988-89, and then moved forward to the creation of a highly stream-lined boat designed from the outset with an AIPS, in this case using a hybrid fuel cell/bat-tery propulsion arrangement based on Siemens PEM fuel cell technology. In 1992, ARGE 212 (a consortium of Howaldtswerke-Deutsche Werft and Thyssen Nord- seewerke, supported by IKL) completed the initial design of the **'Type 212A' class**, and an initial four boats were authorised in July 1994. However, it was only in

SPECIFICATION	
'Type 212A' class	**Torpedo tubes:** six 21-in (533-mm)
Displacement: 1,450 tons surfaced;	tubes (all bow) for 12 DM2A4 wire-
1,830 tons dived	guided torpedoes
Dimensions: length 55.9 m (183 ft 5	**Electronics:** Type 1007 navigation
in); beam 7 m (23 ft); draught 6 m	radar, DBQS-40 passive ranging
(19 ft 8 in)	and intercept sonar, FAS-3 flank
Propulsion: one MTU diesel	and passive towed-array sonar,
delivering 3165 kW (4,245 hp) and	MOA 3070 or ELAK mine-detection
one electric motor delivering	sonar, MSI-90U weapon-control
2890 kW (3,875 shp) to one shaft	system, FL 1800 ESM, and TAU
Performance: speed 12 kts surfaced	2000 torpedo decoy system
and 20 kts dived; range 14805 km	**Complement:** 27
(9,200 miles) at 8 kts surfaced	

July 1998 that the first metal was cut as the programme had been slowed to allow the incorporation of changes (including improved habitability and a greater diving depth) to maximise commonality with two boats ordered by Italy.

The four German boats, which may be complemented by a further eight, are the **U 31** to **U 34**. These are based on forward and after sections produced by HDW at Kiel and TNSW at Emden, with the boats completed alternately at the two yards. The first boat was launched in 2002, and the schedule allows thorough testing of this boat before the other three are finalised.

The design is based on a partial double hull in which the larger-diameter forward section is connected to the narrower-diameter after section (carrying the two liquid oxygen tanks and the hydrogen tankage) by a tapered section accommodating the fuel cell plant. The underwater propulsion can provide a maximum speed of 20 kts declining to 8 kts on just the fuel cells.

The two Italian boats, of which the first is to be called the **Salvatore Todaro**, are being built at Muggiano by Fincantieri, and are scheduled for completion in 2005-2006 to a standard essentially similar to that of the German boats.

Above: key features of the 'Type 212A' class design are the diving planes on the conning tower, the X-configured control surfaces at the stern, and the propeller with seven scimitar-shaped blades.

'Type 214' Patrol submarine

Ordered by Greece and South Korea, the **'Type 214'-class** submarine is basically a development of the 'Type 209'-class design with a hull further optimised for hydrodynamic efficiency and therefore 'stealthiness', but with the 'Type 212A' class's AIPS (Air-Independent Propulsion System) based on the Siemens PEM (Polymer Electrolyte Membrane) fuel cell technology rather than the Stirling system used in

Swedish submarines. Each of the boats boasts two PEM cells, producing 120 kW (161 shp) per module, and this translates into a submerged endurance of 14 days.

In October 1998 the Greek government announced that the Greek navy was to procure four 'Type 214'-class submarines with the local designation **'Katsonis' class**. The first boat is being built by Howaldtswerke of Kiel for planned launch in December

2003 and commissioning in 2005, and the other three are to be completed by the Skaramanga yard of Hellenic Shipyards. The four Greek boats are the **Katsonis**, **Papanilolis**, **Pipinos** and **Matrozos**.

Changes differentiating the 'Type 214' class from the 'Type 212A' class include the location of the diving planes on the forward part of the hull rather than the conning tower, more conventional control surfaces (horizontal and vertical elements rather than an X-configuration) at the stern, eight rather than six swim-out rather than water ram discharge bow tubes (including four fitted for Harpoon anti-ship missiles), a hull made of different materials for a greater diving depth, and

slightly different electronics even though a similar Zeiss optronic periscope is used.

In December 2000 that the South Korean defence ministry selected the 'Type 214' in preference to the French 'Scorpène' design (and the Russian offer of three 'Kilo'-class boats) to meet its 'KS-II' requirement for three submarines. The contract to build the new boats was awarded to Hyundai Heavy Industries rather than Daewoo Shipbuilding and Marine Engineering, which built South Korea's nine 'Chang Bogo' ('Type 1200' subclass of the 'Type 209' class) boats.

The boats are to be built with German technical assistance and are scheduled for completion in 2007, 2008 and 2009.

Above: The advent of their 'Type 214' submarines, derived from the 'Type 209' design with the AIPS developed for the 'Type 212A', will transform the submarine capabilities of the Greek and South Korean navies.

SPECIFICATION	
'Type 214' class **Displacement:** 1,700 tons surfaced; 1,980 tons dived **Dimensions:** length 65 m (213 ft 3 in); beam 6.3 m (20 ft 8 in); draught 6 m (19 ft 8 in) **Propulsion:** two MTU 16V 396 diesels delivering 6320 kW (8,475 shp) and one Siemens Permasyn electric motor delivering unspecified power to one shaft **Performance:** speed 12 kts surfaced and 20 kts dived	**Diving depth:** 400 m (1,315 ft) **Torpedo tubes:** eight 21-in (533-mm) tubes (all bow) for 16 STN Atlas torpedoes and Harpoon anti-ship missiles **Electronics:** navigation radar, bow, flank-array and towed-array sonars, ISUS 90 weapon-control system, ESM, and Circe torpedo decoy system **Complement:** 27

'Uzushio' class
Diesel attack submarine

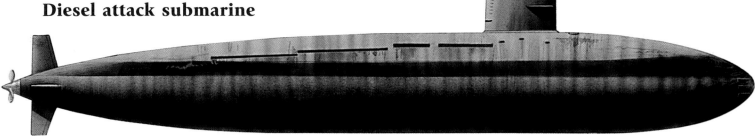

SPECIFICATION

'Uzushio' class
Type: Diesel-powered attack submarine
Displacement: 1,850 tons standard surfaced and 3,600 tons dived
Dimensions: length 72 m (236 ft 3 in); beam 9.90 m (32 ft 6 in); draught 7.50 m (24 ft 7 in)
Machinery: two Kawasaki-MAN V8/V24-30 diesels driving one shaft delivering 2685 kW (3,600 bhp) on the surface and 5369 kW (7,200 bhp) dived
Speed: 12 kts (22 km/h; 14 mph) surfaced and 20 kts (37 km/h; 23 mph) dived
Diving depth: 200 m (656 ft) normal
Torpedo tubes: six 533-mm (21-in) amidships
Basic load: 18 weapons, usually a mix of homing torpedoes
Complement: 80

The increase in Cold War tensions in the 1950s made it necessary for the US and its allies to allow former enemies Germany and Japan to rearm.

The US Navy's submarine stranglehold on the home islands was a major factor in Japan's crushing defeat during World War II. The reborn Japanese navy, originally called the Maritime Safety Agency and latterly known as the Maritime Self-Defence Force to emphasise its purely defensive nature, recognised that fact. As a result, its first priority was anti-submarine warfare.

ASW training

The best defence against submarines is often other submarines. The first MSDF boat was an ex-US 'Gato'-class vessel, followed in the late 1950s by a number of small coastal submarines. Five larger 'Oshio'-class boats followed in the late 1960s, the first Japanese fleet boats to sail since the war. They were conservative in design, and their primary function was to serve as targets for ASW training. Commissioned between 1971 and 1978, the seven boats of the **'Uzushio'sss class** marked a great leap forwards. Influenced strongly by American designs, the boats had an Albacore-type teardrop hull for maximum hydrodynamic efficiency. The bow sonar array meant that the torpedo tubes had to be located amidships, again following US Navy practice.

Double hull

Manufactured from NS-63 high-tensile steel, the 'Uzushios' were double-hulled, and had a diving depth in excess of 200 m (656 ft). They incorporated a certain amount of automation, most notably in the provision of a kind of submarine auto-pilot, combining automatic depth and direction maintenance.

The 'Uzushios' were succeeded in production by the improved and enlarged 'Yuushio'-class, and were retired through the 1990s as they were replaced in service one for one by the 'Harushio'-class boats.

The revolutionary teardrop shape introduced by the US submarine Albacore was a major influence on the design of Japan's first truly modern submarine, the Uzushio.

Right: The 'Uzushio'-class submarine Isoshio enters port. Commissioned in the 1970s, these boats were the foundation of Japan's modern submarine service.

'Yuushio' class Diesel attack submarine

The 10 boats of the **'Yuushio' class** have provided the backbone of the Maritime Self-Defence Force's submarine strength since the 1980s. Essentially an enlarged version of the preceding teardrop 'Uzushio' class, the 'Yuushios' differ primarily in having a deeper diving capability.

The 'Uzushio'-class subs were decommissioned in the 1990s as the new 'Harushio' class was commissioned.

Bow sonar

Of double-hull construction, these boats follow the US Navy nuclear attack submarine practice of having a bow sonar array with the torpedo tubes moved to amidships and angled outwards. The first of the class, **Yuushio** (SS573), entered service in 1980 with the **Mochishio** (SS574), **Setoshio** (SS575), **Okishio** (SS576), **Nadashio** (SS577), **Hamashio** (SS578), **Akishio** (SS579), **Takeshio** (SS580), **Yukishio** (SS581), and **Sachishio** (SS582) following at yearly intervals.

From the *Nadashio* onwards the class was fitted to carry and fire the American Sub-Harpoon anti-ship missile, a capability which was retrofitted to all of the earlier boats except for the *Yuushio* itself. All the boats carry the Type 89 dual-purpose, active-passive torpedoes which have a maximum speed of 55 kts (102 km/h; 63 mph) and a maximum reduced speed range of 50 km (31 miles).

The electronics carried on the Yuushio-class are of the latest design, and include the ZQQ-5 bow sonar (a modified American BQS-4) and the ZQR-1 towed array (similar to the American BQR-15). *Yuushio* was removed from front-line service to become a training boat in 1996.

Last of the line

The last of the 'Yuushios' was

commissioned in 1989. By that time, the first three boats of the follow-on 'Harushio' class had been laid down, with the name-ship commissioning at the end of November 1990. *Harushio* was followed at yearly intervals by *Natsushio, Hayashio, Arashio, Wakashio, Fuyushio*, and by *Asashio* in 1997. As each entered service one of the 'Uzushio'-class boats was paid off.

The 'Harushios' follow the same basic design as the 'Yuushios', but are slightly larger in all dimensions. More attention has been paid to reducing noise internally, and all have anechoic material applied to the outer surfaces. A stronger pressure hull means that operational diving depth has been increased to some 300 m (1,150 ft).

Asashio, the last of the class, was completed to a modified design. Increased systems automation has allowed crew to be reduced from 74 to 71.

Right: The second 'Yuushio'-class boat Mochishio *enters the US Pacific Fleet base as it makes a courtesy visit to Pearl Harbor in the mid 1990s.*

SPECIFICATION	
'Yuushio' class	**Diving depth:** 275 m (900 ft)
Displacement: 2,200 tons standard surfaced and 2,730 tons dived	operational
	Torpedo tubes: six 533-mm (21-in)
Dimensions: length 76 m (249 ft 4 in); beam 9.90 m (32 ft 6 in); draught 7.50 m (24 ft 7¼ in)	amidships
	Basic load: 18-20 torpedoes and anti-ship missiles
Propulsion: two diesels delivering 2535 kW (3,400 hp) to one electric motor driving one shaft	**Electronics:** one ZPS-6 surface-search radar, one ZQQ-5 bow sonar, one SQS-36(J) sonar, one ZQR-1 towed array, one ALR 3-6 ESM suite
Speed: 12 kts (22 km/h; 14 mph) surfaced and 20 kts (37 km/h; 23 mph) dived	**Complement:** 75

Above: Although influenced by US Navy practice, by the time Harushio *was commissioned in 1990, Japanese submarine designs were using mainly home-built systems and equipment.*

Below: Yuushio *conducts an emergency surfacing drill. The name ship of its class has been in use as a training submarine since 1996.*

Above: Sailors prepare to moor as the Mochishio *approaches the dock.*

'Oyashio' class Diesel attack submarine

The **Oyashio**, commissioned in 1998, was the first of five advanced diesel-powered patrol submarines to enter service with the Japan Maritime Self-Defence Force. The new submarines are examples of the changing face of Japanese military equipment acquisition since the establishment of the Self-Defence Forces in the 1950s.

The first generation of equipment was often second hand and generally acquired from the United States. By 1960, however, Japanese industry was up and running after the devastation of World War II, and the second stage saw American equipment or licence-built

Right: Oyashio *is as capable as most nuclear boats. Although slower and with less endurance, its diesel electric powerplant makes it quieter than a 'nuke'.*

Japanese copies of American equipment installed in Japanese-built platforms.

All Japanese

From the late 1970s, an increasing proportion of JMSDF systems has been of Japanese origin. Even where those systems are based on state-of-the-art American or European designs, they have often been upgraded – at great cost – to be even more capable

then the original. The 'Oyashio' class is equipped with Japanese-designed radar and electronics. Its sonar systems are based on American designs, but have been modified to suit Japanese requirements.

Outwardly, the 'Oyashios' have changed a little from preceding Japanese submarines. The revised outer casing gives them something of the look of British nuclear boats, while the fin is of a more efficient hydrodynamic shape.

The new boats share the double hulls and anechoic coating of the previous class, but have been equipped with large flank sonar arrays, which according to some sources account for the increase in displacement over the 'Harushios'.

Future engines

Kawasaki Heavy Industries have been conducting experiments in using Sterling-Cycle air-independent powerplants and fuel cells, and at one stage these were planned for the later 'Oyashios'. It is now likely that such systems, which allow boats to operate submerged for extended periods, will make their appearance in the next class of Japanese submarines.

As the 'Oyashios' are completed they will replace the older 'Yuushio' class boats. The Japanese Defense Agency expects that future world conditions will call for an operational total of 12 to 14 boats. Most of these will be of the 'Oyashio' class as current building plans call for as many as 10 boats to be in service by 2007 or 2008.

SPECIFICATION

'Oyashio' class
Displacement: 2,700 tons standard surfaced and 3,000 tons dived
Dimensions: length 81.70 m (268 ft); beam 8.90 m (29 ft 3 in); draught 7.90 m (25 ft 11 in)
Propulsion: two Kawasaki 12V25S diesels delivering 4100 kW (5,520 hp) to two Fuji electric motors driving one shaft
Speed: 12 kts (22 km/h; 14 mph) surfaced and 20 kts (37 km/h; 23 mph) dived

Diving depth: 300 m (984 ft) operational and 500 m (1,640 ft) maximum
Torpedo tubes: six 533-mm (21-in) amidships
Basic load: 20 Type 89 torpedoes and Harpoon anti-ship missiles
Electronics: one ZPS-6 surface-search radar, one Hughes-Oki ZQQ-5B bow sonar, port and starboard flank sonar arrays, one ZQR-1 (BQR-15) towed array, one ZLR 7 ESM suite
Complement: 69

Left: Oyashio, *commissioned in 1998, is the first Japanese submarine in nearly three decades to have a significantly different hull form and fin.*

'Ula' class Patrol submarine

Since the deletion of the last six of the original 15 'Kobben'-class boats in the second half of the 1990s, the Norwegian navy operates just six submarines in the form of the boats of the **'Ula' class** with diesel-electric propulsion. The boats are named **Ula**, **Uredd**, **Utvaer**, **Uthaug**, **Utstein** and **Utsira**, all but the second of these names having been used for the boats of an earlier 'Ula' class (five British 'U'-class submarines bought from the UK in 1943-46, modernised in 1955-56 and deleted in the first part of the 1960s).

The current 'Ula'-class submarines are intended primarily for coastal operations, and are therefore comparatively small in

*Below: The **Utsira** was the last of the six 'Ula'-class submarines to be completed and was commissioned in April 1992.*

size and limited in their diving depth to some 250 m (820 ft).

German construction

The entire class was ordered from Thyssen Nordseewerke of Emden on 30 September 1982 in a joint Norwegian and West German programme known in the latter country as Project 210, but the option for another two boats of the class was not, in the event, exercised.

Although the boats were completed in the West German yard they did incorporate a measure of Norwegian structural expertise inasmuch as sections of the pressure hulls were fabricated in a Norwegian facility and then shipped to Emden for inclusion into the otherwise German-built boats. The boats were laid down between January 1987 and June 1990, launched between July 1988

SPECIFICATION	
'Ula' class	**Diving depth:** 250 m (820 ft)
Displacement: 1,040 tons surfaced; 1,150 tons dived	**Torpedo tubes:** eight 533-mm (21-in) tubes (all bow) for 14 DM2A3 Seehecht wire-guided active/passive-homing dual-role torpedoes
Dimensions: length 59 m (193 ft 7 in); beam 5.4 m (17 ft 9 in); draught 4.6 m (15 ft 1 in)	
Propulsion: two MTU 16V 396 SB83 diesels delivering 2010 kW (2,695 shp) and one Siemens electric motor delivering 4474 kW (6,000 shp) to one shaft	**Electronics:** one Type 1007 surface search and navigation radar, one passive flank-array sonar; one active/passive intercept, search and attack sonar, and one Sealion ESM system
Performance: speed 11 kts surfaced and 23 kts dived; range 9250 km (5,750 miles) at 8 kts surfaced	**Complement:** 21

and November 1991, and finally commissioned into Norwegian service in the period between April 1989 and April 1992.

Though much of the hull and all of the propulsion machinery are German, the boats were completed with a mix of French, German and Norwegian systems. The basic command and weapon control systems are Norwegian (the torpedo fire-control system being the Kongsberg MSI-90U that is being upgraded and modernised in 2000-05), while the sonars are of French and German origins. The Thomson-CSF low-frequency passive flank-array sonar is of French origin, and is based on piezoelectric polymer technology offering significantly reduced flow noise. The Atlas Elektronik CSU 83 medium-frequency active/passive intercept, search and attack sonar, however, is of German origin.

Another notable feature, designed to reduce the need to incorporate apertures in the pressure hull, is the use of Calzoni Trident modular non-penetrating masts, and the periscopes use Zeiss optics.

Eventful careers

Since entering service, the 'Ula'-class submarines have been found to suffer from noise problems with their machinery, which is a major handicap in submarine operations in which sound is the primary medium for discovering submerged boats. The submarines have undergone quite interesting careers to date. The *Ula*, for example was damaged by a practice torpedo during the boat's trials in 1989, while the *Uredd* in March 1991 was damaged in a docking accident and then in February 1992 suffered a control room fire.

'Götland' class Patrol submarine

Resulting from a research and preliminary design contract placed with the Kockums yard of Malmö in October 1986 for a conventionally powered submarine to replace the obsolescent boats of the 'Sjöormen' class, the design of the boats of the **A19** or **'Götland' class** was derived from that of the A17 or 'Västergötland' class. The three

boats of the class, namely the **Götland**, **Uppland** and **Halland**, were ordered from Kockums in March 1990, but another two projected units were not in the event procured. In September of the following year, before the first boat had been laid down, the programme was temporarily suspended to allow a reworking of the design to incorporate, for

Left: The 'Götland'-class boats are fairly small, but offer excellent capabilities including a sizeable load of modern torpedoes and an extended underwater cruising capability.

Above: The 'Götlands' are very quiet under the water, where their detectability is reduced by silent machinery and an anechoic outer covering.

Below: Commissioned in May 1997, the **Uppland** *was the second of the three 'Götland'-class boats to be completed by the Kockums yard at Malmö.*

Above: Highly reliable boats, the 'Götlands' provide Sweden with effective coastal defence.

two such systems with volume left for the later addition of another two systems should this prove desirable. As it is, the boats can apparently cruise at a submerged speed of 5 kts for several weeks without recourse to snorting.

The boats were laid down in 1992-1994, launched in 1995-96, and commissioned in 1996-97, the lengthening of the hull having resulted in a 200-ton increase in displacement. Another advanced feature of the design was the installation of a periscope with optronic sensors, and this unit is the only mast that penetrates through the pressure hull. The boats' underwater signature is

the first time before the start of fabrication rather than as a retro-fit, an AIPS (Air-Independent Propulsion System), using liquid oxygen and diesel fuel in a helium environment, for much enhanced submerged operating capability. The design of the hull was lengthened by 7.5 m (24 ft 7 in) to allow the incorporation of

⏱	SPECIFICATION
'Götland' class	and 20 kts dived
Displacement: 1,240 tons surfaced; 1,494 tons dived	**Torpedo tubes:** four 533-mm (21-in) and two 400-mm (15.75-in) tubes (all bow) for 12 Tp 613 or Tp 62 wire-guided anti-ship and six Tp 432/451 wire-guided anti-submarine torpedoes
Dimensions: length 60.4 m (198 ft 2 in); beam 6.2 m (20 ft 4 in); draught 5.6 m (18 ft 4 in)	
Propulsion: two Hedemora V12A-15-Ub diesels delivering 4,830 kW (6,480 shp), two Kockums V4-275R Mk 2 Stirling AIPS, and one Jeumont-Schneider electric motor delivering 1350 kW (1,810 shp) to one shaft	**Electronics:** one Scanter navigation radar, one CSU 90-2 passive search and attack sonar with bow and flank arrays, one IPS-19 torpedo fire-control system, and one Manta S ESM system
Performance: speed 10 kts surfaced	**Complement:** 25

being further reduced by the application of anechoic coatings.

Torpedo armament

The torpedo tubes are all located in the bow, and comprise four 533-mm (21-in) tubes over two 400-mm (15.75-in) tubes. The larger units fire anti-ship torpedoes of the swim-out type in the form of the wire-guided Type 613 passive or (since 2000) Type 62 active/passive weapons: the former carries a 240-kg (529-lb) HE warhead to 20 km (12.4 miles) at 45 kts, while the latter carries a 250-kg (551-lb) HE warhead to 50 km (31.1 miles) at a speed of 20-50 kts. Twelve Tp 47 mines can be carried in place of the heavy torpedoes, these swimming out to a predetermined position before laying themselves on the bottom. Another 48 mines can be carried by an external girdle. The smaller torpedo tubes can be tandem loaded with wire-guided Tp 432/451 active/passive ASW torpedoes, each able to carry a 45-kg (99-lb) HE warhead out to 20 km (12.4 miles) at 25 kts.

'Chang Bogo' class Patrol submarine

Up to the 1980s the South Korean navy, faced largely with the threat of North Korean aggression largely through the agency of conventional submarines and small surface ships, concentrated its efforts on the deployment of ex-US surface warships and the development of its overall capability to operate more advanced vessels. The process began to bear fruit toward the end of the 1980s, when a number of more advanced vessels were ordered. Among the new types were the service's first submarines, which were of the West German Type 209 class in its Type 1200 subvariant, which was ordered as the **'Chang Bogo' class** with a diving depth of 250 m (820 ft).

The first order placed late in 1997 covered three boats, one to be completed by Howaldtswerke of Kiel in Germany and the other two by Daewoo at Okpo in South Korea from German-supplied kits. There followed additional three-boat orders placed in October 1989 and January 1994 for boats of South Korean construction, and the entire class comprises the **Chang Bogo**, **Yi Chon**, **Choi Muson**, **Pakui**, **Lee Jongmu**, **Jeongun**, **Lee Sunsin**, **Nadaeyong** and **Lee Okki**. The boats were laid down in the period between 1989 and 1997, launched in the period between 1992 and 2000, and commissioned in the period from 1993 to a final hand-over in 2001.

Turkish similarity

The South Korean boats are generally similar to Turkey's six 'Atilay'-class submarines, and emphasis is therefore placed on the installation of German sensors and weapons. Using the swim-out discharge method (resulting in reduced noise levels) from eight 533-mm (21-in) tubes all located in the bows, the latter comprise 14 SystemTechnik Nord (STN) SUT Mod 2 torpedoes, which are wire-guided weapons with active/passive homing and the ability to carry a 260-kg (573-lb) HE warhead out to a maximum range of 28 km (17.4 miles) at 23 kts or a shorter range of 12 km (7.6 mile) at a speed of 35 kts. The boats can also carry 28 tube-laid mines in place of the torpedoes.

The older boats are being upgraded from a time early in the 21st century, and although details are currently unclear, it is believed that the modernisation will include a hull 'stretch' to the Type 1400 length of some 62 m (203 ft 5 in) with surfaced and submerged displacements of about 1,455 and 1,585 tons respectively, provision for tube-launched UGM-84 Harpoon missiles to enhance the boats' capabilities against surface ships, and possibly the addition of a towed-array sonar for a superior capability for the detection of submerged submarines.

SPECIFICATION	
'Chang Bogo' class	surfaced/snorting and 22 kts dived;
Displacement: 1,100 tons surfaced; 1,285 tons dived	endurance 13900 km (8,635 miles) at 8 kts surfaced
Dimensions: length 56 m (183 ft 9 in); beam 6.2 m (20 ft 4 in); draught 5.5 m (18 ft)	**Diving depth:** 250 m (820 ft) **Torpedo tubes:** eight 533-mm (21-in) tubes (all bow) for 14 SUT Mod 2
Propulsion: diesel-electric arrangement with four MTU 12V 396SE diesels delivering 2840 kW (3,810 shp) and driving four alternators, and one electric motor delivering 3425 kW (4,595 shp) to one shaft	wire-guided active/passive-homing torpedoes or 28 mines **Electronics:** one navigation radar, one CSU 83 hull-mounted passive search and attack sonar, one ISUS 83 torpedo fire-control system, and one Argo ESM system
Performance: speed 11 kts	**Complement:** 33

*Left: The **Pakui** was completed by Daewoo on 3 February 1996, as the fourth of the South Korean navy's 'Chang Bogo'- class conventional submarines. The service plans to operate the boats as a trio attached to each of its three fleets, and further improvement of the boats may be based on an indigenous South Korean development of a US torpedo, the Northrop NP 37.*

'Santa Cruz' class (TR 1700) Attack submarine

Currently the most important submarines of the Argentine navy, the two **'Santa Cruz'-class** diesel-electric boats are the result of a somewhat chequered early history. In November 1977 the Argentine navy contracted with Thyssen Nordseewerke for the building of two **'TR 1700'** type submarines in West Germany and the provision of parts and supervision for the manufacture of four more boats in Argentina at the Astilleros Domecq Garcia facility in Buenos Aires.

As the Argentine navy's plan was originally conceived, the boats to be built in Argentina were to have been two more 'TR 1700' type submarines and two examples of the somewhat smaller 'TR 1400' type. In 1982, however, the contract details were finalised for a class of six 'TR 1700' type submarines and no 'TR 1400' type units.

The two boats built in West Germany are the **Santa Cruz** and **San Juan**, which were laid down in December 1980 and March 1982, launched in September 1982 and June 1983, and commissioned in October 1984 and November 1985 respectively. There were problems with the four boats to be built in Argentina, however, for in 1996, when the initial pair of submarines, destined for completion as the *Santa Fe* and *Santiago del Estero*, were 52 and 30 per cent complete respectively, work ended. In February of that year the dockyard was sold, and what had been completed of the two boats was cannibalised to aid in the maintenance of the two West German-built boats. The same

fate befell the equipment delivered from West Germany for the last two boats that were to have been built in Argentina but were not, in the event, even laid down.

The 'TR 1700' type was of notably advanced concept for its time, and offered both a high underwater speed and a considerable operational diving depth. The standard endurance is 30 days, but the maximum figure is believed to be 70 days. An automatic reloading system is provided for the torpedo tubes, this system performing the reloading of the torpedo tubes in just 50 seconds. The boats also have the capability to carry and land small parties of commando troops for special forces missions.

Both the *Santa Cruz* and *San Juan* are based at Mar del Plata, which is the home of the Argentine navy's small submarine force. Between September 1999 and 2001 the *Santa Cruz* received a mid-life update at a Brazilian yard, and a similar update is planned for the *San Juan* at Puerto Belgrano in Argentina as and when the Argentine economy makes this feasible. The upgrade involves, among other things, the replacement of the submarine's main motors and the

Above: The 'TR 1700' type submarine is still a highly effective design, and the achievement of the service's plan for six such boats would have given the Argentine navy a potent attack force by South American standards.

SPECIFICATION	
'Santa Cruz' class	km (13,825 miles) at 8 kts surfaced
Displacement: 2,116 tons surfaced; 2,264 tons dived	**Diving depth:** 270 m (885 m) operational
Dimensions: length 66 m (216 ft 6 in); beam 7.3 m (24 ft); draught 6.5 m (21 ft 4 in)	**Armament:** six 533-mm (21-in) tubes (all bow) for 22 SST-4 or Mk 37 wire-guided torpedoes, or 34 mines
Propulsion: four MTU 16V652 MB81 diesels delivering 5000 kW (6,705 shp) and one Siemens Type 1HR4525 + 1HR4525 electric motor delivering 6600 kW (8,850 hp) to one shaft	**Electronics:** one Calypso IV navigation radar, one Sinbads fire-control system, one Sea Sentry III ESM system, one CSU 3/4 active/passive search and attack sonar, and one DUUX 5 passive ranging sonar
Performance: speed 15 kts surfaced and 25 kts dived; endurance 22250	**Crew:** 29

updating of the sonar system's active/passive search and passive ranging units.

The torpedoes carried by the 'TR 1700' type submarines are the German SST-4 and US Mk 37 wire-guided types with swim-out

discharge. The former carries a 260-kg (573-lb) warhead to a distance of 12 or 28 km (7.46 or 17.4 miles) at 35 or 23 kts, and the latter delivers a 150-kg (330-lb) warhead to 8 km (4.97 miles) at 24 kts.

'Song' class Attack submarine

The **'Song' class** or **Type 039** is the latest and most advanced diesel-electric attack submarine type to have been designed and built by indigenous Chinese effort. Conceived as the successor to the Chinese navy's ageing force of obsolescent 'Ming'-class (Type 035) and wholly obsolete 'Romeo'-class (Type 033) submarines, which have constituted the core of the service's conventionally powered submarine arm for more than four decades, the 'Song' class is based in design terms on certain Western concepts. These include a low-drag hydrodynamically profiled hull and sail, new cylindrical

bow-mounted sonars, a power-plant centred on the use of four German MTU diesel engines (16V 396 units rather than the 12V493 units originally considered), and a new anti-submarine torpedo of Russian origin.

Another major enhancement contributing to the type's capability for offensive as well as defensive operations is the provision for an anti-ship missile capability. This is in the form of a tube-fired YJ-82 (submarine-launched version of the ship-launched C-801) missile, which can deliver its 165-kg (364-lb) warhead to a range of 40 km (24.9 miles) with the aid

of an inertial platform and active radar terminal seeker.

In overall terms, the 'Song' class reveals a technological standard generally similar to that of Western submarines built during the 1980s.

Pause for reflection

The first boat, **No. 320**, was laid down in 1991 and was launched on 25 May 1994 at the Wuhan Shipyard, but was not commission until June 1999 after the implementation of an exhaustive trials programme to assess the capabilities and, as it turned out, limitations of the design.

It was at this trials stage that the Chinese navy postponed

further construction to allow the rectification of serious performance and design problems, and thus create the initial full-production variant, known as the **Type 039G**. This boat is characterised most obviously by a sail without the stepped-down forward section that in *No. 320* accommodates the bridge with the forward hydroplanes under it.

Production was resumed at the Wuhan Shipyard in 1995, and the first Type 039G boat was launched in November 1999 for commissioning during April 2001 as **No. 321**. By 2003 another three units had been completed.

Teardrop hull

Slightly shorter but beamier than the 'Ming'-class submarine it is designed to succeed, the 'Song'-class boat has a length/beam ratio of 8.91/1, which is slightly less than the 10/1 ratio of the 'Ming'-class submarines but of a decidedly superior hydrodynamic shape. The 'Song'-class submarine is propelled through the water by one large seven-bladed propeller, and the primary machinery is located on shock-absorbent mountings for reduced vibration and therefore minimised underwater noise radiation. The 'stealthiness' of the design is further enhanced by the use of anechoic tiling similar to that of the Russian 'Kilo'-class submarine.

The 'Song'-class submarine has a multi-role combat and command system which provides all the data needed for control of the boat and for the firing of torpedoes and/or missiles. The system is possibly an updated derivative of the combat and command system used in the 'Ming'-class submarines, and is probably of a standard equivalent to that installed in Western submarines in the 1970s.

Mixed armament

As far as weapons are concerned, the 'Song' class is armed primarily with anti-ship cruise missiles and torpedoes. As noted above, the YJ-82 missile is the submarine-launched variant of the C-801 launched underwater from the 533-mm (21-in) torpedo tubes. Boosted by a solid-propellant rocket until it has emerged from the water, whereupon the solid-propellant sustainer takes over, the missile approaches its target as a sea-skimmer and impacts under the guidance of its active radar seeker, the shaped-charge warhead being initiated by a delay-action impact fuse. The six 533-mm tubes, all located in the bows, have a maximum of 16 to 20 Yu-4 (SAET-60) passive homing and Yu-1 (Type 53-51) torpedoes, the total being reduced when the YJ-82 missile is shipped. As an alternative, the submarine can carry tube-launched mines.

Integrated sonar

The 'Song'-class submarine is fitted with an integrated sonar system comprising an active/passive medium-frequency spherical bow-mounted equipment and passive low-frequency reach arrays. The countermeasures suite comprises just the Type 921-A radar warning receiver and direction-finder.

The diesel-electric propulsion arrangement provided to power the 'Song'-class submarine comprises four MTU 16V396 SE diesel engines, four alternators, and one electric motor, the last powering a single shaft.

More units of the 'Song' class, probably to a standard improved to reflect the lessons operational experience with the current boats, may emerge in time.

SPECIFICATION	
'Song' (Type 039G) class	**Diving depth:** not available
Displacement: 1,700 tons surfaced; 2,250 tons dived	**Armament:** six 533-mm (21-in) tubes (all bow) for Yu-4 (SAET-60) and Yu-1 (Type 53-51) torpedoes, or mines, and YJ-82 anti-ship missiles
Dimensions: length 74.9 m (245 ft 9 in); beam 8.4 m (27 ft 6 in); draught 7.3 m (24 ft)	**Electronics:** one surface search and navigation radar, one Type 951-A ESM system, one active/passive search and attack bow sonar, and one passive search flank-array sonar
Propulsion: four MTU 16V396 SE diesels delivering 4540 kW (6,090 shp) and one electric motor delivering power to one shaft	
Performance: speed 15 kts surfaced and 22 kts dived	**Crew:** 60

'Scorpene' class Attack submarine

The **'Scorpene' class** submarine was developed by DCN of France and Izar (formerly Bazán) of Spain, and the first two units were ordered by Chile to be constructed in France and Spain for commissioning in 2004 and 2006 as the *O'Higgins* and *Carrera*, replacing two 'Oberon'-class boats. The Malaysian navy placed a contract for two 'Scorpene'- class submarines in June 2002, the boats to enter service in 2007 and 2008 after construction in France and Spain. France and India are expected to sign an agreement for the latter to build six 'Scorpene'-class boats at the state- owned Mazagon Docks in Bombay, with technical aid from the French DCN and Thales companies. The boats are to be completed on 2010-15 with SM.39 Exocet underwater-launched anti-ship missiles.

As ordered for the Chilean navy, the 'Scorpene'-class submarine will not have a towed-array sonar but will be equipped with flank-array sonar. The six 533-mm (21-in) bow torpedo tubes will in general be capable of launching German SUT torpedoes, F-17 Mod 2, Mk 48 or, in Chilean service, Black Shark 184 Mod 3 torpedoes, as well as the SM.39 Exocet anti-ship missile. The tubes possess a salvo launch capability, and use a positive-discharge system by air turbine pump. The submarine's weapon complement is 18 torpedoes and missiles, or 30 mines, and the handling and loading of weapons are automated.

The SUBTICS combat management system, with up to six multi-function consoles and a central tactical table, is located with the platform-control facili-

Above: The 'Scorpene'-class submarine offers exceptional capabilities, and can be enhanced, either in construction or during retrofit, with AIPS propulsion.

SPECIFICATION	
'Scorpene' class (Chilean standard)	**Diving depth:** 300+ m (985+ ft) operational
Displacement: 1,668 tons dived	**Armament:** six 533-mm (21-in) tubes (all bow) for 18 Black Shark 184 Mod 3 torpedoes
Dimensions: length 66.4 m (217 ft 10 in); beam 6.2 m (20 ft 4 in); draught 5.8 m (19 ft)	**Electronics:** one navigation radar, one SUBTICS fire-control system, one Argo AR 900 ESM system, and one active/passive search and attack hull sonar
Propulsion: four MTU 16V396 SE84 diesels delivering 2240 kW (3,005 shp) and one Jeumont Schneider electric motor delivering 2840 kW (3,810 hp) to one shaft	
Performance: speed 12 kts surfaced and 20 kts dived; endurance 12000 km (7,455 miles) at 8 kts surfaced	**Crew:** 31

ties. SUBTICS comprises a command and tactical data- handling system, a weapon-control system and a suite of integrated acoustic sensors interfaced with the air/surface detection sensors and the navigation system.

Handling operations are effected in the control room. The boat has a high level of automation and system surveillance, with automatic control of the rudders, hydroplanes and propulsion, full-time monitoring of the propulsion and platform installations, full-time centralised surveillance against hazards such as leaks, fires and noxious gases, and the checking of installations critical to submerged safety. When submerged, the 'Scorpene'-class boat has low radiated noise levels, which improves the detection range of its own sensors and reduces risk of detection. These low noise levels are achieved by the use of very advanced hydrodynamics with an albacore bow shape, few external projections, an optimised propeller, suspended decks, the location of equipment on elastic mountings wherever possible, and the use of double elastic mountings for the noisiest systems.

There is provision in the submarine's design for the incorporation of an air independent propulsion system.

'Harushio' class Attack submarine

Since its establishment in the 1950s, the Japanese navy (more formally designated as the Japanese Maritime Self-Defence Force in accordance with the country's post-World War II pacifist constitution) has placed considerable emphasis on the development of a sizeable force of advanced submarines to provide a seaward capability for the destruction of possible maritime invasion forces.

After a number of single- or twin-boat classes that allowed it to develop an initial capability and reacquaint itself with the technology of the time, the JMSDF adopted the 'Oshio' class as its first major submarine force, five such boats being commissioned in 1965-69. There followed seven 'Uzushio'-class boats in 1971-78, and then 10 'Yuushio'-class boats in 1978-88.

By the first half of the 1980s the 'Uzushio' class was obsolescent, and the JMSDF started to plan a successor type. Just as the 'Yuushio' class had been a development of the 'Uzushio' class with improved electronics and a deeper diving capability, the new **'Harushio' class** was schemed as an improved 'Yuushio' class with a towed-array sonar and improved noise-reduction features. Other features of the class include wireless antennae, an anechoic coating for the hull and sail, and a double hull.

The programme was approved in 1986, and the construction of one boat per year was authorised so that the **Harushio**, **Natsushio**, **Hayashio**, **Arashio**, **Wakashio**, **Fuyushio** and **Asashio** were commissioned in the period between November 1990 and March 1997. All of the boats were built at Kobe by Mitsubishi (four boats) and Kawasaki (three boats).

The *Asashio* was completed with a higher level of automation in the machinery and snorting control systems, increasing the displacement slightly and allowing the crew to be trimmed to 71. The boat also had a remote periscope viewer system. In 2001 the boat was also lengthened by 10 m (32 ft 10 in) to allow the retrofit of the Stirling air-independent propulsion system that was to be evaluated for use in later Japanese submarine classes.

Above: The 'Harushio'-class diesel-electric submarines are operated in the seaward defence role, and from 1998 have been complemented by the 'Oyashio'-class boats, of which a total of nine is planned for completion by 2006.

Right: The 'Harushio'-class submarines have distinct teardrop hulls with a lack of excrescences, and considerable operational diving depth.

SPECIFICATION	
'Harushio' class	operational
Displacement: 2,450 tons surfaced; 2,750 tons dived	**Armament:** six 533-mm (21-in) tubes (all bow) for 20 Type 89 wire-guided active/passive homing and Type 80 anti-submarine torpedoes, and Harpoon anti-ship missiles
Dimensions: length 77 m (252 ft 7 in); beam 10 m (32 ft 10 in); draught 7.7 m (25 ft 3 in)	
Propulsion: two Kawasaki 12V25/25S diesels delivering 4120 kW (5,525 shp) and two Fuji electric motors delivering 5370 kW (7,200 shp) to one shaft	**Electronics:** one ZPS 6 surface search and navigation radar, one fire-control system, one ZLR 3-6 ESM system, one ZQQ 5B active/passive search and attack hull sonar, and one ZQR 1 passive search towed-array sonar
Performance: speed 12 kts surfaced and 20 kts dived	
Diving depth: 350 m (1,150 ft)	**Crew:** 75

'Agosta' class Patrol submarine

SPECIFICATION

'Agosta A90' class
Displacement: 1,480 tons surfaced; 1,760 tons dived
Dimensions: length 67.6 m (221 ft 9 in); beam 6.8 m (22 ft 4 in); draught 5.4 m (17 ft 9 in)
Propulsion: two SEMT-Pielstick diesels delivering 2685 kW (3,600 shp) and one electric motor delivering 2200 kW (2,950 shp) to one shaft
Speed: 12.5 kts surfaced and 20.5 kts dived
Diving depth: 300 m (985 ft) operational and 500 m (1,640 ft) maximum
Torpedo tubes: four 550-mm (21.7-in)

with 533-mm (21-in) liners for 23 550-mm (21.7-in) or 533-mm (21-in) anti-submarine and anti-ship torpedoes, or 46 influence ground mines; provision for SM.39 Exocet or UGM-84 Sub-Harpoon underwater-launched anti-ship missiles on French and Pakistani units, respectively
Electronics: one DRUA 23 surface search radar, one DUUA 2A sonar, one DUUA 1D sonar, one DUUX 2A sonar, one DSUV 2H sonar, one ARUR ESM system, one ARUD ESM system, and one torpedo fire-control/action information system
Complement: 54

Left: Now decommissioned, the 'Agosta'-class submarines provided the French navy with a very useful capability for anti-ship operations in shallower waters. The last active French vessel in the class, Ouessant, was decommissioned in 2001.

Designed by the French Directorate of Naval Construction as very quiet but high-performance submarines for operations in the Mediterranean, the boats of the **'Agosta A90' class** are each armed with four bow torpedo tubes that are equipped with a pneumatically rammed rapid-reload system that can launch weapons with the minimum of noise signature. The tubes were of a completely new design which allows the submarine to fire its weapons at all speeds and at any depth down to its maximum operational limit.

The four boats in service with the French navy as its last conventionally powered submarines up to their decommissioning

early in the 21st century were the **Agosta**, **Bévéziers**, **La Praya** and **Ouessant**. All were authorised in the 1970-75 naval programme as the follow-on class to the 'Daphné'-class coastal submarines. *La Praya* was refitted with a removable swimmer delivery vehicle container aft of the sail to replace similar facilities that had been available aboard the *Narval*, lead boat of an obsolete class of six ocean-going submarines deleted during the 1980s.

The Spanish navy received four locally built 'Agosta'-class boats during the early 1980s, namely the **Galerna**, **Siroco**, **Mistral** and **Tramontana** using French electronics as well as

French armament in the form of the L5, F17 and E18 torpedoes. In mid-1978 Pakistan purchased two units (built originally for South Africa but embargoed before delivery) as the **Hashmat** and **Hurmat**, and in 1994 Pakistan ordered three more boats of the improved 'Agosta A90B' class with a number of improved features.

During the 1980s the French boats were revised with the capability to fire the SM.39 underwater-launched variant of the Exocet anti-ship missile, whereas Pakistan looked to the other side of the Atlantic and sought to procure the UGM-84 submarine-launched version of the US Harpoon anti-ship missile.

Left: The Agosta was the lead ship of the last class of conventionally powered submarines built for the French navy. Later in their careers, all were retrofitted to fire the SM.39 Exocet underwater-launched anti-ship missile.

'Daphné' class Patrol submarine

In 1952 plans were requested from STCAN for a second-class ocean-going submarine to complement the larger 'Narval' class. Designated the **'Daphné' class**, the boats were designed with reduced speed in order to achieve a greater diving depth and heavier armament than was

possible with the contemporary 'Aréthuse' design of conventionally powered hunter-killer submarines. To reduce the crew's workload the main armament was contained in 12 externally mounted torpedo tubes (eight forward and four aft), which eliminated the need for a torpedo

room and reloads. Further crew reductions were made possible by adopting a modular replacement system for onboard maintenance. The design was based on the double-hull construction technique with the accommodation spaces split evenly fore and aft of the sail,

below which was the operations and attack centre. A total of 11 units was built for the French navy. The **Daphné**, **Diane**, **Doris**, **Eurydicé**, **Flore**, **Galatée**, **Minerve**, **Junon**, **Vénus**, **Psyché** and **Sirène** entered service between 1964 and 1970. Of these two were lost (the

Once they had reached the ends of their lives and also become obsolete, the 'Daphné'-class submarines were not replaced as the French navy had decided to concentrate on building only nuclear attack submarines for the future. However, the class remains in service with Pakistan (four boats), Portugal (two), South Africa (two) and Spain (four).

Minerve in 1968 and the *Eurydicé* in 1970) with all hands while operating in the western Mediterranean. The remaining boats all underwent an electronics and weapons modernisation from 1970 onwards, but have now all been retired. Another 10 were built for export, Portugal receiving the **Albacore**, **Barracuda**, **Cachalote** and **Delfim**, of which *Cachalote* was sold to Pakistan in 1975 as the

Ghazi. The *Albacore* and *Delfim* remained in service in 2003. Pakistan also has the **Hangor**, **Shushuk** and **Mangro**, armed with Sub-Harpoon. Ordered in 1967, South Africa took delivery of the **Maria Van Riebeeck**, **Emily Hobhouse** and **Johanna Van der Merwe**, of which two remained in service in 2003, renamed as the **Umkhonto** and **Assegaai**. These received a weapons system upgrade

(including sonar) and features to improve habitability in 1988-90. A further four, the **Delfín**, **Tonina**, **Marsopa** and **Narval** were built under licence in Spain and were later updated similar to that which was applied to the French

boats between 1971-81. In 1971 the Pakistani submarine *Hangor* sank the Indian navy's frigate *Khukri* during the Indo-Pakistan war of that year: this was the first submarine attack since the end of World War II.

SPECIFICATION	
'Daphné' class	operational and 575 m (1,885 ft) maximum
Displacement: 869 tons surfaced; 1,043 tons dived	**Torpedo tubes:** 12 550-mm (21.7-in) tubes (eight bow and four stern) for 12 anti-ship and anti-submarine torpedoes, or influence ground mines
Dimensions: length 57.8 m (189 ft 8 in); 6.8 m (22 ft 4 in); draught 4.6 m (15 ft 1 in)	
Propulsion: two SEMT-Pielstick diesel generator sets and two electric motors delivering 1940 kW (2,600 shp) to two shafts	**Electronics:** one Calypso II surface search radar, one DUUX 2 sonar, one DSUV 2 sonar, DUUA 1 and 2 sonars, and one torpedo fire-control/action information system
Speed: 13.5 kts surfaced; 16 kts dived	
Diving depth: 300 m (985 ft)	**Complement:** 54

'Type 206' and 'Type 209' classes Patrol/ocean-going submarines

In 1962 IKL began studies for a follow-on development of its 'Type 205' design. This new **'Type 206'** class, built of high-tensile non-magnetic steel, was to be used for coastal operations and had to conform with treaty limitations on the maximum tonnage allowed to West Germany. New safety devices for the crew were fitted, and the armament fit allowed for the carriage of wire-guided torpedoes. After final design approval had been given, construction planning took place in 1966-68, and the first orders (for an eventual total of 18 units)

were placed in the following year. By 1975 all the boats, **U-13** to **U-30** were in service. Since then the class has been given extra armament in the form of two external GRP containers to carry

a total of 24 ground mines in addition to their normal torpedo armament. From 1988 onwards 12 of the class were modernised with new electronics and torpedoes to form the **'Type 206A'**

class. In 2003, 12 examples remained in German service.

In the mid-1960s IKL also designed for the export market a new boat that became the **'Type 209' class** in 1967. Designed

Right: The basic design of the 'Type 206' class is so versatile customers can opt for different lengths and displacements and an assortment of electronic and armament fits. This is the German navy's U-24.

The Peruvian navy took delivery of a total of six 'Type 209/1200' boats in three batches between 1975-83. The Angamos *(formerly* Casma*), SS 31, can carry a total of 14 American NT-37C dual anti-ship and anti-submarine torpedoes as its main armament in preference to the German weapons normally sold with the vessels.*

specifically for the ocean-going role, the 'Type 209' can, because of its relatively short length, operate successfully in coastal waters. The 'Type 209' and its variants have proved so popular that 50 have been built or ordered by 12 export customers.

Principal variants

The six main variants of the 'Type 209' are the original **54.3-m 'Type 209/1100'** (178 ft 1 in long, 960 tons surfaced and 1,105 tons dived); **56-m 'Type 209/1200'** (183 ft 9 in long, 980 tons surfaced and 1,185 tons dived); **59.5-m 'Type 209/1300'** 195 ft 2 in long, 1,000 tons surfaced and

1,285 tons dived); **62-m 'Type 209/1400'** (203 ft 5 in long, 1,454 tons surfaced and 1,586 tons dived); **64.4-m 'Type 209/1500'** (211 ft 4 in long, 1,660 tons surfaced and 1,850 tons dived); and the smaller coastal **45-m 'Type 640'** (147 ft 7 in long, 420 tons surfaced and 600 tons dived).

The countries which have bought these vessels are Greece (four 'Type 209/1100' and four 'Type 209/1200'), Argentina (two 'Type 209/1200'), Peru (six 'Type 209/1200'), Colombia (two 'Type 209/1200'), South Korea (nine 'Type 209/1200'), Turkey (six 'Type 209/1200' and eight 'Type 209/1400', most of which have

been built locally with German help), Venezuela (two 'Type 209/1300'), Chile (two 'Type 209/1400'), Ecuador (two 'Type 209/1300'), Indonesia (two 'Type

SPECIFICATION

'Type 209/1200' class
Displacement: 1,185 tons surfaced and 1,290 tons dived
Dimensions: length 56 m (183 ft 9 in); beam 6.2 m (20 ft 4 in); draught 5.5 m (18 ft ½ in)
Propulsion: four MTU-Siemens diesel generators delivering 3730 kW (5,000 shp) and one Siemens electric motor delivering 2685 kW (3,600 shp) to one shaft
Speed: 11 kts surfaced and 21.5 kts dived
Diving depth: 300 m (985 ft)

operational and 500 m (1,640 ft) maximum
Torpedo tubes: eight 533-mm (210-in) tubes (all bow) for 14 (typically) AEG SST Mod 4 or AEG SUT anti-ship and anti-submarine torpedoes
Electronics: one Calypso surface search radar, one CSU 3 sonar, one DUUX 2C or PRS 3 sonar, one ESM system, and one Sepa Mk 3 or Sinbad M8/24 torpedo fire-control and action information system
Complement: 31-35

209/1300' plus a further four projected but unlikely to be realised), Brazil (five 'Type 209/1400'), India (four 'Type 209/1500' plus two more projected), South Africa (three 'Type 209/1400') and Israel (three 'Type 640'). Each chose its own equipment fit and crew number according to economic requirements.

During the 1982 Falklands War the Argentine navy's 'Type 209/1200'-class submarine **San Luis** made three unsuccessful torpedo attacks on vessels of the British task force, but the knowledge of the boat's presence tied up considerable British ship and aircraft resources in efforts to find the submarine.

Above: The multiplicity of sensor and snorting masts rising from the sails of the 'Type 209' is notable. This is Tupi, *a 'Type 209 Type 1400' of the Brazilian navy.*

The smallest of the 'Type 209' series variants is the 'Type 640'. Israel ordered three from Vickers of the UK all being commissioned in 1977.

'Ming' class (Type 035) Patrol submarine

Constituting the main strength of the Chinese navy's conventionally powered submarine arm, with up to 23 units completed into the early 2000s, the **'Ming' class** or **Type 035 ('ES5' class** for export) diesel-electric submarine is a development of the Soviet 'Romeo'-class submarine designed in the 1950s. The type is now obsolete by Western standards, but retains a vestigial capability for the patrol and coastal defence roles, and was a relatively inexpensive replacement for China's ageing force of Type 033 ('Romeo'-class) submarines. Some 13 of the boats are allocated to the North Sea Fleet, based at Lushun, Qingdao and Xiapingdao, while the others are allocated to the South Sea Fleet.

After building the Type 033 boats in the 1960s and then undertaking a number of improvements to the class, the Chinese decided in 1967 to develop an improved submarine, although still based on the Soviet original. The task was allo-

cated to the 701 Shipbuilding Institute at Wuhan, and the Wuhan Shipyard was selected to build the boats of the new class. The aim was a boat offering higher submerged speed and longer range than the 'Romeo' and Type 033 submarines, and the first of the new class was laid down in October 1969, launched in July 1971 and commissioned in April 1974.

The first two or three boats, the last completed in 1979, were **'ES5C/D'-class** three-shaft prototypes that were scrapped in the late 1980s. The full production standard then appeared in the **'ES5E' class**, which introduced a number of changes and was produced at the rate of some two boats per year from 1988 to 1995, when the North Sea fleet had some 12 such boats in service.

Production resumed

It was planned at this stage to follow the Type 035 with the Type 039 ('Song' class) as the Chinese navy's new diesel-elec-

tric submarine, but delays in the programme for the newer boat meant that construction of the Type 035 was resumed in 1997, these later units being allocated to the South Sea Fleet. These late-production boats were completed to the **Type 035G** standard, which may have been offered for export as the **'ES5F' class**. This standard introduced a number of enhancements suggested by operational experience with the older boats, and also introduced the French DUUX 5 passive ranging and intercept sonar, an improved fire-control system, an upgraded

command system providing the data required for more effective handling and torpedo launching, and black anechoic tiling on the outside of their hulls to reduced underwater noise and therefore detectability.

One of the Type 035G boats is believed to have a hull 2 m (6 ft 7 in) longer than the other members of the class, but the significance of this change has not been revealed.

It is worth noting that while some sources claim two-shaft propulsion for the 'Ming' class, others state that a single-shaft arrangement is used.

SPECIFICATION	
'Ming' class	**Diving depth:** 300 m (985 ft) operational
Displacement: 1,584 tons surfaced; 2,113 tons dived	**Torpedo tubes:** eight 533-mm (21-in) tubes (six bow and two stern) for 18 Yu-4 (SAET-60) passive-homing and Yu-1 (Type 53-51) torpedoes, or for 32 mines
Dimensions: length 76 m (249 ft 4 in); beam 7.6 m (25 ft); draught 5.1 m (16 ft 9 in)	
Propulsion: two Shaanxi 6E 390 ZC1 diesels delivering 3880 kW (5,205 hp) and two electric motors powering two shafts	**Electronics:** one 'Snoop Tray' surface search and navigation radar, one 'Pike Jaw' active/passive hull sonar, and one DUUX 5 passive ranging and intercept sonar
Performance: speed 15 kts surfaced and 18 kts dived; endurance 14825 km (9,210 miles) at 8 kts snorting	**Complement:** 57

'Tumleren' class (Type 207) Attack submarine

In 1959 the Norwegian defence ministry ordered from Rheinstahl-Nordseewerke of Emden a class of 15 **Type 207** coastal submarines based on the

West German navy's Type 205 class, but with a stronger hull for deeper-diving capability and, partially reflecting US funding for 50 per cent of the cost, revised

equipment including the Mk 37 wire-guided torpedo. These 'Kobben'-class boats entered service in 1964-67. Norway also borrowed a German boat for

Below: The cylindrical fairing above the bow of the 'Tumleren'-class coastal attack submarine carries the passive search and attack sonar.

training, and had one of her own submarines modified for officer training with its hull lengthened by 1 m (3 ft 3 in) and a second periscope added.

Six of the boats were upgraded in 1989-1991 with more modern electronics and new fire-control equipment, and over the same period three of the class were recommissioned into Danish service as replacements for the four 'Delfinen'-class boats. Bought under a 1986 contract, the boats were the *Utvaer*, *Uthaug* and *Stadt*. The last was so badly damaged when it ran aground in 1987, however, that it was scrapped and replaced in the Danish contract by the *Stadt*.

In Danish service the three boats became the **Tumleren**, **Saelen** and **Springeren** of the '**Tumleren' class**. Before being recommissioned into the Danish navy in October 1989, October 1990 and October 1991 respectively, the boats were upgraded at the same Norwegian yard, the

Urivale Shipyard in Bergen. The process was centred on the structural lengthening of the hull by 1.6 m (5 ft 3 in), in the process increasing the displacement from the Norwegian figures of 370 tons standard and 530 tons full load.

While under unmanned tow in the Kattegat during December 1990 the *Saelen* sank, but was recovered and had her refurbishment and upgrade completed with the aid of spares taken from the ex-Norwegian *Kaura*. The latter was handed over to Denmark for the purpose in October 1991 and cannibalised, allowing the *Saelen* to re-enter Danish service in August 1993.

As part of their reconditioning before they entered Danish service, the three boats also received a complete overhaul of their propulsion systems, and in electronic terms were upgraded with new and more capable fire-control, ESM, navigation and communications equipment. Further improvement came in

Above: The **Tumleren** *is caught by the camera as it surfaces. The three boats of the 'Tumleren' class will probably remain in service until replaced by new construction, possibly with the design being considered by Denmark, Norway and Sweden in the Viking programme.*

1992-93, when the new Atlas PSU NU passive search and attack sonar was installed in place of the original equipment. Another modification, which at first sight might seem strange in a Danish submarine, was the 1990 installation in the *Saelen* of an air conditioning and battery cooling system, but this reflected the commitment of the Danish

navy to provide one submarine for NATO operations in the Mediterranean.

In Danish service the boats are optimised for the attack rather than patrol task, and in this role their primary target-acquisition sensors are the sonar and the Pilkington Optronics CK 34 search periscope. Targets are then engaged with the Swedish

SPECIFICATION	
'Tumleren' class	km (5,750 miles) at 8 kts snorting
Displacement: 459 tons surfaced; 524 tons dived	**Diving depth:** 200 m (655 ft) operational
Dimensions: length 47.4 m (155 ft 6 in); beam 4.6 m (15 ft 1 in); draught 4.3 m (14 ft 1 in)	**Torpedo tubes:** eight 533-mm (21-in) tubes (all bow) for eight Tp 613 wire-guided passive-homing torpedoes
Propulsion: two MTU 12V493 AZ80 diesels delivering 900 kW (1.210 hp) and one electric motor delivering 1270 kW (1,705 hp) to one shaft	**Electronics:** one Furuno 805 surface search radar, one PSU NU passive search and attack sonar, one Tactic fire-control system, and one Sea Lion ESM system
Performance: speed 12 kts surfaced and 18 kts dived; endurance 9250	**Complement:** 24

FFV Tp 513 anti-ship torpedo. This is capable of delivering its 240-kg (529-lb) HE warhead to a maximum range of 25 km (15.5 miles) at a speed of 30 kts, though use over shorter distances allows the torpedo to exploit its 45-kt maximum speed. The Tp 513 is wire guided, and its own seeker is of the passive acoustic-homing type.

Left: A distinctive feature of the 'Tumleren'-class submarine is the sail, which has an angled-back front and side fairings for the rearward extension.

'Narhvalen' class Attack submarine

Needing a coastal attack submarine to supplement and complement its indigenously designed 'Delfinen' class, of which four examples (the last funded by the US) had been commissioned in 1958-64, Denmark secured from the West German submarine design house IKL a licence to manufacture an improved version of the Type 205 submarine already in service with the West German navy. Modified to a limited extent to ensure that it fully satisfied Denmark's particular requirements, the design was used by the Royal Dockyard in Copenhagen for the construction of the two **'Narhvalen'-class** boats. Named **Narhvalen** and **Nordkaperen**, these were laid down in 1965-66, launched in 1968-69, and were commissioned in February and December 1970 respectively.

Propulsion systems

In their early form, the boats were powered by two diesels and one electric motor, each half of the diesel-electric propulsion arrangement delivering 11125 kW (1,510 hp) for surfaced and submerged speeds of 12 and 17 kts respectively. They had active as well as passive sonar, and a complement of 22. With Denmark's 1986 purchase of three 'Kobben'-class coastal submarines that had become surplus to the requirements of the Norwegian navy, the decision was made to upgrade the two 'Narhvalen'-class boats to a comparable standard. Work on the Narhvalen started in late

Right: Now decommissioned, the 'Narhvalen'-class submarines gave the Danish Navy long and useful service, latterly to a virtual 'Tumleren'-class standard.

SPECIFICATION	
'Narhvalen' class	**Diving depth:** 200 m (655 ft) operational
Displacement: 420 tons surfaced; 450 tons dived	**Torpedo tubes:** eight 533-mm (21-in) tubes (all bow) for eight Tp 613 wire-guided passive-homing torpedoes
Dimensions: length 44 m (144 ft); beam 4.55 m (14 ft 9 in); draught 3.98 m (13 ft 9 in)	
Propulsion: two MTU 12V493 TY7 diesels delivering 1680 kW (2,250 hp) and one electric motor delivering 895 kW (1,200 hp)	**Electronics:** one Furuno 805 surface search radar, one PSU NU passive search and attack sonar, one Tactic fire-control system, and one Sea Lion ESM system
Performance: speed 12 kts surfaced and 17 kts dived	**Complement:** 24

1993 and was completed in February 1995, while the same programme was implemented on the Nordkaperen between the middle of 1995 and the middle of 1998. The work included a propulsion system overhaul, new periscopes, an optronic mast from the French company Sagem, an upgraded

ESM system from the British company Racal, general improvements to the radar, and a modern sonar system from the German company Atlas.

The two boats were relegated to a secondary role after the 2000 arrival of the Kronborg (ex-Swedish Näcken), and were finally decommissioned in 2002.

'Enrico Toti' class Patrol submarine

The 'Enrico Toti' class was designed specifically for the shallow water areas found around the Italian coastline. Armed with four bow torpedo tubes for the wire-guided A184 heavyweight torpedo, the four vessels had a submerged dash speed of 20 kts, but could sustain 15 kts for one hour.

As the first indigenously built Italian submarine design since World War II, the **'Enrico Toti' class** had a chequered start as the plans had to be recast several times from their origins during the mid-1950s in an American-sponsored NATO project for a small anti-submarine boat. Stricken or decommissioned in the period between 1991 and 1993, the four units were the **Attilio Bagnolini**, **Enrico Toti**, **Enrico Dandolo** and **Lazzaro Mocenigo**, which

entered service in 1968-69 for use in the notoriously difficult ASW conditions encountered in the central and eastern regions of the Mediterranean. For these operations the boats' relatively small size and minimum sonar cross section stood them in good stead. The main armament was originally four Kanguru anti-submarine and four anti-ship torpedoes, but then revised to six examples of the 533-mm (21-in) Whitehead Motofides A184 wire-guided dual-role anti-

submarine and anti-ship weapon with active/passive acoustic homing that features enhanced ECCM to counter decoys launched or towed by a target. With a launch weight of 1300 kg (2,866 lb), a large HE warhead

and a range in the order of 20 km (12.4 miles), the electrically powered A184 would have been used by the 'Enrico Totis' at natural 'chokepoints' to attack much larger opponents such as Soviet SSNs or SSGNs.

*Below: Third of the 'Enrico Toti'-class boats was the **Enrico Dandolo**, which shows off the characteristic **IPD 64** active sonar system housing on the bow in this view. The crew for the relatively small boats of this class was four officers and 22 other ranks.*

SPECIFICATION	
'Enrico Toti' class	**Diving depth:** 180 m (591 ft)
Displacement: 535 tons surfaced; 591 tons dived	operational and 300 m (984 ft) maximum
Dimensions: length 46.2 m (151 ft 8 in); beam 4.7 m (15 ft 5 in); draught 4 m (13 ft 1 in)	**Torpedo tubes:** four 533-mm (21-in) tubes (all bow) for six A184 torpedoes, or 12 ground influence mines
Propulsion: two diesels and one electric motor delivering 1641 kW (2,200 shp) to one shaft	**Electronics:** one 3RM 20/SMG surface search radar, one IPD 64 sonar, one MD 64 sonar, torpedo
Performance: speed 14 kts surfaced and 15 kts dived; range 5550 km (3,450 miles) at 5 kts surfaced	fire-control and action information system, and ESM system **Complement**: 26

'Sauro' class Patrol submarine

During the early 1970s it became clear to the Italian navy that a new submarine type was required for defence against amphibious landings and for ASW and anti-shipping tasks in the local area. The result was the Italcantieri design for the **'Sauro' class**, whose first two units were the **Nazario Sauro** and **Carlo Fecia di Cossato**,

the US-developed HY-80 steel, which provides a deeper diving depth than was possible with the preceding 'Enrico Toti'-class boats. The main armament is the A184 wire-guided dual-role torpedo. The *Sauro* and *Marconi* were deleted in 2001 and 2002 respectively.

In March 1983 and July 1988 two additional pairs of boats

Above: The boats of the 'Sauro' class are welded from HY-80, a US-developed high-tensile steel, and thus possess a usefully greater diving depth than the earlier 'Totis'. Nazario Sauro decommissioned in 2001.

Left: Salvatore Pelosi is one of the sub-class of four 'Improved Sauros'. A Harpoon or Exocet capability may be added to the last two of these vessels. The current armament options are limited to the 12 Whitehead A184 torpedoes normally carried for the boats' six 533-mm (21-in) bow tubes. Alternatively, mines can be stowed.

Left: Leonardo da Vinci *was modernised in 1993 to receive new batteries of greater capacity, and improved habitability.* **Fecia di Cossato** *was similarly upgraded in 1990.*

displacements of 1,653 tons surfaced and 1,862 tons dived with a length of 66.4 m (217 ft 10 in). Uprated machinery provides surfaced and dived speeds of 11 and 19 kts respectively.

which entered service in 1980 and 1979 respectively following major problems with their batteries. A further two units, the **Leonardo da Vinci** and the **Guglielmo Marconi** were then for commissioning in 1981 and 1982. The class has a single pressure hull with external ballast tanks at the bow and stern, and a buoyancy tank in the sail. The pressure hull is made from

were ordered to the **'Improved Sauro' class** design, and these were delivered in 1988-89 and 1994-95 by Fincantieri as the **Salvatore Pelosi**, **Giuliano Prini**, **Primo Longobardo** and **Gianfranco Gazzana Priaroggia**. The first pair have displacements of 1,476 tons surfaced and 1,662 tons dived with a length of 64.4 m (211 ft 3 in), and the second pair have

SPECIFICATION

'Sauro' class
Displacement: 1,456 tons surfaced; 1,631 tons dived
Dimensions: length 63.9 m (209 ft 8 in); beam 6.8 m (22 ft 4 in); draught 5.7 m (18 ft 8 in)
Propulsion: three diesel engines delivering 2395 kW (3,210 shp) and one electric motor delivering 2720 kW (3,650 shp) to one shaft
Performance: speed 12 kts surfaced and 20 kts dived; range 20385 km (12,665 miles) at 11 kts surfaced

and 465 km (290 miles) at 4 kts dived
Diving depth: 250 m (820 ft) operational and 410 m (1,345 ft) maximum
Torpedo tubes: six 533-mm (21-in) tubes (all bow) for 12 A184 torpedoes or 24 ground mines
Electronics: BPS 704 surface search radar, IPD 70 and Thomson sonars, fire-control and action information system, and ESM
Complement: 45

'Zwaardvis' & 'Walrus' classes
Patrol submarines

Ordered in the late 1970s, the two 'Walrus'-class submarines are much improved versions of the 'Zwaardvis' design with more modern electronics, greater automation and therefore a smaller crew.

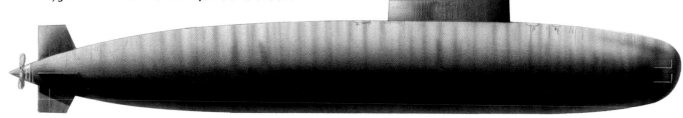

Based on the US Navy's teardrop-hulled 'Barbel' class of conventional submarine, the Dutch **Zwaardvis** and **Tijgerhaai** of the **'Zwaardvis' class** were ordered in the mid-1960s. Because of the requirement to use indigenous Dutch equipment wherever possible, the design was modified to include the placement of all noise-producing machinery on a false deck with spring suspension for silent running. The two submarines entered service with the Dutch navy in 1972 and were decommissioned in 1994-95. A buyer is still sought for the boats.

At the same time the need began to arise to start the design of a new class to replace the boats of the elderly 'Dolfijn' and 'Potvis' classes. The new design evolved as the **'Walrus' class**, which was based on the basic hull form of the 'Zwaardvis' with similar dimen-sions and silhouette but with more automation allowing a significant reduction in the number of crew needed, more modern electronics, X-layout control surfaces and fabrication in the French MAREI high-tensile steel allowing a 50 per cent increase in the maximum diving depth.

Above: Although fitted for the Sub-Harpoon SSM, the 'Walrus' class does not carry these weapons. The lead ship of the class is illustrated.

Left: For their time the 'Zwaardvis' class of conventionally powered submarines were capable boats well suited to the demands of the Dutch navy for littoral defence. Both vessels underwent an upgrade in 1988-90.

The first unit, the **Walrus**, was laid down in 1979 in Rotterdam (where all the boats were built) for commissioning in 1986 and the **Zeeleeuw** a year later for service entry in 1987. A further two, the **Dolfijn** and **Bruinvis**, were laid down in 1986 and 1988 for commission-ing in 1993 and 1994.

In 1987-88 Taiwan received two **'Improved Zwaardvis'** or **'Hai Lung'-class** units **Hai Lung** and **Hai Hu**. These are planned to carry Hsiung Feng II SSMs.

SPECIFICATION
'Walrus' class

Displacement: 2,390 tons surfaced; 2,740 tons dived
Dimensions: length 67.7 m (222 ft 1 in); beam 8.4 m (27 ft 7 in); draught 6.6 m (21 ft 8 in)
Propulsion: three diesel engines delivering 4700 kW (6,300 shp) and one electric motor delivering 5150 kW (6,910 shp) to one shaft
Performance: speed 13 kts surfaced and 20 kts dived; range 18500 km (11,495 miles) at 9 kts snorting
Diving depth: 450 m (1,476 ft) operational and 620 m (2,034 ft) maximum
Torpedo tubes: four 533-mm (21-in)

tubes (all bow) for 20 Mk 48 dual-role wire-guided torpedoes, or 40 influence ground mines, or Sub-Harpoon underwater-launched anti-ship missiles
Electronics: one ZW-07 surface search radar, one TSM 2272 Eledone Octopus active/passive bow sonar, one Type 2026 towed-array passive sonar, one DUUX 5 passive ranging and intercept sonar, GTHW torpedo/missile fire-control system, Gipsy data system, SEWACO VIII action information system, and ARGOS 700 ESM
Complement: 52

SPECIFICATION
'Zwaardvis' class

Displacement: 2,350 tons surfaced; 2,640 tons dived
Dimensions: length 66 m (216 ft 6 in); beam 8.4 m (27 ft 7 in); draught 7.1 m (23 ft 4 in)
Propulsion: three diesel engines delivering 3130 kW (4,200 shp) and one electric motor delivering 3725 kW (4,995 shp) to one shaft
Performance: speed 13 kts surfaced and 20 kts dived
Diving depth: 300 m (984 ft) operational and 500 m

(1,640 ft) maximum
Torpedo tubes: six 533-mm (21-in) tubes (all bow) for 20 Mk 37C anti-submarine and Mk 48 dual-role wire-guided torpedoes, or 40 influence ground mines
Electronics: one Type 1001 surface search radar, one low-frequency sonar, one medium-frequency sonar, one WM-8 torpedo fire-control/action information system, and one ESM system
Complement: 67

'Sjöormen' class Patrol submarine

The first of the modern type of submarines for the Swedish navy was the **'Sjöormen' class** designed in the early 1960s by Kockums, Malmö and built by that company (three units) and Karlskronavarvet (two units). The class comprised the *Sjöormen*, *Sjölejonet*, *Sjöhunden*, *Sjöbjörnen* and *Sjöhästen*. With an 'albacore' type hull for speed and a twin-deck arrangement the class was extensively used in the relatively shallow Baltic, where its excellent manoeuvrability and silent-running capabilities greatly aided the Swedish navy's ASW operations. The control surface and hydroplane arrangements were the same as those fitted to the latter Swedish submarine classes, and it was these together with the hull design that allowed the optimum manoeuvrability characteristics to be used throughout the speed range, though they were

Below: The **Sjölejonet** *of the 'Sjöormen' (sea serpent) class runs on the surface in the submarine's major operating area of the Baltic. In such a region speed and manoeuvrability is of greater importance than diving depth, since much of the sea is relatively shallow.*

The five vessels of the 'Sjöormen' class were designated the Type A12 by their builders. Fitted with X-configuration stern planes for increased manoeuvrability, they carried four 533-mm (21-in) and two 400-mm (15.75-in) calibre torpedo tubes for anti-ship and ASW torpedoes respectively. Four vessels transferred to Singapore.

SPECIFICATION	
'Sjöormen' class **Displacement:** 1,125 tons surfaced and 1,400 tons dived **Dimensions:** length 51 m (167 ft 4 in); beam 6.1 m (20 ft); draught 5.8 m (19 ft) **Propulsion:** four diesels delivering 1566 kW (2,100 shp) with one electric motor driving one shaft **Speed:** 15 kts surfaced and 20 kts dived **Diving depth:** 150 m (492 ft) operational and 250 m (820 ft) maximum	**Torpedo tubes:** four 533-mm (21-in) bow and two 400-mm (15.75-in) bow **Basic load:** 10 Type 61 533-mm (21-in) anti-ship wire-guided torpedoes or 16 influence ground mines, plus four Type 431 anti-submarine wire-guided torpedoes **Electronics:** one Terma surface search radar, one low-frequency sonar, one torpedo fire-control/action information system, and one ESM system **Complement:** 18

Right: The Sjöbjörnen *shows the sail-mounted hydroplanes which increased the vessel's underwater manoeuvring capabilities. The class could, at medium speeds submerged, out-turn most of the Western and Warsaw Pact ASW vessels it was likely to encounter in the Baltic.*

more noticeable at the lower end: for example, a 360° turn could be achieved in five minutes within a 230-m (755-ft) diameter circle at a speed of 7 kts underwater; if the speed was increased to 15 kts the same turn would take only two and a half minutes, which meant the class could easily out-turn most of the Warsaw Pact ASW escorts encountered in the Baltic, as well as most of the NATO escorts.

Sjöbjörnen was modified and upgraded for tropical conditions 1996-97 and re-launched as **Challenger** on 26 September 1997, as one of four submarines of the **'Challenger' class** on order for the Republic of Singapore Navy. The other vessels comprise **Centurion** (ex-*Sjöormen*), **Conqueror** (ex-*Sjölejonet*) and **Chieftain** (ex-*Sjöhunden*) and together will form 171 Squadron. The weapons options for the reconditioned boats comprises a combination of FFV Type 613 anti-ship torpedoes (10 carried) and FFV Type 431 ASW torpedoes (four).

'Näcken' class Patrol submarine

Since World War II Sweden has placed considerable emphasis on the possession of a small but highly capable force of conventional submarines as a key element in the preservation of its long coastline against the incursions of other nations' surface

Above: Sweden's 'Näcken'-class submarines were extremely capable boats by the standards of their day, their wire-guided torpedoes providing high capability against surface ships as well as submarines. The lead unit is illustrated.

Right: The 'Näckens' were typical diesel-electric 'submersibles', with limited submerged endurance, until the addition of air-independent propulsion in the lead boat. Neptun and Najad are seen at Karlskrona.

and underwater forces for the purposes of reconnaissance and/or aggression. The Swedish navy's first post-war submarines were the six boats of the 'Hajen' class, built during the 1950s on the basis of the German Type XXI class design: the design data were derived from the *U-3503*, which its crew scuttled off Göteborg on 8 May 1945 and which the Swedes salvaged.

From 1956 the Swedes followed with six examples of the indigenously designed 'Draken' class, and in 1961 the Swedish government approved plans for five more advanced submarines of the Type A12 or 'Sjöormen' class. This latter introduced a teardrop-shaped hull with two decks and X-configured stern planes.

'Sjöormen' successor

The Swedish navy considers the effective life of its conventional submarines to be something in the order of 10 years, and in the early 1970s raised the matter of a class to succeed the 'Sjöormen' class from a time later in the same decade. The Swedish government gave its approval to the request in 1972, and the Swedish defence ministry was therefore able to contract in March 1973 with Kockums of Malmö (two boats) and Karlskronavarvet naval dockyard (one boat) for the three **Type A14** or **'Näcken'-class** diesel-electric submarines. The boats were all laid down in 1976 and launched between April 1978 and August 1979 for commissioning between April 1980 and June 1981 as the **Näcken**, **Neptun** and **Najad**. The Baltic, which is the primary operational theatre for Sweden's submarine

arm, is shallow, so the diving depth of the 'Näcken'-class boats was fixed at some 150 m (500 ft). The boats were based on the same type of teardrop-shaped two-deck hull as the 'Sjoormen' class, and were completed with Kollmorgen periscopes from the US as well as the Data Saab NEDPS combined ship control and action information system.

In 1987-88 the *Näcken* was lengthened by 8 m (26 ft 3 in) to allow the installation of a neu-

trally buoyant section containing two liquid-oxygen tanks, two United Stirling Type V4-275 closed-cycle engines and the relevant control system, this air-independent propulsion arrangement boosting the submerged endurance to 14 days and in effect making the boat a true submarine rather than just an advanced submersible.

Danish service

From the early 1990s the boats were upgraded to a partial

SPECIFICATION	
'Näcken' class (upgraded)	**Diving depth:** 150 m (492 ft) operational
Displacement: 1,015 tons surfaced; 1,085 tons dived	**Torpedo tubes:** four 533-mm (21-in) and two 400-mm (15.75-in) tubes (all bow) with eight and four torpedoes respectively; up to 48 mines can be carried in an external girdle
Dimensions: length 57.5 m (188 ft 8 in); beam 5.7 m (18 ft 8); draught 5.5 m (18 ft)	
Propulsion: one MTU 16V 652 MB80 diesel delivering 1290 kW (1,730 shp), two Stirling engines and one Jeumont Schneider electric motor delivering 1340 kW (1,800 shp) to one shaft	**Electronics:** Terma navigation radar, IPS-17 (Sesub 900C) fire-control system, AR700-S5 ESM, and Thomson-Sintra passive sonar with bow and flank arrays
Performance: speed 10 kts surfaced and 20 kts dived	**Complement:** 27

Above: The submarines of the 'Näcken' class were characterised by their good fire-control system, the relevant data being derived from the passive sonar and single Kollmorgen periscope.

'Västergötland' class standard in their electronics. but were discarded from a time later in the same decade. The sole surviving boat is the **Kronborg** of the Danish navy, which was the *Näcken* until transferred in August 2001, after a refit by Kockums, under a lease to buy or return (in 2005).

The boat is armed with wire-guided torpedoes, the 533-mm (21-in) Type 613 passive anti-ship weapons attaining 45 kts over a range of 20 km (12.4 miles), and the 400-mm (15.75-in) Type 431 active/passive anti-submarine weapons having a speed of 25 kts over the same range.

'Romeo' class
Diesel-electric submarine

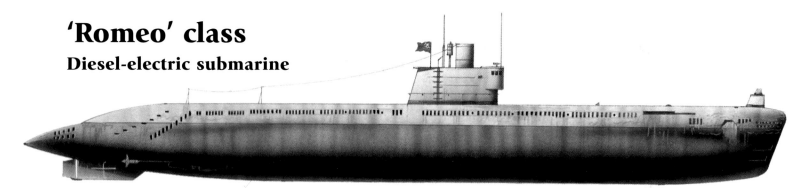

Although it was the Soviets who built the first **'Romeo' class** (**Project 633**) submarines in 1958 at Gorky, as an improvement on their 'Whiskey' design, the construction coincided with the successful introduction of nuclear propulsion into Soviet submarines. As a consequence, only 20 of these diesel electric powered boats were actually completed out of the 560 boats originally planned.

Chinese production

However, the design was passed to the Chinese as part of the development of their weapons production industry, and the class was built in China from 1962, the first boats being completed at the Wuzhang shipyard

under the local designation **Type 033**. Three further shipyards, located at Guangzhou (Canton), Jiangnan (Shanghai) and Huludao, then joined the programme to give a maximum yearly production rate of nine units during the early 1970s.

A total of 84 'Romeos' was constructed by the Chinese. However, it is now thought that only 31 remain in service with the People's Liberation Army Navy, with a further nine vessels in reserve. A total of four were exported to Egypt during 1982-84, and these have since been fitted with Sub Harpoon missiles. North Korea is believed to operate 22 'Romeo'-class boats, some of which were locally built

The Chinese adopted the Soviet 'Romeo' class as their main submarine production type and exported the type to North Korea. Today numbers of PLAN 'Romeo' ships are decreasing, and construction ceased in 1987 in favour of the 'Ming' class.

SPECIFICATION
Type 033 'Romeo' class

Displacement: 1,475 tons surfaced and 1,830 tons dived
Dimensions: length 76.6 m (251 ft 3 in); beam 6.7 m (22 ft); draught 5.2 m (17 ft 1 in)
Propulsion: two diesels delivering 2.94 MW (4,000 shp) with two electric motors driving two shafts
Speed: 15.2 kts surfaced and 13 kts dived
Range: 14,484 km (9,000) miles at 9 kts surfaced
Torpedo tubes: eight 533-mm (21-in), six located in the bows and two at the stern
Basic load: 14 533-mm (21-in) anti-ship or anti-submarine torpedoes (including Yu-4 and Yu-1 weapons) or 28 mines
Electronics: one 'Snoop Plate' or 'Snoop Tray' surface search radar, one Thomson Sintra interception sonar (some vessels), one high-frequency Herkules or Tamir 5 active/passive search and attack hull-mounted sonar
Complement: 54 (10 officers)

Below: With only a few 'Romeo' class units left in service, the Soviet navy transferred surplus vessels to Algeria, Bulgaria, Egypt and Syria. Algeria's boats were on loan and were used to train naval personnel in submarine operations. The Algerian navy have since replaced the boats with the 'Kilo'-class.

with Chinese assistance from 1976. Bulgaria operates a single Soviet-built vessel named **Slava**.

Of the original Soviet boats, all of them had been decommissioned by 1987. Two boats were loaned to Algeria in 1982-83 for a five-year period as training boats,

before Algeria's acquisition of more modern 'Kilo'-class submarines. In physical appearance both the Chinese and Soviet 'Romeos' are essentially identical, except that the Soviet boats tend to have extra sonar installations around the bow.

'Foxtrot' class
Diesel-electric submarine

Built in the periods 1958-68 (45 units) and 1971-74 (17 units) at Sudomekh for the Soviet Union, the **'Foxtrot' class (Project 641)** has proved to be the most successful of the post-war Soviet conventional submarine designs, a total of 62 entering service with the Soviet navy. Two were subsequently struck off as a result of damage sustained in accidents, one of them apparently caused by a collision with the Italian liner *Angelino Lauro* in the Bay of

Naples on 10 January 1970, after which the unit was seen later at a Soviet naval anchorage off Morocco with 8 m (26 ft 2 in) of its bow missing. All four Soviet navy fleet areas operated 'Foxtrot'-class diesel-electric submarines , and the Mediterranean and Indian Ocean squadrons regularly had units attached to them as part of their subsurface forces.

The first foreign recipient of the type was India, which took eight brand new boats between

A total of up to 79 'Foxtrot'-class units were built from 1958 onwards in several subgroups. Surprisingly, even after this period of time the basic design is still being built for the export market, with new-build ships transferred to India, Libya and Cuba (three boats received between 1979-84), albeit with downgraded electronic systems.

1968 and 1975, although it now only deploys two of the vessels. India was followed by Libya, with six units received between 1976 and 1983, of which two remain operational. Poland intended to operate two vessels, **Wilk** and **Dzik**, until 2003, while a single boat remains in the Russian navy. Export versions differed from the standard Soviet units by having export-grade electronic and weapon fits, although the eight Indian navy units (received 1968-75) were of a very similar standard to the Soviet vessels. Like all Soviet conventional and nuclear

submarine classes, the 'Foxtrots' were fitted to carry the standard Soviet 15-kT yield anti-ship torpedo as part of its weapons load, but liners for 400-mm (16-in) ASW torpedoes were not apparently fitted. The Soviet 'Foxtrots' were built in three distinct subclasses that differed only in the propulsion plant. The last group is thought to have served as prototypes for the follow-on 'Tango' design. The submerged non-snorkelling endurance of the class is estimated to have been around 5 to 7 days when operating at very low speeds (2-3 kts).

Below: Of the 62 'Foxtrot' boats which entered service with the Soviet navy, a single boat remains in service with the Russian navy. This, the last of the class, is used for basic ASW training. Another four units were transferred to the Ukraine in 1997.

SPECIFICATION	
'Foxtrot' class	at 2 kts dived
Displacement: 1,952 tons surfaced and 2,475 tons dived	**Torpedo tubes:** 10 533-mm (21-in) located as six at the bows and four at the stern
Dimensions: length 91.3 m (299 ft 5 in); beam 7.5 m (24 ft 6 in); draught 6 m (19 ft 7 in)	**Basic load:** 22 533-mm (21-in) anti-ship and anti-submarine torpedoes or 32 mines
Propulsion: three Type 37-D diesels delivering 4.4 MW (6,000 shp) with three electric motors driving three shafts	**Electronics:** one 'Snoop Tray' or 'Snoop Plate' surface-search radar, one 'Pike Jaw' high-frequency passive/active search and attack hull sonar, one 'Stop Light' ESM system
Speed: 16 kts surfaced and 15 kts dived	**Complement:** 75 (12 officers)
Range: 32186 km (20,000) miles at 8 kts surfaced; 612 km (380 miles)	

'Tango' class
Diesel-electric submarine

Built as the Soviet navy's interim long-range successor to the 'Foxtrot' class in the Black Sea and Northern Fleet areas, the first unit of the **'Tango' class** (**Project 641B**) was completed at Gorky in 1972. A total of 18 were constructed in two slightly different versions, the later type being several metres longer than the first, perhaps due to the installation of ASW missile equipment. The bow sonar installations appear similar to those fitted to the latter classes of contemporary Soviet nuclear attack submarines, while

Production of the 'Tango' class was completed in 1982. The design succeeded the 'Foxtrot' and offered increased battery storage capacity and more advanced electronics systems. The hull was also more streamlined than that of the 'Foxtrot', making it more suitable for submerged operations.

SPECIFICATION	
'Tango' class	**Torpedo tubes:** six 533-mm (21-in) located in the bow
Displacement: 3,100 tons surfaced and 3,800 tons dived	**Basic load:** 24 533-mm (21-in) anti-submarine and anti-ship torpedoes, or equivalent load of mines
Dimensions: length 91 m (298 ft 6 in); beam 9.1 m (29 ft 9 in); draught 7.2 m (23 ft 6 in)	**Electronics:** one 'Snoop Tray' surface-search radar, one medium-frequency active/passive search and attack hull-mounted sonar, one high-frequency active attack hull-mounted sonar, one 'Brick Group' or 'Squid Group' ESM system
Propulsion: three diesels delivering 4.6 MW (6,256 shp) with three electric motors driving three shafts	
Speed: 13 kts surfaced and 16 kts dived	**Complement:** 62 (12 officers)
Diving depth: 250 m (820 ft) operational and 300 m (984 ft) maximum	

Above: The casing and fin of the long-range 'Tango'-class submarines are fitted with a continuous acoustic coating, and at least one vessel was completed with a towed sonar tube in the stern and a reel mounted in the casing forward of the fin.

the propulsion plant was the same as that tested on the last subgroup of the 'Foxtrot' design. The battery capacity was much higher than in any preceding Soviet conventional submarine class as a result of the increased pressure hull volume. This allowed an underwater endurance in excess of a week before snorkelling was required. Coupled with the new armament and sensor fit, this made the 'Tangos' ideal for use in 'ambush' operations against Western nuclear submarines at natural 'chokepoints'. Construction of this class has now stopped. However, four 'Tango'-class boats remain in service. These are operated by the Russian navy's Northern Fleet at Polyarny and were inherited from the Soviet navy. The current condition of these vessels is unknown.

Left: The 'Tango' class prototype with its characteristic raised forecasing was first identified at the July 1973 Sevastopol Naval Review in the Black Sea. Directly ahead of the 'Tango' is a 'Whiskey Twin Cylinder' boat.

'Oberon' class Patrol submarine

The 'Oberon'-class boats were considered to be among the quietest conventional submarines ever built, and continued to serve on with the Royal Navy into the 1990s as training boats.

SPECIFICATION	
'Oberon' class	operational and 340 m (1,115 ft) maximum
Displacement: 2,030 tons surfaced; 2,410 tons dived	**Armament:** eight 21-in (533-mm) tubes (six bow, two short stern) for 22 or, in British boats, 18 torpedoes
Dimensions: length 90 m (295 ft 3 in); beam 8.1 m (26 ft 6 in); draught 5.5 m (18 ft)	
Propulsion: two diesels delivering 2745 kW (3,680 shp) and two electric motors delivering 4475 kW (6,000 shp) to two shafts	**Electronics:** one Type 1006 surface search radar, one Type 187 sonar, one Type 2007 sonar, one Type 186 sonar, one torpedo fire-control/action information system, and one ESM system
Speed: 12 kts surfaced; 17.5 kts dived	
Diving depth: 200 m (656 ft)	**Complement:** 69

Left: HMS Olympus is seen against the icy background of a Norwegian fjord. The 'Oberon'-class boats were optimised for operations in shallow waters such as these fjords.

Above: Australia's fleet included six 'Oberon' boats. Canadian and Australian units were modernised to a standard higher than that of the Royal Navy's boats.

Built in the late 1950s to the mid-1960s as the follow-on design to the 'Porpoise' class, the **'Oberon'-class** submarine was outwardly identical to its predecessor while internally there were a number of differences. These included the soundproofing of all the equipment for silent running and the use of a higher-grade steel for the hull to allow a greater maximum diving depth. A total of 13 units was commissioned into the Royal Navy between 1960 and 1967 as **HMS Oberon**, **HMS Odin**, **HMS Orpheus**, **HMS Olympus**, **HMS Osiris**, **HMS Onslaught**, **HMS Otter**, **HMS Oracle**, **HMS Ocelot**, **HMS Otus**, **HMS**

Opossum, **HMS Opportune** and **HMS Onyx**. The *Oberon* was later modified with a deeper casing to house equipment for the initial training of personnel for the nuclear submarine fleet, and several other units were subsequently modified for the same role. The *Opossum* later operated with a new GRP bow sonar dome and was used as a trials vessel for an integrated combat operations centre that was under development for use in future submarine classes. The *Orpheus* was also fitted with a special five-man lock-out diving chamber in its forecasing for covert operations, and for training by the Special Boat Squadron and SAS

Above: Unlike the US, which abandoned diesel-electric submarines, the UK valued conventional vessels such as the 'Oberon' class for the hunter-killer role in the Greenland-Iceland-UK gap and for clandestine duties.

Regiment. The *Onyx* served in the South Atlantic during the Falklands War on periscope beach reconnaissance operations and for landing special forces, and while performing these duties rammed a rock, which caused a live torpedo to become stuck in one of the bow tubes. This weapon had to be removed in dry dock after *Onyx* had returned to Portsmouth. The two shortened 21-in (533-mm) stern tubes, designed for Mk 20S anti-escort torpedoes, were subsequently converted to carry additional stores.

The 'Oberon' design was also sold to other navies. Chile bought the **O'Brien** and **Hyatt**; Brazil the **Humaita**, **Tonelero** and **Riachuelo**; Canada the **Ojibwa**, **Onondaga** and **Okanagan**; and Australia the **Oxley**, **Otway**, **Onslow**, **Orion**, **Otama** and **Ovens**. The type is obsolescent, and most of the boats have been retired. The *O'Brien* was the sole ship still in service in 2003.

'Guppy' class Patrol submarine

At the end of World War II Nazi Germany was poised to introduce a new fleet of U-boats. The Type XXI class were potentially revolutionary. Standard U-boats were essentially submersibles rather than true underwater weapons platforms; they spent as much time as possible on the surface as their submerged speed was very slow, slower even than many of the lumbering merchant ships they were trying to sink. The Type XXIs were faster underwater than on the surface,

indeed, they could out-run many of the warships that might be hunting them. Built too late, and often to shockingly bad production standards, they had no effect on the war. However, the Allies were impressed by their potential; several navies commissioned captured Type XXIs into service

Left: Snorkel-equipped 'Guppy'-class submarines were typical of the fast US underwater fleet that was built up as part of the race with the USSR for control of the seas. Each such boat was capable of a two-month patrol, covering 22240 km (13,820 miles) without refuelling. At the top and bottom are the USS Pickerel and USS Cubera respectively.

and elements of their design were incorporated into many post-war submarine classes.

The US Navy developed Project 'GUPPY' (Greater Underwater Propulsive Power) as a conversion programme in which current submarines were provided with greater battery capacity (at the cost of four reload torpedoes, some fresh water tanks, and magazine space) and streamlined topside with their superstructures remodelled and guns removed. Though snorkels were not fitted to the **'Guppy I'-class** prototypes, **USS Odax** and **USS Pomodon**, all subsequent conversions had them. On trials the *Pomodon* made 18.2 kts submerged. The streamlining made a great difference, the snorkel-equipped

'Guppy II' class needing only about 44 per cent of the power of the standard fleet boat, submerged, at 10 kts. Twelve 'Guppy II' conversions were approved in 1947, and in 1951 there was approval of 12 **'Guppy IA'-class** conversions (including two for the Netherlands) as well as 16 austere **'Fleet Snorkel'** conversions with the hull unchanged but the original superstructure replaced by a 'Guppy' fin with a snorkel fitted. By this time the boats' ASW training role had been eclipsed by a conventional attack submarine function.

Snorkel-equipped fleet boats could be distinguished by their raked bows, whereas those of the 'Guppy' boats were rounded; underwater they could not make much more than the 10 kts of a

Above: A Lockheed P-3 Orion patrol aircraft exercises with a 'Guppy' in the Gulf of Mexico in May 1967. The submarine is the USS Chopper, a 'Guppy IA', originally launched in 1945 as a 'Balao'-class boat.

fleet boat, though they could snorkel at 6.5 kts (compared to 7.5 and 9.5 kts for a 'Guppy IA' and 'Guppy II' respectively.

Some 16 more fleet submarines became **'Guppy IIA'-class** conversions under a 1952 programme. These had improved sonar performance with one main engine removed to permit the relocation of auxiliary machinery farther away from the sonar transducers. Two of the 'Guppy IIA'-boats were used as underwater targets, but were easily convertible back to the 'Guppy IIA' standard. Under the

FRAM (Fleet Rehabilitation And Modernization) programme, nine 'Guppy IIs' were rebuilt to the **'Guppy III'-class** standard with a 3.05-m (10-ft) lengthening for a plotting room and longer conning tower, together with new fire-control systems for the Astor (Mk 45) nuclear ASW torpedo. They also received a new plastic fin similar to that of the nuclear submarines. In the 1960s US yards converted several fleet boats (including a number already transferred abroad) to the late 'Fleet Snorkel' layout with the plastic fin.

'Guppy' conversions were transferred to several friendly nations: Argentina, Brazil, Peru and Venezuela in South America, Greece, Italy, Spain and Turkey in Europe, and Taiwan in Asia.

SPECIFICATION	
'Guppy IIA' class	**Speed:** 16 kts surfaced; 18 kts dived
Displacement: 1,848 tons surfaced; 2,440 dived	**Armament:** 10 21-in (533-mm) tubes (six bow, four stern) for 24 torpedoes
Dimensions: length 93.6 m (307 ft); beam 8.2 m (27 ft); draught 5.2 m (17 ft)	**Electronics:** BQR-2, BQS-3 and SQR-3 sonars; one Type 1006 surface search radar, one Type 187 sonar, one Type 2007 sonar, one Type 186 sonar, one torpedo fire-control/action information system, and one ESM system
Propulsion: Fairbanks-Morse diesel engines delivering 2557 kW (3,430 shp) and two electric motors delivering 3579 kW (4,800 shp) to two shafts	**Complement:** 85

Left: A US submarine squadron visits Portsmouth in June 1962. The front row comprises the 'Guppy IIs' USS Dogfish, USS Halfbeak, USS Tirante and the 'Tench C1' USS Torsk. The second row comprises USS Sablefish ('Balao' class), USS Trutta ('Guppy IIA'), USS Sennett ('Balao') and USS Irex ('Tench').

Submarine Weapons

Mk 60 CAPTOR and Mk 67 SLMM
Submarine-launched mines

The aluminium-case **Mk 60 CAPTOR** encapsulated torpedo mine is the US Navy's principal offensive anti-submarine warfare barrier weapon for use in the vicinity of deep-water routes where enemy submarines are likely to travel without escort.

CAPTOR (the name indicating encapsulated torpedo) is fitted with a detection and control unit (DCU) that is capable of detecting and classifying submarine targets over an estimated range of 1 km (0.62 miles) but gated to ignore surface traffic. There is, however, no identification friend or foe (IFF) system, so friendly submarine units must be warned of any laying or spots where CAPTORS have already been deployed. The current operational life of the mine is believed to be six months underwater before self-neutralisation devices are activated.

Above: The active component of CAPTOR consists of a Mk 46 Mod 4 lightweight torpedo armed with a 43.5-kg (96-lb) shaped-charge warhead.

Left: 'Los Angeles'-class attack submarines can carry two Mk 67 mines in place of one standard 21-in (533-mm) torpedo. The Mk 67 mine gives US submarines the ability to lay mines in heavily defended waters.

Below: CAPTOR mines can be deployed by vessels using an over-the-side ship-mounted boom or crane to ensure the correct orientation of the torpedo in the water.

Target detection

The initial target detection is carried out by a passive sonar, while the optimum release time for the Mk 46 Mod 4 homing torpedo payload (which is built with the latest Mod 5 NEARTIP improvements implemented) is determined by a second (active) ranging set. CAPTORS may be laid by surface ship, submarine or aircraft, the first platform requiring only an over-the-side boom or crane with a capacity of 1247 kg (2,750 lb) to ensure correct orientation of the mine when it hits the water. Any submarine with standard 21-in (533-mm) torpedo tubes can lay a CAPTOR, while aircraft deploy a parachute-equipped version.

Likely wartime airborne delivery platforms during the Cold War included SAC B-52Hs, US Navy P-3C Orions and possibly C-130 Hercules transport aircraft.

After several years of problems the CAPTOR became fully operational in 1979 and remained in service at the beginning of the 21st century.

Mk 67 SLMM

The **Mk 67 SLMM** dual anti-ship/anti-submarine weapon was designed to provide the US Navy submarine force with a capability for covert laying of ground influence mines in heavily defended and/or relatively inaccessible shallow waters. The platform used to perform the SLMM (submarine-

SPECIFICATION	
Mk 60 CAPTOR	**Mk 67 SLMM**
Dimensions: length air-/surface-launched 3.68 m (12 ft 1 in) or submarine-launched 3.51 m (11 ft 6 in); diameter 533 mm (21 in)	**Dimensions:** length 4.09 m (13 ft 5 in); diameter 485 mm (19 in)
Weight: air-/surface-launched 1184 kg (2,610 lb) or submarine-launched 1069 kg (2,356 lb)	**Weight:** 753 kg (1,660 lb)
	Warhead: estimated 159-227 kg (350-500 lb) HE
Payload: Mk 46 Mod 4 torpedo	**Performance:** speed 18 kts; maximum depth 100 m (330 ft); range 16.5 km (10.3 miles)
Maximum depth: 915 m (3,000 ft)	

launched mobile mine) operation is a modified Mk 37 torpedo with its warhead and homing systems replaced by all the components needed to turn the weapon into a ground mine.

Single and multi-influence fusing systems were developed for this weapon and the later mines of the Quickstrike programme. Since 1987, US submarines have been able to

carry two Mk 67s in place of each standard 21-in (533-mm) weapon offloaded. Originally several submarine classes up to the 'Los Angeles' class were fitted for minelaying.

However, the US Navy's minelaying abilities has now been transferred to the boats of the 'Virginia' class. These nuclear attack submarines were launched in 2004.

French lightweight torpedoes L4 and L5

The electric-powered **L4** air-launched torpedo is in service with the French navy for use with helicopters and fixed-wing aircraft, and it also armed the Malafon stand-off ASW missile prior to its retirement. Entering service in 1964, the L4 was the first French torpedo designed as part of the NATO weapons standardisation program, and as such it has a calibre of 533 mm (21 in). Fitted with an active acoustic-homing system, the L4 describes a circular search path upon entering the water until its seeker acquires the target. The warhead is detonated either by an impact fuse or a proximity acoustic influence fuse. French navy L4 torpedoes have been modernised to improve their shallow-water performance, and their target capability against submarines moving at speeds of between 0 and 20 kts is increased from periscope depth to around 300 m (984 ft) deep cruising. A version for surface ship launch was also developed: this has a length of 3.3 m (10.83 ft) and a weight of 570 kg (1,257 lb).

Above: The L4 air-launched torpedo can function in shallow water against submarines manoeuvring at speeds of up to 20 kts. It also provided the warload for the Malafon ASW missile system, and a ship-launched version was also designed.

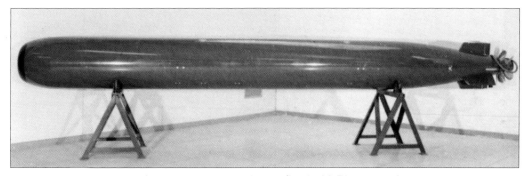

Above: The L5 series of multi-purpose torpedoes is fitted with Thomson-CSF active/passive homing heads, although the Mod 1 is intended for surface vessel use and the heavier Mod 3 version (shown here) equips submarines.

Multiple roles

The next of the L-series torpedoes to enter service, during the early 1970s, was the electric-powered **L5**. The weapon was made available in four principal versions. The dual-purpose ASW/anti-ship **L5 Mod 1** is carried by surface ships, while the similar-role but heavier **L5 Mod 3** is used by submarines, including France's SSBNs of the 'L'Inflexible' and 'Le Triomphant' classes and the 'Rubis'-class nuclear-powered attack submarines. A single-role variant, the anti-submarine **L5 Mod 4**, was

also derived from the Mod 1 and is intended for use solely by surface ships; this weapon arms France's destroyers and frigates. A further version of this last mentioned type was subsequently developed for the export market as the **L5 Mod 4P** multi-role torpedo.

All versions are fitted with a Thomson CSF active/passive guidance system and are capable of various attack profiles, including direct and programmed searches using either of the acoustic homing techniques avail-

able. Known operators of the L5, other than France, include the Belgian navy (the L5 Mod 4 arms frigates of the 'Weilingen' class), Spain (the L5 Mod 3 arms

'Agosta' submarines) and Turkey (aboard ex-French navy frigates of the 'D'Estienne d'Orves' class). The production of the current L5 models is undertaken by ECAN.

SPECIFICATION	
L4	**L5**
Dimensions: diameter 533 mm (21 in); length 3.033 m (9 ft 11 in), or 3.13 m (10 ft 3 in) with parachute pack	**Dimensions:** diameter 533 mm (21 in); length 4.4 m (14 ft 5 in)
Weight: 540 kg (1,190 lb)	**Weight:** Mod 1 1000 kg (2,205 lb); Mod 3 1300 kg (2,866 lb); Mod 4 920 kg (2,028 lb); Mod 4P 930 kg (2,050 lb)
Warhead: 104-kg (229-lb) HE	**Warhead:** 150-kg (331-lb) HE
Performance: speed 30 kts; range 5.5 km (3.4 miles)	**Performance:** speed 35 kts; range 9.25 km (5.75 miles)

French heavyweight torpedoes L3 and F17

The electric-powered 550-mm (21.65-in) calibre **L3** ship- or submarine-launched heavyweight ASW homing torpedo entered service with the French navy in 1960 and was designed by the Direction Technique des Constructions Navales (DTCN) to attack submerged targets at depths up to 300 m (984 ft) and at speeds from 0 to 20 kts. It is fitted with an AS-3T active acoustic guidance system that has a detection range of about 600 m (1,969 ft) in ideal condi-

tions, and the torpedo's warhead is detonated by an electromagnetic proximity fusing system. A 533-mm (21-in) version of the L3 with the same performance was made available for export, length and weight being 4.318 m (14.17 ft) and 900 kg (1,984 lb). Apart from France, several of the countries (including Spain) which bought 'Daphné'-class submarines also obtained the larger-calibre weapon, as did Uruguay to equip its ex-French navy frigates.

Above: Built by Sintra-Alcatel, the L3 is a conventional ship- or submarine-launched active acoustic-homing anti-submarine torpedo. Unusually, it has a diameter of 550 mm (21.65 in) but has been offered in the standard 533-mm (21-in) diameter for export. It was formerly in widespread French naval service.

The **F17** was the first wire-guided heavyweight torpedo to be used by the French navy. Designed for use against surface ships from submarines, the weapon can be employed either in the wire-guided mode or in an autonomous passive homing mode, the capability for instant switching between the two modes being provided on a control panel aboard the launch platform.

Terminal attack phase

The terminal attack phase is normally of the passive acoustic type under the torpedo's own internal control. A dual-purpose surface- or submarine-launched variant, the **F17P**, was also developed for the export market, and was bought by Saudi Arabia for use aboard frigates of the 'Madina' (Type F2000S) and 'Arrivad' (Type F3000S) classes, and by Spain for use aboard its submarines of the 'Agosta' and modernised 'Daphné' classes. The F17P version differs from the basic F17 torpedo in having an active/passive acoustic-homing seeker with completely autonomous operation if required.

SPECIFICATION	
F17	**L3**
Dimensions: diameter 533 mm (21 in), length 5.91 m (19 ft 4⅔ in)	**Dimensions:** diameter 550 mm (21.65 in); length 4.3 m (14 ft 1 in)
Weight: 1410 kg (3,108 lb)	**Weight:** 910 kg (2,006 lb)
Warhead: 250-kg (529-lb) HE	**Warhead:** 200-kg (441-lb) HE
Performance: speed 35 kts; range 18 km (11.18 miles)	**Performance:** speed 25 kts; range 7.5 km (4.66 miles)

Above: The wire-guided F17 heavyweight torpedo is a submarine-launched anti-shipping weapon, although an automatic homing head is standard. The F17P is a development capable of ship or submarine launch, and in addition to wire guidance is equipped for active or passive acoustic homing. The terminal attack phase is usually autonomous. The latest version of the latter type is the F17P Mod 2.

Left: A French navy 'Agosta'-class boat makes its way through the waves. These submarines can carry 16 F17 torpedoes and at the beginning of the 21st century the class served in two versions with the navies of Pakistan (F17P torpedoes) and Spain (F17P later replaced by L5 Mod 3 torpedoes).

German torpedoes Seal, Seeschlange, Seehecht, SST and SUT types

These AEG-Telefunken (now STN Atlas) weapons are a complete family of heavyweight torpedoes. The basic electric-powered dual-speed **DM2A1 Seal** and **DM1 Seeschlange** (the latter upgraded for service re-entry in 1985 as the **DM2A3** and **DM2A4 Seehecht** with improved guidance and propulsion respectively) were developed for the German navy, primarily for its Type 205/206 submarines, whilst the Seal is also employed on some light forces' missile craft. There is a high degree of commonality between the weapons, the major difference being that the smaller ASW Seeschlange has only half the propulsive battery capacity of the anti-ship Seal and dual-role Seehecht. An active/passive homing head is fitted with a wire-guidance system that allows rapid changes in speed, attack pattern and guidance mode in changing tactical situations.

Weapon variants

The Seal was then taken as the model for the **Special Surface Target (SST)** torpedo in baseline **SST-3** and shorter-range **SST-4** variants, which except for certain features unique to German operational requirements are comparable in dimensions, construction and capabilities to their predecessors. Used as the standard anti-ship weapon sold with export Type 209 submarines and German missile craft, the SST-4 is found in various NATO and South American navies, and was

Above: A missile-armed fast attack craft of the German navy's Type 143 class makes a test launch of an AEG-Telefunken DM2A1 Seal torpedo. One of a family of weapons, the Seal was designed for the engagement of surface targets, and has been shipped on Type 142 and Type 143 surface craft as well as aboard Type 206 submarines.

used by the Argentine submarine *San Luis* during the 1982 Falklands War in abortive attacks on Royal Navy ships.

The Seal was then developed to produce the **Surface and Underwater Target (SUT)** export torpedo. As a dual-purpose weapon for surface ship, submarine and shore launch, the SUT has the same shallow-water/deep-diving capabilities of the other members of the family plus the same contact and magnetic proximity fusing systems. Like the SST-4 it is in production for export with Type 209 submarines.

Right: The Surface and Underwater Target (SUT) torpedo, seen being loaded aboard one of the widely exported Type 209 submarines, is the most versatile of the AEG-Telefunken heavyweight torpedo range. It is a dual-purpose weapon, wire-guided for greater accuracy.

SPECIFICATION	
DM2A1 Seal	**Weight:** 1370 kg (3,020 ft)
Dimensions: diameter 533 mm (21 in); length 6.08 m (19 ft 11¼ in) or 6.55 m (21 ft 6 in) with wire guidance casket	**Warhead:** 250-kg (551-lb) HE **Performance:** speed 23 or 33 kts; range 28 or 12 km (17.4 or 7.46 miles)

Italian torpedoes Whitehead A184, A244 and A290

The **A184** is a dual-purpose ASW/anti-ship heavyweight wire-guided torpedo produced by Whitehead Motofides and carried by submarines and surface ships of the Italian navy, and has also been exported to Taiwan for use on its 'Guppy II' and 'Hai Lung'-class submarines until replaced by the German SUT. The panoramic active/passive acoustic-homing head controls the torpedo's course and depth in the final attack phase while the initial wire guidance uses the launch platform's own sonar sensors to guide the weapon up to the point of acoustic acquisition. Like most modern electrically powered torpedoes the A184 is fitted with a silver-zinc battery and has dual-speed capabilities (low speed for the passive hunting phase and high speed for the active attack phase). To complement the A184 and replace the American Mk 44 for operations in the notoriously difficult ASW environment of the Mediterranean, the lightweight **A244** was developed with a 324-mm (12.75-in) diameter. This is an electrically powered weapon suitable for use by aircraft, helicopters and surface ships in normal and shallow waters. In its original form it was fitted with a

Selenia AG70 homing head, but the later **A244/S** variant has a CIACIO-S advanced homing seeker. Using special signal-processing technique, this allows both active and passive operations which can discriminate between a real target and decoys. The A244 and A244/S have been sold to a number of countries including India, Argentina, Ecuador, Iraq, Indonesia, Libya, Nigeria, Venezuela, and Peru. Whitehead is currently man-

ufacturing, as successor to the A244 series, high-performance **A290** capable of speeds of 50 kts, which uses advanced

seeker technology derived ultimately from that of the A244/S weapon, together with pump-jet propulsion.

Above: Designed for launch from surface ships, helicopters and aircraft, the A244 is capable of both active and passive operations in a wide variety of attack patterns in both deep and shallow waters. The weapon was also adapted as a possible warload for the Ikara anti-submarine missile system. The A244 torpedo is powered by a lead/acid rather than silver/zinc battery.

SPECIFICATION	
A244/S	**Warhead:** 34-kg (75-lb) HE
Dimensions: diameter 324 mm (12¾ in); length 2.75 m (9 ft ¼ in)	**Performance:** speed 30 kts; range 6.5 km (4 miles)
Weight: 235 kg (518 lb)	

Right: The A184 is a modern heavyweight product of one of the world's oldest torpedo manufacturers. As with most modern torpedoes, it is electrically powered, in this instance to a maximum speed of 36 kts, and has a maximum range of 10.9 km (6.77 miles) at that speed.

Swedish torpedoes FFV Tp42 and Tp61 series

Originally intended as the successor to the Swedish navy's Tp41, the **Tp42** is the base model of a whole series of lightweight 400-

mm (15.75-in) torpedoes built by FFV (now Saab Bofors Dynamics) for the home and export markets. The **Tp422** basic model entered

service in mid-1983 primarily for ASW operations from the navy's small fleet of Boeing-Vertol 107 helicopters. It is unique among

Western lightweight weapons in that it is capable of wire guidance after an air-launched delivery. The terminal attack phase is carried out by a passive sonar system. Propulsion is by an electric battery of the silver-zinc type, while the warhead is fitted with both proximity and contact fuses.

Variable speed

The torpedo can be set to run at one of two speeds which are changeable after launch either via the guidance wire or as an instruction preprogrammed into the seeker unit. The similar **Tp423** is believed to be intended for launch from surface ships and submarines against submarine or ship targets. The export version of the Tp422/423 is known as the **Tp427**, and this has internal and guidance changes which effectively introduce different sonar and proximity fuse frequencies in order not to compromise Swedish navy settings.

In 1984 the Swedish navy initiated a product improvement programme that led to the **Tp432**. This was designed round digital microprocessor guidance units, and was optimised for attacks on the new generation of Soviet conventional submarines operating quietly in shallow waters. A new three-speed selectable propulsion system and increased guidance wire capacity improved the maximum range of the weapon, at the slowest speed, by 33 per cent in comparison with the earlier Tp42 models. The equivalent export version is designated **Tp43X0**, which is able to use alternative

propulsion systems if required. The lightest of the whole Tp432/43X0 family is the **Tp45** helicopter-launched variant which weighs 280 kg (617 lb), and because it has a smaller battery capacity this has a maximum range in the order of 15-20 km (9.3-12.4 miles) at the slowest speed setting.

Designed for use against surface ship targets, the **Tp61** entered service in 1967 as a wire-guided heavyweight torpedo, without terminal guidance, for use by surface ships, submarines and coastal defence batteries. In 1984 the longer-range **Tp613** entered service as the Tp61's successor with essentially the same propulsion system and a terminal homing seeker that makes

Above: Norway acquired the improved Tp613 torpedo in place of the Tp61 already operated. The later weapon equips the 'Hauk'-class fast attack craft, but not submarines such as Uthaug, seen here, of the now retired 'Kobben' class or the identically named S304 of the newer 'Ula' class, which uses the DM2A3 Seehecht torpedo.

use of an onboard computer to oversee the attack and, if necessary, to initiate previously programmed search patterns at the target's predicted location. The computer also guides the torpedo to the latter point and initiates a search even if the guidance wire is broken. The torpedo's thermal propulsion system combines hydrogen peroxide with ethanol to power a 12-cylinder steam motor which produces an almost invisible wake signature. Compared with modern electrically powered weapons moving at similar speed, the maximum range attainable is between three and five times greater.

The earlier Tp61 is in service with Norway, whilst the Tp613 was more recently ordered by Denmark and Norway. For other nations there is the **Tp617** export version which differs from the Tp613 only in internal software changes to give sonar and proximity fuse settings different from those used in the Swedish weapons. Each Tp61 series torpedo can be left in its tube for up to four months without requiring overhaul.

The latest Saab Bofors Dynamics heavyweight weapon is the **Torpedo 2000**, which is a wire-guided type offering great resistance to countermeasures, high speed and long range.

Left: The advantage of the lightweight torpedo is that it can give a significant anti-submarine capability to the smallest of helicopters. The Tp422 has been launched from the Swedish navy's AB 206 helicopters, although the KV 107 (Japanese licence-built Boeing-Vertol 107) is the usual platform for this weapon.

SPECIFICATION	
Tp432/43X0	**Weight:** 280 to 350 kg (617 to 772 lb)
Dimensions: diameter 400 mm (15¾ in); length 2.6 m (8 ft 6⅛ in) or 2.85 m (9 ft 4¼ in) with wire guidance section	**Warhead:** 45-kg (99-lb) HE **Performance:** speed 15, 25 or 35 kts; range 30, 20 or 10 km (18.64, 12.43 or 6.21 miles)

Soviet sea mines Chokepoint weapons

The Soviet navy was a firm believer in the utility of the sea mine: many surface ships and submarines had a minelaying capability, and the laying of mines in and off harbours was entrusted to Soviet naval aircraft. The Western concern for deep minehunting was inspired by reports in the mid-1970s of two new mine types: the **RVM** rocket-propelled and **UEP** anti-submarine mines. The Soviets then introduced a torpedo mine similar in concept to the US CAPTOR and also a submarine-fired mobile mine.

The **AMD**, **KMD**, **KMK** and **MKD** were air-, surface ship- and submarine-laid ground mines suffixed by a figure indicating their weight in kilogrammes, and the known influence mechanisms were of the magnetic, acoustic, pressure and combination types. The original AMD appeared in World War II as an air-dropped version of the earlier MKD magnetic ground mine, itself the first modern Soviet ground mine. An AMD-II was reported in 1950 (the KMD being a surface ship-laid variant). There was no AMD-III, but an more modern AMD-IV was first reported in 1954. Supposed inventory strengths were 18,000 each of the AMD-500 and AMD-1000 and 35,000 of the AMD-IV. The AMD-P-V reported in 1988

Left: Seeming not obviously hostile in intent, intelligence gatherers such as the Cuban Isla de la Juventud are ideally suited to the task of laying small and clandestine minefields in key regions.

Above: Technicians work on M08/39 mines, a type created on the basis of the M08 in 1939 and used by the Soviet navy until well into the 1960s. The weight was 592 kg (1,305 lb) rather than the M08's 575 kg (1,268 lb).

(12,000 units) may have been a successor type.

The **KRAB** designation was used for moored acoustic influence mines, with a 250-kg (551-lb) HE charge. The type entered service in 1949 and a more modern version was intro-

duced in 1960. KRAB mines can be moored in 600 m (1,970 ft) of water with the weapon at no more than 150 m (500 ft). It was inventoried at 10,000 units.

The **MAG** designation was used for a moored ASW antenna mine modified from

SPECIFICATION	
M08/39	**KB1**
Dimensions: diameter 0.9 m (35.4 in); maximum case length 6.096 m (20 ft)	**Dimensions:** diameter 0.9 m (35.4 in); maximum case length 9.144 m (30 ft)
Charge weight: 115 kg (253.5 lb)	**Charge weight:** 230 kg (507 lb)
Maximum laying depth: 130 m (427 ft)	**Maximum laying depth:** 275 m (902 ft)

MKB standard and on occasion fitted with impact horns. The maximum laying depth was 450 m (1,475 ft) with the case at between 2.5 and 45 m (8 and 148 ft), and the antennae were 24 and 35 m (79 and 115 ft) long for the upper and lower units for a swept depth of 60 m (197 ft). Some 10,000 units were held.

The **MKB-3** was a standard moored contact mine, the successor to the classic **M08**. It had a 200-kg (441-lb) charge and five chemical horns, and inventory was reckoned at 30,000.

Appearing in 1969, the **RVM 'Cluster Bay'** was a rocket-propelled rising mine: it listened for a target and then engaged its active sonar for depth and speed determination. The rocket fired the weapon straight up, a pre-set fuse detonating it at the estimated target depth. The inventory of 15,000 included the **A-RVM** air-dropped model and **G-RVM** with a torpedo payload. The mine was moored at a maximum depth of 750 m (2,460 ft) with the case at no more than 300 m (985 ft).

Inventoried at 10,000, the **UDM** was a universal influence mine laid by aircraft, surface ships and possibly also by submarines. The total weight of some 1000 kg (2,205 lb)

included a 650-kg (1,433-lb) charge. In its magnetic version, the mine released a sensor which floated closer to the surface. The UEP **'Cluster Gulf'**

was an anti-submarine 480-kg (1,058-lb) anti-submarine type whose 30-kg (66-lb) charge was triggered by differentials in underwater electric potential.

Above: The M08 series of moored horn mines dates from 1908, and was produced in vast numbers by Russia and the USSR, and also by several of the latter's client states such as North Korea.

Soviet torpedoes Anti-ship and anti-submarine weapons

Soviet torpedoes, like their Western counterparts, could be categorised into heavy and lightweight models for specific purposes. Of the former, two calibres are known: the standard 533 mm (21 in) and the newer 650 mm (25.6 in). The 533-mm versions were thought to have been evolved from German World War II designs, and included straight- and pattern-running surface- and submarine-launched steam- and electric-powered models for anti-ship use, as well as acoustic/passive-homing weapons for both anti-ship and anti-submarine service. Surprisingly, most large modern surface combatants had multi-tube launchers for the ASW acoustic-homing versions. There was also a special 15-kT yield nuclear-armed 533-mm torpedo without terminal homing in service on many of the submarines designed for use against high-value surface targets such as

aircraft carriers and VLCC (Very Large Crude Carrier) vessels. Similarly the huge 9.14-m (30-ft) long 650-mm **Type 65** anti-ship torpedo was introduced on board later generations of nuclear attack submarines for use against surface ship targets. It was believed to use wake-homing guidance methods and, with selectable 50- or 30-kt speeds, had ranges of 50

and 100 km (31 and 62 miles) respectively. With ranges like these, the Type 65 was used to supplement the pop-up anti-ship cruise missile weapons of 'Charlie'-class SSGNs, and the type's availability for the first time allowed Soviet SSNs to fire torpedoes from outside the ASW screen of a convoy.

For air, shipboard and submarine ASW used at close

range a 400-mm (15.75-in) electric-powered lightweight torpedo was used for many years. This was later supplemented and then supplanted for use aboard ASW aircraft and helicopters by a larger 450-mm (17.7-in) weapon which was believed to have a larger warhead, greater range and upgraded guidance packages combining to increase lethality.

Above: The Vitse-Admiral Kulakov is the second of the large ASW destroyers of the 'Udaloy' class. In addition to its ASW missiles and helicopters, it is armed with two quadruple 533-mm (21-in) torpedo tubes, one of which is visible astern of the aft funnel structure.

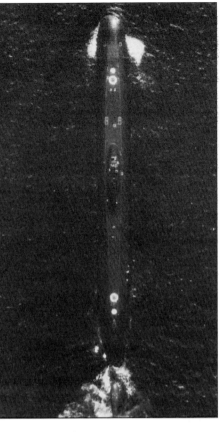

Left: Photographed by a US Navy F-14 fighter, this 'Victor I'-class SSN had fouled the towed-array sonar of a 'Spruance'-class destroyer off the coast of Georgia. These large boats were probably fitted with long-ranged 533-mm (21-in) torpedoes, permitting attacks from considerable stand-off range.

SPECIFICATION	
Type 53-56	**Type 65-73**
Type: free-running or wake-homing ship/submarine-launched torpedo	**Type:** free-running submarine-launched anti-ship torpedo
Dimensions: diameter 533 mm (21 in); length 7.7 m (25 ft 3¼ in)	**Dimensions:** diameter 650 mm (25.6 in); length 11 m (36 ft 1 in)
Weights: total 2000 kg (4,409 lb); warhead 400 kg (882 lb)	**Weights:** total 4000+ kg (8,818+ lb); warhead nuclear
Performance: range/speed 8000 m (8,750 yards) at 50 kts or 13000 m (14,215 yards) at 40 kts	**Performance:** range/speed 50 km (31 miles) at 50 kts

Both the air-launched weapons used parachutes to slow their water entries.

According to some reports there was also a short 400-mm

Below: The 'Alfa'-class submarine was considerably shorter than other Soviet SSN designs, so it was not fitted with the massive and very long-ranged 650-mm (25.6-in) torpedo used by other late-generation SSNs such as the 'Sierra'- and 'Akula'-class boats.

anti-ship torpedo for first-generation 'Hotel-', 'Echo-' and 'November-'class nuclear submarines in their stern tubes. The later-generation nuclear submarine classes apparently had several of their standard 533-mm torpedo tubes fitted with liners to fire the ASW version of the same weapon.

The standard fusing system fitted to Soviet torpedoes was an active magnetic proximity device to ensure detonation under the target's hull, so as to break its back, with a secondary contact unit for detonation after a direct hit.

Below: The backbone of the Soviet surface vessel anti-submarine force, the 'Krivak'-class frigate is, like all major Soviet vessels, fitted with torpedo tubes. The eight 533-mm (21-in) tubes abaft the bridge, in quadruple mountings to port and starboard, fire acoustically-homing torpedoes.

Stingray Lightweight torpedo

Designed to supplement the American Mk 46 Mod 2 and to replace the Mk 44 torpedoes in British service, the **Stingray** lightweight torpedo was the sequel of the abortive Ministry of Defence in-house lightweight Mk 30 and Mk 31 programmes, which were cancelled in 1970. The Stingray is the first British torpedo to be developed entirely by private industry (Marconi, now BAE Systems), and the weapon incorporates a number of technical innovations. The weapon is capable of being

launched from helicopters, aircraft and surface ships over a wide range of speeds and sea states and, as a result of its unique guidance system, can be used satisfactorily in both shallow and deep waters with an equally high single-shot kill probability. The former was demonstrated during a development trial shot when a Stingray dropped from a RAF Nimrod of No. 42 Squadron hit and sank the decommissioned conventional submarine HMS *Porpoise*. Although deployed operationally

Above: The Stingray can be carried by many types of fixed- and rotary-wing aircraft, such as the Britten-Norman Defender series machine seen here.

Below: The Stingray is slowed before its entry into the water by a drag chute, which then breaks away, allowing the torpedo to reach a submerged speed of 45 kts.

Above: A Stingray anti-submarine torpedo is launched from a frigate of the Royal Navy. The torpedoes are surface ship-launched from modified versions of the US Mk 32 triple tubes.

SPECIFICATION	
Stingray	**Warhead:** 45-kg (99-lb)
Dimensions: diameter 324 mm	shaped-charge HE
(12.75 in); length 2.6 m (8 ft 6 in)	**Performance:** speed 45 kts; range
Weight: 266.9 kg (588.5 lb)	8000 m (8,750 yards)

aboard several ships during the 1982 Falklands War, the Stingray was not fired in anger, and did not enter full-scale service with the Royal Navy and Royal Air Force until 1983. Since then the weapon has been sold to Thailand and Egypt. In terms of general performance it is similar to the Mk 46 though, it seems, the British torpedo has a slightly deeper diving depth of 800 m (2,625 ft). The Stingray also possesses an onboard digital computer coupled to a multi-mode multi-beam active/passive sonar that effectively makes it a 'smart' weapon. Propulsion is by an electrical pumpjet with a battery activated by sea water that ensures no speed loss as the depth increases. The warhead is of the directed-energy shaped-charge variety rather than blast type to ensure the penetration of a Soviet submarine's double-hull construction.

Mk 24 Tigerfish Heavyweight torpedo

The origins of the **Mk 24 Tigerfish** heavyweight torpedo can be found as far back as 1959, in a British torpedo project codenamed 'Ongar'. By 1970 it was realised that the technology involved could not be handled solely by the in-house service approach of the Royal Navy Torpedo Factory, which was closed, and the task was entrusted to Plessey, from 1972 onward. This was five years after the originally envisaged in-service date. As a result of development and engineering problems the first version of the Tigerfish, the **Mk 24 Mod 0**, entered limited fleet service in 1974 with less operational capability than originally desired. It was only granted its full Fleet Weapon Acceptance certificate in 1979 after protracted evaluation.

To rectify the problems Plessey initiated development of a product-improved version, the **Mk 24 Mod 1**, during 1972 but this also encountered technical problems and finally entered limited service only in mid-1978. By 1981 sufficient update kits were available to upgrade all the earlier Mod 0 weapons to this standard. Designed for submarine use against submerged (Mod 0 and 1) and surface (Mod 1) targets, the dual-speed Tigerfish torpedo is electrically powered and is guided over the initial stage of its run by means of wire dispensed from

Right: Tigerfish packs a considerable punch in terms of its warhead, but has been the subject of criticism for its lack of reliability (largely as a result of its batteries), control problems and a tendency to dip and thus break the guidance wire linking it with the FCS of the launch submarine.

Left: A Mk 24 Tigerfish heavyweight torpedo is readied for lowering into the torpedo room of a British submarine. This weapon was designed for use only by submarines.

stub wings, and is guided in the above fashion up to the point at which its own three-dimensional active/passive sonar seeker head and computer can take over for the terminal phase of the mission, namely the attack on the target.

A programme that reached fruition in 1986, when the **Mk 24 Mod 2** weapon entered service, was handled by Marconi (now BAE Systems) to improve reliability to some 80 per cent or more from the Mk 24 Mod 1's figure of only 40 per cent. In 1990 the Cardoen company of Chile was licensed to produce the Tigerfish for Brazil, Chile and Venezuela, but it is thought that only Brazil uses the torpedo.

SPECIFICATION	
Mk 24 Tigerfish	**Warhead:** 340-kg (750-lb) HE
Dimensions: diameter 533 mm (21 in); length 6.464 m (21 ft 2½ in)	**Performance:** speed 24 or 35 kts; range 27430 or 21030 m (30,000 or 23,000 yards) at 24 or 35 kts
Weight: 1551 kg (3,420 lb)	

both the submarine and the torpedo itself, using data derived from the launch platform's passive sonar sets. The torpedo is roll-stabilised by extending mid-body

Spearfish Heavyweight torpedo

Left: A Spearfish torpedo is loaded on board a trials vessel. The guidance system makes use of features developed for the Stingray, and the directed-energy warhead is notably advanced.

Below: Personnel prepare to lower a Spearfish into a submarine for firing trials, which revealed the torpedo's very high speed.

Designed by Marconi (now BAE Systems) to meet Naval Staff Requirement 7525, which followed feasibility studies in 1977-79, the **Spearfish** is an advanced-capability wire-guided heavyweight dual-role torpedo to provide a capability against later generations of Soviet submarines offering high speed and deep-diving capability. The torpedo uses a new hydrogen ammonium perchlorate/Otto-

powered Sundstrand 21TP01 turbine engine with a pumpjet outlet to achieve speeds in excess of 60 kts (more than 70 kts on trials). The warhead is of the directed-energy shaped-charge type to penetrate double-hull construction.

To ensure that the weapon contacts the target's hull before the warhead is triggered, the guidance system uses technology developed for the Stingray lightweight torpedo.

The onboard computer's decision-making algorithms enable the torpedo to make its own tactical decisions during an engagement, optimising the homing modes to the underwater environment encountered and also to the target's use of decoys and manoeuvring patterns.

Work on the development prototypes began in 1982, the first in-water trials taking place in the following year. The pro-

SPECIFICATION	
Spearfish	**Warhead:** 300-kg (661-lb) HE
Dimensions: diameter 533 mm (21 in); length about 5.94 m (19 ft 6 in)	**Performance:** speed 80+ kts; range (1981 version) about 21030 m
Weight: 1849 kg (4,077 lb)	(23,000 yards) at 60+ kts

gramme was delayed by changes in the requirement, and in the late 1980s Marconi produced about 100 pre-production torpedoes before the bidding process was reopened in 1989 to include Dowty and BAe proposals. In the 1990s

the programme was suspended in the hopes of attracting international collaboration and/or adoption.

A major limitation is much slowed speed at great depths because of pumpjet back-pressure limitations.

Mk 44, Mk 46 and Mk 50 Lightweight anti-submarine torpedoes

The **Mk 44 Mod 0** lightweight torpedo was selected for production in 1956, and in the following year became the payload for the new ASROC ASW missile as well as the standard US Navy lightweight torpedo for ship- and air-launched applications. The weapon was electrically powered, using a battery activated by sea water, and had an active homing seeker with a detection range of 585 m (1,920 ft). A slightly modified version, the **Mk 44 Mod 1**, was produced at a later date, and this model differed only in internal details. Several countries procured the weapon, but most later replaced it with the Mk 46, although some, like the UK, kept some stocks as the Mk 44 provided better shallow-water performance than its successor. The US Navy replaced

it completely from 1967 onwards by the Mk 46.

Acoustic homing

The active/passive acoustic-homing **Mk 46** programme began in 1960, the first production rounds of the air-launched **Mk 46 Mod 0** variant being delivered in 1963. The new torpedo achieved twice the range of the Mk 44, could dive deeper (460 m/1,500 ft by comparison with 300 m/ 985 ft) and was 50 per cent faster (45 kts rather than 30 kts) because of the use of a new type of propulsive system. In the Mod 0 this

More than 9,000 Mk 46 lightweight torpedoes have been produced by Honeywell for service with the US Navy and the naval forces of more than 20 other countries. The weapon can be launched from aircraft, ships and the ASROC missile.

was a solid-fuel motor, but as a result of maintenance difficulties it had to be changed to the Otto-fuelled thermo-chemical cam engine in the follow-on **Mk 46 Mod 1**. The latter first entered service in 1967 for use in ASROC, surface ship and some air-launched applications, and the

Mk 46 Mod 2 first appeared in 1972. There was no Mod 3, so the next variant to see service was the **Mk 46 Mod 4** intended specifically for use as the payload for Mk 60 CAPTOR mines. As a result of Soviet submarine developments, primarily in the area of anechoic hull coatings to degrade

Above: A Mk 46 torpedo is launched from one of the Mk 32 triple torpedo tubes currently fitted to all of the cruisers, destroyers and frigates of the US Navy.

Left: The development of the anti-submarine helicopter, together with the lightweight homing torpedo, has immensely extended ASW radius. This Mk 46 torpedo, dropped by an SH-3A Sea King, is parachute-retarded for slow impact with the water.

Left: A Recoverable Exercise Torpedo is fired from the guided missile destroyer USS Donald Cook (DDG 75). Based on operational torpedoes, exercise weapons have reduced fuel loads together with instrumentation packages enabling them to be tracked in real time on live firing ranges.

SPECIFICATION	
Mk 44	**Warhead:** 43.1-kg (95-lb) HE
Dimensions: diameter 12.75 in	**Performance:** speed 40/45 kts; range
(324 mm); length (Mod 0) 2.54 m	11 km (6.8 miles) at 15-m (50-ft)
(8 ft 4 in) or (Mod 1) 2.57 m (8 ft 5 in)	depth or 5.5 km (3.4 miles) at 457-m
Weight: (Mod 0) 192.8 kg (425 lb) or	(1,500-ft) depth
(Mod 1) 196.4 kg (433 lb)	
Warhead: (Mod 0) 34-kg (75-lb) HE or	**Mk 50 Barracuda**
(Mod 1) 33.1-kg (73-lb) HE	**Dimensions:** diameter 12.75 in
Performance: speed 30 kts; range 5.5	(324 mm); length 2.9 m (9 ft 6 in)
km (3.4 miles)	**Weight:** 362.9 kg (800 lb)
	Warhead: 45.4-kg (100-lb)
Mk 46	shaped-charge HE
Dimensions: diameter 12.75 in	**Performance:** speed 55/60 kts; range
(324 mm); length 2.6 m (8 ft 6 in)	up to 20 km (12.4 miles) depending
Weight: (Mod 0) 257.6 kg (568.1 lb) or	on depth
(Mod 1, 2, 4 and 5) 230.4 kg (508 lb)	

active sonar acoustic transmissions, however, the US Navy had to develop a modification kit. This contained new guidance and control units, engine improvements and an enhanced sonar transducer to restore the 33 per cent loss in the 550-m (1,800-ft) detection range suffered by Mk 46s when faced by such coatings. Known by the title **NEARTIP** (NEAR-Term Improvement Program), the **Mk 46 Mod 5** was procured both as new-build weapons and as conversions of the earlier Mod 1 and Mod 2 weapons.

Apart from the US Navy, other users of the Mk 46 have included Australia, Brazil, Canada, France, Germany, Greece, Indonesia, Iran, Israel, Italy, Morocco, the Netherlands, New Zealand, Pakistan, Saudi Arabia, Spain, Turkey, Taiwan and the UK.

Falklands War

The Mk 46 was used operationally by the Royal Navy on several occasions in the Falklands War with inconclusive results, although the threat of the Mk 46 did help in the damaging and subsequent grounding of the Argentine submarine Santa Fe off South Georgia.

The replacement for the Mk 46 in US Navy service from the early 1990s is the **Advanced Light Weight Torpedo** (**ALWT**), designed by Honeywell/Garrett and given the designation **Mk 50 Barracuda** following a competitive evaluation against the McDonnell Douglas Mk 51. Fitted with a directed-energy shaped-charge warhead, the Mk 50 is roughly the same size and weight as the Mk 46 but faster at 55+ kts and able to dive deeper (to 600 m/ 1,970 ft). It also has a new stored chemical-energy propulsion system with a closed-cycle steam turbine in conjunction with a pump-jet arrangement. An onboard computer and advanced active/passive sonar give the weapon 'smart' capability similar to that of the British Stingray.

Mk 37 Heavyweight anti-submarine and anti-ship torpedo

Designed by Westinghouse, the **Mk 37 Mod 0** heavyweight torpedo entered service in 1956 as an underwater- and surface-launched ASW acoustic-homing free-running torpedo. Fitted with studs along its sides, the 19-in (483-mm) calibre Mk 37 could be fired from the standard 21-in (533-mm) torpedo tube. As operational experience built up with the weapon, many Mod 0 torpedoes were refurbished and modified to bring them up to **Mk 37 Mod 3** standard. Although useful in the ASW role, these free-running weapons, which could dive to 300 m (985 ft), were not suited to very long sonar detection ranges as during the torpedo's run to a predicted target location it was possible that the target could perform evasive manoeuvres taking it out of the 640-m (2,100-ft) acquisition range of the weapon's seeker head. Thus wire guidance was fitted to the Mk 37 to produce the **Mk 37 Mod 1**, which entered service in 1962 aboard US submarines. This was followed by the updated **Mk 37 Mod 2** conversion of Mod 1 weapons. The standard US Navy submarine-launched ASW torpedo for some 20 years, the Mk 37 last saw American service aboard the diesel-electric boat USS Darter. The Darter carried these torpedoes until it was stricken in December 1989.

Mk 67 mobile mine

Many of the obsolescent Mk 37 torpedoes were converted to Mk 67 submarine-launched mobile mine shells, while others were put through major upgrades before sale to other countries. The first such modification, in the mid-1970s, resulted in the **NT37C** with a new thermo-chemical propulsion system (based on that of the Mk 46) and an anti-ship capability option. The NT37C served with Canada and Israel. In 1979 Honeywell acquired from Northrop the rights to the NT37C, and at the request of several NATO navies developed the weapon to the **NT37E** standard allowing the addition of kits to produce **NT37E Mod 2** and **NT37E Mod 3** conversions of the basic Mk 37 variants. In general terms these new vari-

SPECIFICATION	
Mk 37	**NT37E**
Dimensions: diameter 19 in (483 mm);	**Dimensions:** diameter 19 in (483 mm);
length (Mod 0 and 3) 3.52 m (11 ft 6	length (Mod 2) 4.51 m (14 ft 8 in) or
in) or (Mod 1 and 2) 4.09 m (13 ft 5	(Mod 3) 3.95 m (12 ft 7 in)
in)	**Weight:** (Mod 2) 748 kg (1,650 lb) or
Weight: (Mod 0 and 3) 649 kg (1,430	(Mod 3) 640 kg (1,412 lb)
lb) or (Mod 1 and 2) 767 kg (1,690 lb)	**Warhead:** 150-kg (330-lb) HE
Warhead: 150-kg (330-lb) HE	**Performance:** speed 22.4 or 33.6 kts;
Performance: speed 16 or 24 kts;	range (Mod 2) 21.7 km (13.5 miles) or
range (Mod 0 and 3) 16.5 or 7.3 km	(Mod 3) 18.3 km (11.4 miles)
(10.25 or 4.5 miles) or (Mod 1 and 2)	
8.7 km (5.4 miles)	

Left: Dutch seamen manoeuvre a NATO-standard NT37 torpedo into one of the forward tubes of a 'Dolfijn'-class submarine. The original Mk 37 entered service in the 1950s, but progressive modifications by Westinghouse and Northrop upgraded the weapon's capability to an enormous extent.

Above: In its anti-ship version the NT37 could be programmed to explode on impact or by the action of an acoustic proximity fuse. Adjustment of the running depth ensured detonation immediately under the target, so breaking the ship's back. Had the trial torpedo seen here been armed, the explosion would have occurred immediately under the ship's engines.

ants displayed 40, 150, 80 and 100 per cent increases in speed, range, endurance and seeker detection range respectively over the original Mk 37 models.

At least 16 countries used the various versions of the Mk 37 family of torpedoes.

The last navies to operate the NT37 series of torpedoes were those of Argentina ('Salta'/Type 209 submarines now with German weapons), Brazil ('Humaita' submarines), Peru ('Dos de Mayo' submarines), Spain ('Baleares' frigates), Taiwan ('Hai Lung' and 'Hai Shih' submarines now with German weapons), Turkey ('Atilay'/Type 209, 'Hizir Reis', 'Ikinci Inonu' and 'Burak Reis' submarines), and Venezuela ('Sábalo'/Type 209 submarines now also with German weapons). These and other navies are also thought to retain at least some of these obsolete torpedoes as emergency 'war stock'.

Mk 48 Heavyweight anti-submarine and anti-ship torpedo

Two versions of this torpedo were produced to engage sub-merged targets moving at 35 kts: the **Mk 48 Mod 0** powered by a gas turbine and then refined to **Mk 48 Mod 2** standard with added anti-ship capability, and the **Mk 48 Mod 1** dual-role torpedo with an Otto-fuelled piston (swashplate) engine and a different acoustic homing system for service from 1972.

The **Mk 48 Mod 3** had the same 760-m (2,500-ft) depth capability as the Mod 1 but intro-duced a new two-way TELCON (rather than one-way) wire-guid-ance communication link that allowed the torpedo head to transmit its search data back to the launch platform for more accurate processing to produce what was in effect track-via-tor-pedo guidance.

The next production standard was the **Mk 48 Mod 4**. This had the same TELCON facilities of the Mod 3, speed and diving depth increased to 55 kts and 915 m (3,000 ft) respectively, and an additional fire-and-forget mode which could be initiated if the tor-

Built to replace the Mk 14 and Mk 37 torpedoes, the Mk 48 has been successively upgraded to improve its capabilities.

pedo's own noise masked the launch submarine's passive sonar detection sets.

Because of advances in Soviet submarines' capabilities in the area of speed and diving depth, an **ADCAP** (ADvanced CAPability) version of the Mk 48, the **Mk 48 Mod 5**, entered development in the mid-1970s for service from 1988. A higher-powered sonar improves target acquisition range and reduces the effect of decoys and anechoic coatings. The sonar is electrically steered to reduce the torpedo's need for manoeuvre in the search phase. A larger fuel load gives the new variant a longer range and an under-ice capability. The latest **Mk 48 Mod 6** introduces further ADCAP improvements.

SPECIFICATION	
Mk 48 Mod 5	
Dimensions: diameter 21 in (533 mm); length 5.79 m (19 ft)	**Performance:** speed (Mod 1 and 3) 48 kts, (Mod 4) 55 kts, or (Mod 5) 60 kts; range (Mod 1 and 3) 32 km
Weight: 1676 kg (3,695 lb)	(20 miles), (Mod 4) 28 km (17.5 miles),
Warhead: 294.5-kg (650-lb) HE	or (Mod 5) 38 km (23.75 miles)

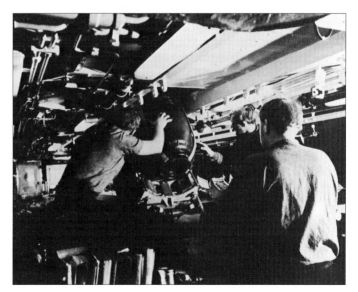

Above: Crewmen aboard the 'Sturgeon'-class nuclear attack submarine USS Pargo carefully receive a Mk 48 Mod 1 torpedo into the torpedo room. Most current US Navy SSNs have reduced torpedo armament to allow for Sub-Harpoon and Tomahawk missiles.

Anti-Submarine Weapons

Keeping the submarine at bay

The formidable strike range of submarines armed with long-range torpedoes, and later with missiles, has led to the creation of shipborne anti-submarine weapons of greater lethality and increasingly long range.

*Above: The nuclear depth charge's power is evident as the destroyer **USS** Agerholm is dwarfed by the 1962 detonation, several miles away, of a nuclear-armed **RUR-5A ASROC**.*

There are two ways in which ASW projectiles destroy a target. Proximity weapons, such as the depth charge, must be large enough to damage a submarine at a distance, which can be enlarged by the use of nuclear depth charges. Contact weapons can be smaller but must either be guided onto their targets or used in very large numbers to ensure a kill. A homing torpedo is an intermediate case, since its effective homing volume may rival that of a nuclear depth charge.

Development

Improvements in submarine weapon systems from the late

*Right: The **RUR-5A ASROC** was a stand-off delivery system for depth charges or, as shown here, for torpedoes.*

Right: The forecastle of the 'Kiev' class carried AShMs and a gun as well as an RBU-6000 12-tube ASW rocket launcher and a single-arm launcher for nuclear-armed RPK-1 Vikhr ASW rockets.

1950s meant that a ship carrying conventional depth charges, mortars (such as the British three-barrel Limbo with a range of 1000 m/ 1,095 yards), or simple rocket systems such as the US Navy's Weapon Alfa (firing a 25-kg/55-lb projectile to 900 m /985 yards) might not be able to get within range of a hostile submarine before the latter was able to fire its torpedoes. In the 1960s the development of submarine-launched anti-ship missiles magnified the problem. Some way had to be found to deliver an anti-submarine weapon to greater distances.

Most large modern warships carry helicopters, usually armed with homing torpedoes, which can engage a submarine many miles from the parent ship. But the helicopter is not ideal in every case: while it can pursue a contact for long periods, it takes some time to reach an operational area from launch. The US Navy recognised the problem early, and in 1952 the US tested a RAT (Rocket-Assisted Torpedo). The idea was that the weapon would be launched under rocket power to the general area of the target, dropping its homing torpedo payload which would then search for the submarine.

However, the two initial RAT designs had unsatisfactory ballistic characteristics and failed to achieve the needed accuracy. A redesigned RAT-C was initiated in 1955: combined with a requirement for a rocket-boosted nuclear depth charge, the name was changed to ASROC. A solid-

propellant rocket boosted the unguided weapon on a ballistic trajectory, range being determined by a timer set before launch. At the predetermined moment, the motor was separated and the payload fell into the water: a depth charge simply plunged into the water, while a homing torpedo was lowered by parachute. The payload options of the original RUR-5A ASROC were the 10-kT W44 nuclear depth charge or the Mk 44 homing torpedo. In September 1989, at the end of the Cold War, ASROC's nuclear capability was removed. By the 1990s the RUR-5A was being replaced by the RUM-139 VL-ASROC (Vertical Launch ASROC), which is the ASROC modified for launch from the Mk 41 Vertical Launch

Above: Limbo was a bulky three-barrel mortar. It was one of the last of the old-style depth charge throwers, which gave vessels the ability to attack submarines several hundred metres away.

System. Similar weapons were developed in Australia and France as the Ikara and Malafon respectively. More recently, France and Italy

have developed the capable Milas system, which is faster and has a greatly increased range than its predecessors. The system combines

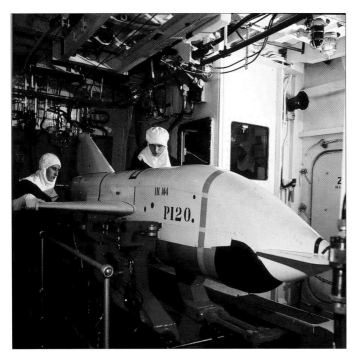

Above: Carried by Royal Navy destroyers and ASW frigates, Ikara was a small winged vehicle with a homing torpedo carried underneath its body.

Above: A 'Petya'-class escort vessel mounts a pair of RBU-6000 launchers abaft and above the main gun. The RBU is a mortar which fires salvoes of ASW rockets out to a range of six kilometres.

long-range detection, high precision, and the ability to deliver an advanced homing torpedo to 35 km (22 miles) within three minutes of initiating launch.

The Soviets developed a wide range of stand-off ASW weapons in much the same categories as those of Western navies, but Soviet and current Russian systems tend to be larger, have longer range and carry much heavier loads. Soviet and Russian RBU series mortar systems can fire single rounds or salvoes out to ranges in excess of 4000 m (4,375 yards), and the latest versions can fire decoy rockets to divert homing torpedoes.

Soviet missiles

Soviet ASW missiles are also large. The RPK-2 Viyoga (SS-N-15 'Starfish') can deliver a torpedo or a nuclear depth charge to a range of 45-50 km (27-31 miles). The command-guided RPK-3 Metel (SS-N-14 'Silex') can carry a homing torpedo or a special homing warhead; in the latter case the whole missile is guided onto a target by the launch vessel's fire control. The massive RPK-6 Vodopod (SS-N-16 'Stallion') can carry a torpedo or 10/12-kT nuclear warhead to a range estimated at more than 100 km (62 miles), and can also be used against surface ships. Deployed around 1980, it has also been adapted for submarine launch as the RPK-7 Vodopei.

The latest Russian ASW weapon is the RPK-9 Medvedka (SS-N-29). Similar to ASROC, this is designed for launch from smaller surface combatants. The basic variant of the system comprises two four-tube launcher modules.

SUBROC: SUBMARINE-LAUNCH ASROC

Entering service in 1965, the UUM-44A SUBROC was the submarine-launched counterpart of the RUR-5A ASROC. Fired from one of the submarine's standard torpedo tubes on the basis of data provided by the submarine's own sensors and fire-control system, the inertially guided SUBROC ignited its rocket motor when well clear of the submarine for a short horizontal distance before pitching up to emerge from the water and adopt its maximum 56-km (35-mile) course to the target area, where a 5-kT W55 nuclear depth charge was released.

Anti-submarine torpedoes
Weapons in the underwater war

Anti-submarine warfare (ASW) remains one of the key factors in the control of the sea, but it has changed considerably since the end of the Cold War. However, torpedoes remain perhaps the most potent of ASW weapons.

Existing ASW capabilities in the major naval powers were created to counter the Soviet submarine force in a global, deep-water conflict. However, the collapse of the USSR has seen a new world order arise, and the major threat to surface forces now comes from quiet diesel- or air-independent-powered boats, operating in coastal or littoral waters. The submarine is a deadly weapon, and as increasingly capable vessels are becoming available at an affordable price, defence against sub-surface attack is a priority for all seagoing nations. Further, since the Russian navy has continued to maintain nuclear submarines with global reach, the 'Cold War' threat, though numerically smaller, must still be considered.

Despite the advance of technology, ASW remains an extremely difficult mission, which rarely has simple or elegant solutions. There are three fundamental truths about ASW. Firstly, it is critically important to any strategy of sea control, power projection, and direct support to land campaigns – exactly the kinds of operations which have been prominent for much of the last decade.

Secondly, ASW is the ultimate team sport. It requires a complex combination of very different resources to work in a highly variable physical environment, which ranges from coastal shallows to the ocean depths. It requires con-

Above: The Mk 46 torpedo is designed to attack high-performance submarines, and may be considered the backbone of the US Navy's ASW inventory. This lightweight torpedo is launched from triple Mk 32 Surface Vessel Torpedo Tubes (SVTTs) onboard US Navy warships. Mk 46 can also be launched by aircraft and ASROC missiles, and forms the payload of the CAPTOR mine.

tributions from intelligence sources, oceanography research, complex command and control, the use of multiple sensor technologies, and a wide variety of underwater weapons.

Finally, ASW is hard. During the Falklands War, the Argentine diesel boat *San Luis* operated in the vicinity of the British task force for more than a month. Despite the deployment of five nuclear attack submarines, 24-hour airborne ASW operations, and expenditures of precious time, energy, and ordnance, the British never once detected the Argentine submarine. The move to coastal operations has increased the problems. Acoustic reverberation, poor sound propagation, local ship

Right: MILAS is typical of modern stand-off ASW weapons and can be armed with an MU 90 or Mk 46 lightweight torpedo. The long range of such systems means the launch ship can attack a submarine while outside of enemy torpedo range.

traffic, false targets, and seabed 'clutter' all make torpedo operations more difficult in this noisy operating environment, and the need for more capable guidance and control becomes critical.

Torpedoes have replaced the depth charge as the primary ASW weapon of surface vessels. Modern torpedoes usually carry their own sonar, able to home in on the sound generated by a hostile submarine. However, they are

usually guided into the vicinity of the target by wires connecting them to the launch platform. They can be delivered in a variety of ways: lightweight weapons can be fired from torpedo tubes on warships, dropped from helicopters or maritime aircraft, or can form the payload of a long-range missile.

Heavyweight torpedoes are the primary ASW weapon of submarines.

There are several new approaches under study to build more intelligent guidance and control systems for the torpedo. In addition to improved signal and tactical data processing, progress is being made in connectivity

Below: The Mk 46 Mod 5 torpedo, launched here from the destroyer **USS Preble**, *has an improved shallow-water performance and is also capable of attacking surface targets.*

between submarines and weapons, intelligent controllers, and ultra-broadband sonar arrays. Acoustic and fibre-optic communications will improve connections between weapon and launch platform, allowing the torpedo to act as an improved sensor for the fire-control systems, giving an improved tactical picture for combat control systems. Torpedoes themselves are becoming more intelligent, using neural nets and fuzzy logic to more accurately predict a target's movements.

Developing a truly stealthy torpedo will provide more approach-and-attack options for submarines. A stealth weapon that cannot be heard until very late in the encounter will delay the threat's detection of the torpedo and impair its ability to respond effectively with either countermeasures or return fire. This will greatly increase the probability of killing the enemy and avoiding a potentially lethal counter-attack.

Future technology

As these new torpedo technologies take shape, they promise some dramatic departures from the configuration of current weapons. Pushing the speed envelope, for example, will greatly affect torpedo performance and resulting effectiveness – the ability to kill a target before it can react provides a distinct advantage.

Anti-torpedo torpedoes will provide future ships and submarines with an additional defensive capability. Their primary mission is to destroy incoming torpedoes that may have evaded a countermeasure field. A 6.25-in (158.7-mm) diameter self-protection weapon is currently the subject of a US Navy study for the defence of surface ships and submarines. The Advanced High Speed

Above: Spearfish is the Royal Navy's primary submarine-launched heavyweight torpedo and the latest version is capable of a speed in excess of 80 kts, although this is much reduced at great depths.

Underwater Munition (AHSUM) program has already demonstrated the effectiveness of such high-speed underwater 'bullets'. Fired from an underwater gun, these projectiles have successfully broken the speed of sound in water (1500 metres/ 4.921 ft per second) over short distances. Future operational systems are likely to be used as last-ditch defences, in the same way that the CIWS serves against air and missile threats above the surface.

Torpedo payloads will also see improvement in the future. Warheads will be capable of multi-mode detonation, offering both purely explosive effect and directed detonation. They will provide higher lethality and use increasingly energetic materials. This will give the torpedo more destructive power and provide the potential for weapons to be smaller and lighter, with increased range capability or room for additional sensors and signal processing.

AIPS: THE QUIET ALTERNATIVE

An air-independent propulsion system (AIPS) such as that employed by the Swedish navy's 'Gotland' class, increases a non-nuclear submarine's submerged endurance to weeks rather than days, and offers a quiet alternative to battery power. On a normal diesel-electric boat the batteries require frequent recharging which means using the noisy diesel generators. AIPS-equipped boats present a new challenge to both detection equipment and torpedoes.

Hunting The Submarine

Submarine sensors

The submarine sensor had a vital role in the nuclear-armed game of cat and mouse that was played out between Allied and Soviet submarines in the tense days of the Cold War.

Underwater warfare is unlike any other form of conflict. A duel between submarines is a bit like that between two men, blindfold in a darkened room. Both carry loaded revolvers, but the only clues to each other's position come from the sounds the opponent makes: the rustle of shoes on the carpet or of moving clothes, or at close range the sound of breathing.

Sound is the only sense that is of any real use under water. Light, radio and radar penetrate the ocean poorly or not at all. Sound, on the other hand, can travel great distances. The first underwater sensors developed in the early years of this century were simple hydrophones. By using an array of several such listening devices, submarines could be detected at distances of thousands of yards, and even the general direction of their movement might be determined.

ASDIC and sonar

During World War II, active sound systems like the British ASDIC and the American sonar were developed. They used bursts of sound, or 'pings', which produced echoes. These echoes were then detected as they

Above: The 'Vanguard'-class SSBN boats feature a Type 2043 hull-mounted sonar system. This can be configured to act in both active and passive modes.

bounced back off targets, in much the same way that radar uses radio waves to detect aircraft. Sonar, which was originally an acronym for SOund Navigation And Ranging, has become the generic term for any underwater use of echo-location, and has even been compared to the navigation techniques

used by whales and dolphins.

The art of anti-submarine warfare would be especially useful during the Cold War in the north Atlantic. Huge resources were invested by both the Western powers and

the Soviets to develop increasingly sophisticated sonar systems and anti-sonar countermeasures. One such example was the US SOund SUrveillance System (SOSUS) line – a network of

Left: When operating at surface level, the 'Vanguard'-class boats use, among other systems, a Kelvin-Hughes Type 1007 I-band radar navigation system.

undersea microphones laid across the seabed at the Bering Straits. It was designed to listen for Soviet missile boats and hunter-killer submarines entering and leaving their home port of Murmansk. Once a positive 'fix' had been identified, NATO hunter-killer submarines would then follow the Soviet boat. In response, Soviet submarine commanders invented a manoeuvre

Below: With their huge destructive force, the 'Vanguard'-class submarines represent a powerful nuclear deterrent.

dubbed the 'Crazy Ivan'. Upon discovering that it was being followed by a Western submarine, the Soviet boat would suddenly rotate 180°, doubling back on itself and driving at high speed towards its pursuer, an intensely nerve-racking experience for the Allied boat.

One of the Soviet navy's primary missions throughout the Cold War was the detection and destruction of NATO submarines, in particular ballistic missile boats (SSBNs). Hunter-killer boats were also targeted, however. The purpose behind this was twofold; not only did the Soviets want to destroy the threat to their shipping and submarines, but they also wanted to allow their own SSBNs to disperse in order to fire their missiles. The tense nature of anti-submarine combat made the north Atlantic one of the most terrifying theatres of the Cold War.

Sonar clutter

Technology has made sonar effective beyond the wildest dreams of its early operators, but the sea remains a confusing place. In spite of all the highly-advanced sensor and computerised signal processing equipment that make up a modern sonar system, the performance of that system will vary greatly depending on the conditions. For one thing, sound does not travel in straight lines under water. Much also depends upon transient ocean conditions, such as water temperature and salinity, and confusing echoes can be generated by factors including the sea bed, storm waves, schools of fish or pods of whales.

A basic fact of sonar operations is that the lower the sound frequency, the further it will travel. However, there is a trade-off between range and discrimination. Small, high-frequency sonars have limited range, but are useful for providing detailed information in specialist situations, such as mine-hunting or when operating under ice. Lower-frequency sonars have longer range but provide less detailed information about targets. In general, the larger the sound generator, the lower the frequency it can generate. This may go some way to explaining why modern submarines and ASW vessels are much larger than earlier vessels.

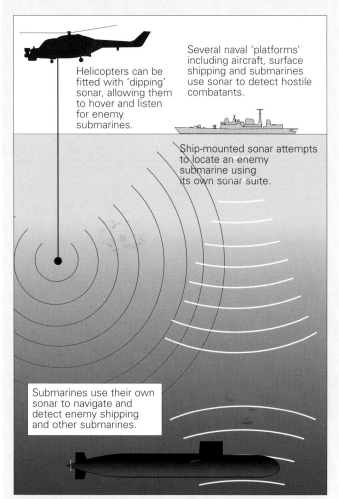

SONAR: LISTENING FOR THE ENEMY

Helicopters can be fitted with 'dipping' sonar, allowing them to hover and listen for enemy submarines.

Several naval 'platforms' including aircraft, surface shipping and submarines use sonar to detect hostile combatants.

Ship-mounted sonar attempts to locate an enemy submarine using its own sonar suite.

Submarines use their own sonar to navigate and detect enemy shipping and other submarines.

Arguably one of the most vital naval war-fighting tools ever invented, sonar is used across most naval platforms for the detection and destruction of submarines and surface shipping. During the Cold War, naval helicopters would become particularly useful for submarine detection. They were able to 'dip' a sonar sensor into the water and listen for submarines. They could be deployed on ships far away from their home ports and had the added advantage of being able to fly quickly from place to place, covering a wide area in a relatively short amount of time. The helicopter brought a quiet revolution to anti-shipping and submarine warfare.

ASW destroyers and frigates usually have a large bow sonar – often indicated by a sharply-raked stern – that is used as an early-warning system, with helicopters being used to close in precisely on the contact using their own higher frequency dipping sonars. Despite efforts to develop new submarine detection systems, sound remains the primary method of detection. Nevertheless, ASW aircraft also use an additional search technique called Magnetic Anomaly Detection.

Left: 'Vanguard'-class submarines are fitted with a Thales CH91 attack periscope and a Thales CK51 search periscope. Both of these feature a TV camera and a normal optical channel.

ASW helicopters
Submarine killing helicopters

During the Cold War years the ASW helicopter was a vitally important part of any naval force. With the changing threats of the modern world, many such aircraft are adding littoral and multi-role taskings to their basic ASW mission.

Above: This RCN HO4S-3 demonstrates its dipping sonar. Helicopters typically dip the sensor many times during a search, using it in lieu of the sonobuoys that fixed-wing ASW types use.

Below: NH Industries NH 90 (illustrated) and EH Industries EH 101 represent the pinnacle of current ASW helicopter design. Mission equipment varies according to customer needs.

ASW (anti-submarine warfare) was the very first active combat duty of the earliest helicopters in World War II. Those machines were embarked aboard surface warships but could not do more than search for submarines with the human eye, and on occasion carry a depth charge weighing about 181 kg (400 lb). By the 1950s much more powerful helicopters could carry heavier loads of weapons, and Bell built a small number of single-engined, tandem-rotor

Left: This Agusta-built SH-3D wears special markings to celebrate 30 years of Italian Sea King operations, such has been the longevity of the SH-3 in the demanding ASW role.

sensors needed to find the submarine and the weapons to destroy it, and thus do what is called a hunter/killer job. The main sensors are radar; sonobuoys, which are in effect 'underwater radar', using high-intensity sound waves; and MAD which detects the extremely small distortion of the terrestrial magnetic field caused by the presence of a large mass of metal such as a submerged submarine. Sonobuoys are probably the most important sensor, and unlike other aircraft the helicopter has the choice of dropping small buoys into the sea or of dunking a single very large buoy on the end of a cable.

The chief helicopter ASW weapon is the homing torpedo. Being able to match the speed of a target sub, an ASW helicopter is usually able to launch its torpedo closer to the target than either a surface vessel or fixed-wing aircraft could.

Above: Where helicopters employ magnetic anomaly detection (MAD) devices, these are typically in the form of towed MAD birds. Here a JMSDF SH-60J demonstrates its AN/ASQ-81 towed 'bird'.

HSL-1 machines, which were designed purely for the ASW role. The HSL-1s were not particularly useful, and as with other classes of helicopter, the whole picture was transformed by the switch to turbine engines.

Modern ASW helos

With abundant power available, the modern ASW helicopter can carry both the

ASW HELICOPTER TACTICS: THE HELICOPTER VERSUS THE SUBMARINE

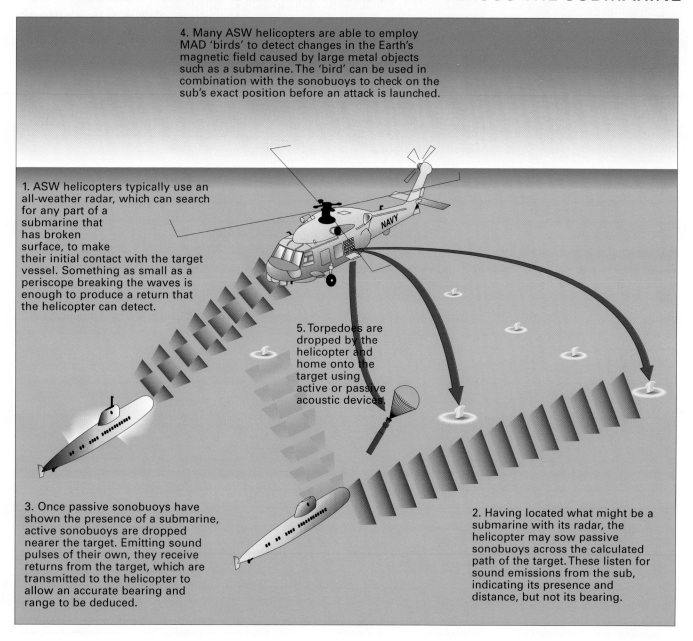

4. Many ASW helicopters are able to employ MAD 'birds' to detect changes in the Earth's magnetic field caused by large metal objects such as a submarine. The 'bird' can be used in combination with the sonobuoys to check on the sub's exact position before an attack is launched.

1. ASW helicopters typically use an all-weather radar, which can search for any part of a submarine that has broken surface, to make their initial contact with the target vessel. Something as small as a periscope breaking the waves is enough to produce a return that the helicopter can detect.

5. Torpedoes are dropped by the helicopter and home onto the target using active or passive acoustic devices.

3. Once passive sonobuoys have shown the presence of a submarine, active sonobuoys are dropped nearer the target. Emitting sound pulses of their own, they receive returns from the target, which are transmitted to the helicopter to allow an accurate bearing and range to be deduced.

2. Having located what might be a submarine with its radar, the helicopter may sow passive sonobuoys across the calculated path of the target. These listen for sound emissions from the sub, indicating its presence and distance, but not its bearing.

Right: ASW helicopters exist in various disparate forms. Taiwan is one of a handful of operators flying the MD 500MD/ASW (above) from its ships. Note the nose-mounted search radar and towed MAD 'bird'. Provision is made for torpedo carriage between the fuselage and the heightened undercarriage. At the other end of the scale, the EH 101 Merlin HM.Mk 1 (left) entered Royal Navy service in 1998 and became fully operational in 2003.

Helicopter Anti-Submarine Warfare Sensors and systems

Helicopter ASW is a complex science involving multiple sensors and well-trained operator. Here, the key sensors and techniques are described, with reference to Canadian Armed Forces operations.

Number 443 Squadron CAF operates the CH-124A as an active sonar-dipping platform. Its primary sensor is the Tethered Sonar Sub-System (TSSS) employing the Bendix AN/AQS-502 sonar (internationally known as the AN/AQS-13). This medium-frequency sonar is able to function in active, passive, or underwater communications modes. Although old, it is an adequate sonar that was intended to be used primarily in the open ocean environment. Current output is rated at 5,000 watts. Three frequencies can be emitted, and the pulse width for each frequency can be changed.

The CH-124A does not have a sonobuoy processing capability, but it can receive signals from sonobuoys on 31 different radio frequency channels. The CH-124 generally carries three types of sonobuoys.

The AN/SSQ-47B is an active sonobuoy that provides only range information when it receives an echo return from a contact; this is ascertained with the aid of a stopwatch. Crew members aurally monitor these sonobuoys to determine which are in contact. Up to four sonobuoys can be aurally monitored by the aircrew, one per crew member. At least three sonobuoys must be in contact to localise a contact and determine tracking information, elicited by triangulation methods.

The AN/SSQ-53D/E Directional Frequency Analysis and Recording (DIFAR) passive sonobuoy, and the AN/SSQ-62C Directional Command Activated Sonobuoy System (DICASS) sonobuoy can also be dispensed. Signals are processed by nearby ships operating with the helicopter. Conversely, the CH-124B helicopter is a sonobuoy- processing platform, and does not carry a dipping sonar.

The single-frequency Litton Canada AN/APS-503 I-band multi-mode surveillance radar is also standard equipment and a rather primitive FLIR Systems 2000G FLIR is nose mounted when operational requirements dictate.

AESOP responsibilities

The Airborne Electronic Systems Operator (AESOP) is responsible for the proper use of the sonar, radar and FLIR. Contact information acquired by the sonar or radar is electronically transferred to the AN/ASN-123 Tactical Doppler. Contacts then need to be tracked by the Tactical Coordinator (TACCO) to discern what the target could be. The TACCO and AESOP stations are next to each other on the starboard side of the aircraft, directly behind the pilot and co-pilot.

The ability to properly identify a target essentially comes down to training and recognition of a contact's

track and speed. A team effort is always used in identifying targets, whether it be the TACCO analysing acquired target information from the AESOP, or pilot and co-pilot assistance for verifying targets in visual range. In contrast, modern ASW helicopter sensor suites, such as that fielded on the US Navy's Sikorsky MH-60R Seahawk, are able to acquire, track, identify, and integrate by way of data fusion any sonar, radar, IFF, and ESM contacts automatically.

Effective anti-submarine warfare does not necessarily entail destroying a hostile submarine. ASW tactics do, however, require keeping a hostile submarine at a place where it cannot fire at friendly assets. This is achieved by keeping it deep and/or distant. Part of ASW helicopter tactics dictate establishing an active sonar or sonobuoy field, creating an acoustic barrier between a submarine and friendly assets. This serves to localise areas for a helicopter to search within, and also serves to cut off avenues of approach for a submarine. A submarine skipper would thus be required to conduct a risk assessment to determine whether he is willing to attack a target. ASW helicopters are very effective in creating these screens for friendly assets. This effectiveness is greatly enhanced when CH-124s work in conjunction with fixed-wing

CP-140 Aurora long-range patrol aircraft, and/or towed array equipped surface combatant vessels.

Random dipping

Random dipping is used as an effective means of searching an Area of Probability (AOP). This method is used to confuse a submarine's tactical picture, making it more difficult to formulate a firing solution on friendly assets. The AESOP may also change sonar parameters during each dip, or from one dip to the next, to further confuse any submarine in the area.

When tasked to search for a possible contact, sonobuoys may be used as an effective means for area coverage. The benefits of dropping sonobuoys are speed, and route denial by creating an acoustic barrier. This avails the helicopter to search other areas, hopefully in cooperation with other friendly ships and aircraft.

Mission planning

Planning for a mission takes place well before the actual flight. Helicopter ASW crews onboard ship will typically brief the mission objectives, weather, threat assessment, aircraft state, water-space management, and emergency procedures. Additionally, a bathythermograph reading supplied by the ship will also be reviewed. This reading gives a record of water temperature in relation to depth. This knowledge is essential

to agitate the water sufficiently with a sonar signal in search of hostile submarines.

Water temperature varies with depth, causing invisible temperature layers. When a sonar transducer (also known as a 'ball') sends out its pulse, that pulse seeks a water layer where the sound speed refracts towards colder water. The factors affecting this propagation are temperature, salinity and pressure. Submarines use these layers to hide in, primarily because sonar pulses do not diffuse very well through adjacent layers. To identify different temperature levels, the sonar transducer is fitted with a temperature sensor. This allows best sonar ball depths to be calculated by the AESOP for the prevailing water conditions.

To ideally search a body of water for a submarine, a sonar-dipping ASW helicopter would lower its sonar transducer into as many different temperature layers as possible. During a busy target prosecution, the crew would need to determine if and when to attempt this time-consuming procedure.

Once a submarine is

Above: Having been licence built abroad and manufactured in some numbers at home, Sikorsky's Sea King is one of the world's classic military helicopters. For anti-submarine warfare (ASW), it is fitted with the sensors and armament required to detect, localise, track, identify and prosecute submerged hostile submarines.

located, there are a number of attack methods an ASW helicopter could use. Attacking a submarine can be a self-initiated evolution, or can be a vectored/guided event. Torpedoes can be dropped from the helicopter in forward flight, in the hover, or while dipping. On the Ch-124A a maximum of two Alliant Techsystems Mk 46 Mod 5 fire-and-forget torpedoes can be mounted. Prior to release, various attack parameters must be set; these include torpedo search depth, seabed floor depth (for shallow water operations), and a selection of active or passive homing. To effect a successful attack, an ASW helicopter crew would always prefer to work in conjunction with other ASW assets.

INSIDE THE CH-124: CANADIAN ANTI-SUBMARINE OPERATING ENVIRONMENT

Operating with a four-person crew, two configurations of the CH-124 (A and B) are operated by the Canadian Forces. Internal stores can be carried in 30 chutes located in the aft cabin floor. Six chutes are capable of loading various sonobuoys, Mk 58 marine location markers, and Thiokol LUU-2B/B illumination flares, while 24 smaller chutes are intended for C2A1 smoke markers and electronic Sound Underwater Signalling (SUS) devices.

Below: In addition to the sonobuoy chutes seen here in the cabin floor, two racks can be mounted inside the aircraft for a maximum of 18 additional sonobuoys.

Below: The TACCO and AESOP sit alongside each other at these two stations, with the AESOP furthest away in this image. Note the dated display units and switch gear of the veteran Canadian Forces ASW helicopter.

Below: The CH-124A has approximately 152 m (500 ft) of cable on its sonar transducer reeling machine. A number of variables are considered in deciding how deep to lower a transducer. These variables primarily take into account target considerations, water temperature, and the time it takes to lower/raise a sonar transducer to the preferred search depth.

Aérospatiale Dauphin, HH-65A Dolphin and Eurocopter Panther Multi-role naval helicopters

The first version of the **Aérospatiale Dauphin** developed for naval warfare was based on the twin-engined **Dauphin 2** and built for the US Coast Guard. This **SA 366G** or **HH-65A Dolphin** was built for the SAR role. Subsequently, Aérospatiale developed the versatile **AS 365F** from the the AS 365N, intended primarily for the anti-ship role. The type is also available in SAR configuration, as well as with a more advanced ASW capability.

Eurocopter Panther

The first order for the type was placed by Saudi Arabia, which received 24 examples in two subvariants now designated in the **Eurocopter AS 565 Panther** military series as the **AS 565SC** (four for the SAR role, later redesignated **AS 565MB**) and the **AS 565SA** (20 anti-ship helicopters, later redesignated **AS 565SB**). Other small export orders were received, Israel designating its AS 565SAs **Atalef**, or bat.

Eurocopter offers two naval variants of the AS 565: the unarmed **AS 565MA** (replaced from 1997 by the **AS 565MB**) for the SAR and sea surveillance roles, and the **AS 565SB** for the ASW as well as anti-ship roles.

Above: The SA 365 Dauphin is employed by French naval aviation units for shipboard duties, including small ships ASW/utility work, as well as land-based SAR. This is an example from Flotille 23S, a former ship-based 'Pédro' unit.

Below: Three SA 365Fs were acquired by the Aéronavale for plane-guard duties. The helicopters now service the nuclear-powered aircraft carrier Charles de Gaulle.

Below: This AS 565SB has the type's maximum load of four AS.15TT anti-ship missiles, as well as anti-ship radar with its antenna in a radome beneath the helicopter's nose.

SPECIFICATION
Eurocopter AS 565SA Panther **Type:** two-seat light naval utility helicopter optimised for the anti-ship and anti-submarine roles **Powerplant:** two Turboméca Arriel 1M1 turboshaft engines each rated at 558 kW (749 shp) **Performance:** maximum cruising speed 274 km/h (170 mph) at sea level; initial climb rate 420 m (1,378 ft) per minute; service ceiling 4575 m (15,010 ft); hovering ceiling 2600 m (8,530 ft) in ground effect and 1860 m (6,100 ft) out of ground effect; radius 250 km (155 miles) with four AShMs	**Weights:** empty 2240 kg (4,938 lb); maximum take-off 4250 kg (9,370 lb) **Dimensions:** main rotor diameter 11.94 m (39 ft 2 in); length 13.68 m (44 ft 10¾ in) with rotor turning; height 3.98 m (13 ft ¾ in); main rotor disc area 111.97 m² (1,205.26 sq ft) **Armament:** up to 600 kg (1,323 lb) of disposable stores, generally comprising four AS.15TT light anti-ship missiles or two Mk 46 lightweight ASW torpedoes **Payload:** up to 10 passengers or 1700 kg (3,748 lb) of freight in the cabin, or 1600 kg (3,527 lb) of freight carried as a slung load

Aérospatiale SA 321 Super Frelon SAR and transport helo

Delivery of 16 SA 321Ja Super Frelons to the Chinese navy took place between 1975 and 1977 and was expanded with licence-built Changhe Z-8s.

To meet a French armed services requirement for a medium transport helicopter, Sud-Aviation flew the prototype **SE.3200 Frelon** (hornet) on 10 June 1959. Powered by three Turmo IIIB turboshafts, the SE.3200 had large external fuel tanks that left the interior clear for a maximum 28 troops, and a swing-tail fuselage to simplify cargo loading. However, development was terminated in favour of a larger and more capable helicopter designed in conjunction with Sikorsky and Fiat. What was to become Western Europe's largest production helicopter emerged with a rotor system of Sikorsky design, and with a watertight hull suitable for amphibious operation. Two military prototypes of the Super Frelon were built, the **SA 3210-01** troop transport, and the **SA 3210-02** maritime version for the Aéronavale on 28 May 1963.

Four pre-production aircraft were built under the new designation **SA 321 Super Frelon**. These were followed in October 1965 by production **SA 321G** ASW helicopters for the Aéronavale. Apart from ship-based ASW missions, the SA 321G also carried out sanitisation patrols in support of 'Rédoutable'-class ballistic missile submarines. Some were modified with nose-mounted targeting radar for Exocet

AShMs. Five **SA 321Ga** freighters, originally used in support of the Pacific nuclear test centre, were transferred to assault support duties. In 2003, the surviving Aéronavale Super Frelons are assigned to transport duties including commando transport, VertRep and SAR.

Exports

Six radar-equipped **SA 321GM** helicopters were delivered to Libya in 1980-81. The SA 321G was also modified for air force and army service. Designated **SA 321H**, a total of 16 was delivered from 1977 to the Iraqi air force with radar and Exocets. These aircraft were used in the Iran-Iraq conflict and the 1991 Gulf War, in which at least one example was destroyed.

The **SA 321Ja** was a higher weight version of the commer-

cial **SA 321J**, of which the People's Republic of China navy received 16 aircraft fitted with targeting radar. Non-amphibious military export versions included 12 **SA 321K** transports for Israel, 16 similar **SA 321L** transports for South Africa and eight **SA 321M** SAR/ transports for Libya.

When French production ended in 1983 a total of 99 Super Frelons had been built,

Above: France's SA 321 Super Frelons are retained in service for SAR and heavylift transport, for which their long-range capability proves useful.

but production continued in China under licence-agreement as the **Changhe Z-8**. Eight Israeli aircraft were re-engined with T58 engines and were later sold to Argentina.

SPECIFICATION	
Aérospatiale SA 321G Super Frelon **Type:** medium SAR and transport helicopter **Powerplant:** three Turboméca Turmo IIIC7 turboshafts each rated at 1201 kW (1,610 shp) **Performance:** maximum cruising speed at sea level 248 km/h (154 mph); maximum rate of climb at sea level 300 m (984 ft) per minute; service ceiling 3100 m (10,170 ft); hovering ceiling 1950 m (6,400 ft) in ground effect; range	1020 km (633 miles) with a 3500-kg (7,716-lb) payload **Weights:** empty 6863 kg (15,130 lb); maximum take-off 13000 kg (28,660 lb) **Dimensions:** main rotor diameter 18.9 m (62 ft); length overall, rotors turning 23.03 m (75 ft 6½ in); height overall 6.76 m (22 ft 2¼ in); main rotor disc area 12.57 m² (135.27 sq ft) **Payload:** maximum payload 5000 kg (11,023 lb)

Westland Lynx Multi-role naval helicopter

Left: Germany's Lynx Mk 88 fleet is being upgraded to the Mk 88A 'Super Lynx' standard shown.

The first Lynx prototype flew on 21 March 1971, and the Royal Navy's **Lynx HAS.Mk 2** was the first production variant to fly, in February 1976. It was equipped for a wide range of shipboard missions including ASW, SAR, ASV, recce, troop transport, fire support, communication and fleet liaison, and VertRep.

The basic Lynx has one of the world's most advanced flight control systems and comprehensive navaids, systems which served it well during over 3,000 hours of combat operations off the Falklands in 1982. During this campaign the Sea Skua AShM was also brought into action for the first time.

The RN received the first of 23 upgraded **Lynx HAS.Mk 3** aircraft in March 1982, and converted its HAS.Mk 2s to this standard. Among the improved systems were Gem 41-1 engines. The **Lynx HAS.Mk 3ICE** designation covers a few downgraded aircraft for utility work on the Antarctic patrol vessel HMS *Endurance*. Subsequently, seven HAS.Mk 3s were procured with secure speech facility and other upgrades as **HAS.Mk 3S** machines. Eighteen aircraft were upgraded to **Lynx HAS.Mk 3GM (Gulf Mod)** standard with improved cooling, and carried IR jammers and ALQ-167 ECM pods during Desert Storm. The final RN version added a central tactical system and a flotation bag (**Lynx HAS.Mk 3CTS**). The definitive upgraded aircraft is the **Lynx HMA.Mk 8**, or export **Super Lynx**.

Super Lynx

Most of the RN's Lynx, plus the survivors of 26 French navy **Lynx HAS.Mk 2(FN)** helicopters, received new high-efficiency composite British Experimental Rotor Programme (BERP) main rotor blades.

The definitive Mk 8 has BERP blades and a reverse-direction tail rotor to improve yaw control at higher take-off weights. Other changes include a nose-mounted Sea Owl passive identification thermal imager turret, MAD, INS and GPS systems, Orange Crop ESM and a Yellow Veil jamming pod.

Many Mk 8 features are incorporated in the export Super Lynx, which has found several buyers for new or upgraded machines.

SPECIFICATION

Westland Lynx HAS.Mk 2
Type: twin-engined naval helicopter
Powerplant: two Rolls-Royce Gem 42-1 turboshafts each rated at 846 kW (1,135 shp)
Performance: maximum continuous cruising speed at optimum altitude 232 km/h (144 mph); maximum rate of climb at sea level 661 m (2,170 ft) per minute; combat radius 178 km (111 miles) on a SAR mission with 11 survivors
Weights: empty 2740 kg (6,040 lb); maximum take-off 4763 kg (10,500 lb)
Dimensions: main rotor diameter 12.8m (42 ft); fuselage length 11.92 m (39 ft 1¼ in); height 3.48 m (11 ft 5 in); main rotor disc area 128.71 m² (1,385.44 sq ft)
Armament: pylons for two Mk 44, Mk 46 or Sting Ray torpedoes, two Mk 11 depth charges or four Sea Skua AShMs, plus one FN HMP 0.5-in (12.7-mm) machine-gun for self protection. An ALQ-167 ECM pod can also be carried

---

France's HAS.Mk 2(FN) machines (illustrated) have been upgraded to Mk 4(FN) standard, but will be retired from 2004/05.

EH Industries EH 101/Merlin ASW helicopter

This pre-production Merlin HM.Mk 1 was initially used for trials with the Type 23 frigate HMS Norfolk. It then moved onto sonobuoy drop trials and was fitted with full Merlin avionics.

The **EH 101** has its roots in the Westland WG.34 design that was adopted in late 1978 to meet the UK's Naval Staff Requirement 6646 for a replacement for the Westland Sea King. Work on the WG.34 was cancelled before a prototype had been completed, however, opening the way for revision of the design to meet Italian navy as well as Royal Navy requirements. European Helicopter Industries Ltd was given a formal go-ahead to develop the new aircraft in 1984.

The EH 101 is a three-engined helicopter with a five-bladed main rotor. Much use is made of composites throughout, although the fuselage itself is mainly of aluminium alloy. Systems and equipment vary with role and customer. For the Royal Navy, which calls its initial variant of the EH 101 the **Merlin HM.Mk 1**, IBM is the prime contractor in association with Westland and provides equipment as well as overall management and integration. Armament on the Merlin com-prises four Marconi Sting Ray torpedoes, and there are also two sonobuoy dispensers.

Merlin HM.Mk 1

The initial Royal Navy requirement for 50 Merlins to operate from Type 23-class frigates, 'Invincible'-class aircraft carriers, ships of the Royal Fleet Auxiliary and other ships or land bases has been reduced to 44, with delivery starting late in 1998 rather than in 1996, as hoped. These British helicopters are each powered by RTM 322 turboshafts, whereas the Italian helicopters (16 on order, out of a requirement for 36) each have the alternative powerplant of three 1278-kW (1,714-shp) General

Electric T700-GE-T6A turboshafts, assembled in Italy. Earlier CT7 commercial variants of the General Electric engine were used to power the prototypes, the first of which was a Westland-built machine that achieved its maiden flight on 9 October 1987. A similar Agusta-built basic model flew in Italy on 26 November 1987.

Next to fly in Italy, on 26 April 1989, was a prototype of the Italian ASW version, followed in the UK by a basic ASW version on 15 June and then the definitive Merlin prototype on 24 October of that year. The second prototype was lost in an accident on 21 January 1993, resulting in a suspension of all flight-testing

Left: Merlin HM.Mk 1 equipment includes GEC Ferranti Blue Kestrel 360° search radar, GEC Avionics AQS-903 processing and display system, Racal Orange Reaper ESM and Ferranti/Thomson-CSF dipping sonar.

SPECIFICATION	
EH Industries Merlin HM.Mk 1	**Dimensions:** main rotor diameter
Type: one/two-crew shipborne and	18.59 m (61 ft); length 22.81 m
land-based anti-submarine and	(74 ft 10 in) with the rotors turning;
utility helicopter	height 6.65 m (21 ft 10 in) with the
Powerplant: three Rolls-Royce/	rotors turning; main rotor disc area
Turboméca RTM 322-01 turboshaft	271.51 m² (2,922.60 sq ft)
engines each rated at 1724 kW	**Armament:** up to 960 kg (2,116 lb) of
(2,312 shp)	disposable stores carried on the
Performance: cruising speed	lower sides of the fuselage, and
278 km (173 mph) at optimum	generally comprising four homing
altitude; hovering ceiling 3810 m	torpedoes
(12,500 ft) in ground effect; range	**Payload:** up to 45 troops, or up to
1056 km (656 miles)	16 litters plus a medical team, or
Weights: empty 10500 kg	up to 3660 kg (12,000 lb) of freight
(23,149 lb); maximum take-off	carried internally or as a slung load
14600 kg (32,188 lb)	

until 24 June that year. The RTM 322 engines were first flown in the fourth prototype during July 1993, and subsequently fitted to the fifth prototype.

Canada ordered 35 of the naval version as the **CH-148 Petrel**, to meet its New Shipborne Aircraft requirement for a Sea King replacement. Assembled and fitted out by IMP Group Ltd in Canada, these EH 101s were to have been powered by 1432-kW (1,920-shp) CT7-6A1 turboshaft engines. The deal was hard-fought, subject to constant scrutiny and not unimportant to the chances of the EH 101's long-term success.

Right: Merlin HM.Mk 1 options include the Exocet, Harpoon, Sea Eagle and Marte Mk 2 AShMs, as well as the Stingray torpedo (as here).

Deliveries were scheduled to begin early in 1998, although an increasingly bitter argument over the costs versus acquisition of less complex aircraft saw the EH 101 become a campaign issue in the Canadian elections of 1993. The pro-EH 101 Conservative government was subsequently ousted in favour of a Liberal administration which, true to its election pledge, cancelled the entire programme. Then, in

January 1998, the Canadian government placed a new order for 15 examples of the revised AW320 Cormorant version for the SAR role, for delivery between 2000 and 2003.

Further development of the EH 101 could result in variants including an airborne early warning version of the type, which might be required by both the Italian navy and the Royal Navy.

NH Industries NH90 ASW/ASV helicopter

SPECIFICATION

NH Industries NH 90 NFH
Type: three/four-crew shipborne ASW/surface ship helicopter
Powerplant: two RTM 322-01/9 turboshaft engines each rated at 1566 kW (2,100 shp) or two General Electric/Alfa Romeo T700-T6E turboshaft engines each rated at 1521 kW (2,040 shp)
Performance: (estimated) maximum cruising speed 291 km/h (181 mph); initial climb rate 660 m (2,165 ft) per minute; hovering ceiling 3300 m (10,820 ft) in ground effect, or 2600 m (8,540 ft)

out of ground effect; radius 90 km (56 miles) for a loiter of 3 hours 18 minutes
Weights: empty 6428 kg (14,171 lb); maximum take-off 10000 kg (22,046 lb)
Dimensions: main rotor diameter 16.30 m (53 ft 5½ in); length 19.56 m (64 ft 2 in) with the rotors turning; height 5.44 m (17 ft 10 in) with the rotors turning; main rotor disc area 208.67 m² (2,246.18 sq ft)
Armament: up to 1400 kg (3,086 lb) of disposable stores carried on two lateral hardpoints

Above: The NH90 NFH helicopter is scheduled to enter French service in 2004-05, Italian service in 2005, German service in 2007 and operational Dutch service from 2007.

In 1985 five European nations signed a memorandum of understanding covering a 'NATO helicopter for the 1990s', or **NH 90**. The UK dropped out of the programme in 1987, leaving only France, Germany, Italy and

the Netherlands in the project by means of NH Industries, established in 1992 to control the programme.

Two initial versions were planned, the **NH 90 NFH (NATO Frigate Helicopter)** for the autonomous ASW and anti-surface vessel roles with ASW torpedoes or AShMs and 360° search radar under the cabin as key elements in a fully integrated mission system, and the **NH 90 TTH**.

The NH 90 has a four-bladed main rotor and its powerplant of two turboshaft engines is installed to the rear of the main rotor and gearbox. The landing gear is fully retractable and the flightdeck is laid out for operation by a crew of two.

NH 90 NFH

NH 90 NFH is being developed under Agusta leadership, and its advanced mission suite includes radar, dipping sonar, FLIR, MAD, an ESM system and an ECM system, with weapons carried on two lateral hardpoints. Power is provided either by two RTM 322-01/9s or two General Electric T700-T6Es.

Development of the NH 90 was suspended in May 1994 but resumed in July the same year after a short but rigorous effort to reduce cost escalation, and the first of five flying and one ground-test prototypes was the French-assembled PT 1 that first took to the air on 18 December 1995 with RTM 322 engines. The PT 2 second prototype was also assembled in France and first flew on 19 March 1997 as the initial machine with a fly-by-wire control system (initially analogue but later the definitive digital type). The third, fourth and fifth prototypes were assembled in France, Germany and Italy.

The overall helicopter totals required were trimmed from the original 726 to 647 in July 1996 and then to 642 in 1998 and the number of naval helicopters now likely to be acquired includes 27 for the Aéronavale (which may also acquire 27 TTH aircraft to replace its Super Frelons), 38 for Germany, 56 for Italy, and 20 for the Netherlands. NH Industries has also secured export orders from Norway, while Sweden hopes for large export sales. There have been considerable delays in the signature of the production contract for the NH 90, which was originally scheduled for 1997 but finally took place in March 2000, when an initial 244 helicopters were ordered for the armed forces of the four partner nations. The first NH 90s seem likely to enter service in the period 2004-2007.

Westland Wasp Multi-role naval helicopter

Though its development can be traced back to the **Saro P.531**, first flown in 1958, the **Westland Wasp HAS.Mk 1** emerged in October 1962 as a highly specialised machine for flying missions from small ships, such as frigates and destroyers with limited deck pad area. The missions were ASW and general utility, but the Wasp was not sufficiently powerful to carry a full kit of ASW sensors as well as weapons, and thus in this role relied on the sensors of its parent vessel and other friendly naval forces. In the ASV role the Wasp was autonomous, and though it had no radar, it could steer the AS12 wire-guided missile under visual conditions over ranges up to 8 km (5 miles). Other duties included SAR , liaison, VIP ferrying, casevac, ice reconnaissance and photography/ survey. The stalky quadricycle landing gear had wheels that castored so that, while the machine could be rotated on deck, it could not roll in any direction even in a rough sea. Sprag (locking) brakes were fitted to arrest all movement. Provision was made for various hauldown systems such as Beartrap to facilitate alighting on small pads in severe weather.

Wasp service

Deliveries to the Royal Navy began in 1963, and a few were flown in Operation Corporate in the South Atlantic right at the end of their active lives when most had been replaced in RN service by the Lynx. Wasp HAS.Mk 1s operated from eight ships in that campaign, all assigned to No. 829 Squadron, FAA. Most were used in reconnaissance and utility missions, though several operated in the casevac role. Three, two from HMS *Endurance* and one from the frigate HMS *Plymouth*, engaged the Argentine submarine *Santa Fe* and holed its conning tower with AS12s which passed clean through before exploding. Other Wasps served with the Australian, Brazilian, New Zealand and South African navies. In late 2003 the Wasp remained a front-line type with Indonesia and Malaysia, although the later was retiring its aircraft in favour of Fennecs.

SPECIFICATION	
Westland Wasp HAS.Mk 1	**Weights:** empty 1566 kg (3,452 lb);
Type: light multi-role ship-based	maximum take-off 2495 kg
helicopter	(5,500 lb)
Powerplant: one 529-kW (710-shp)	**Dimensions:** main rotor diameter
Rolls-Royce Nimbus 503 turboshaft	9.83 m (32 ft 3 in); length overall
Performance: maximum speed with	12.29 m (40 ft 4 in); height 3.56 m
weapons 193 km/h (120 mph);	(11 ft 8 in); main rotor disc area
cruising speed 177 km/h (110	75.90 m² (816.86 sq ft)
mph); range 435 km (270 miles)	**Armament:** two Mk 44 AS
	torpedoes or two AS12 AShMs

Right: The Westland Wasp took a long time to see action. In service with the Royal Navy for nearly 20 years, Wasps were very active during the Falklands War, just in the twilight of their careers.

Mil Mi-14 'Haze' Naval helicopter family

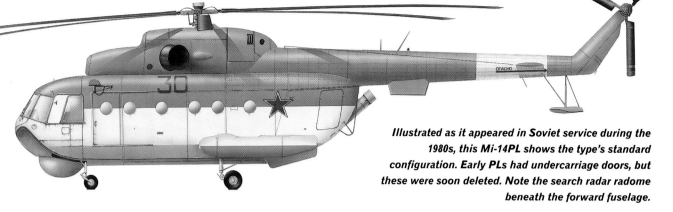

Illustrated as it appeared in Soviet service during the 1980s, this Mi-14PL shows the type's standard configuration. Early PLs had undercarriage doors, but these were soon deleted. Note the search radar radome beneath the forward fuselage.

In order to produce a replacement for the large numbers of Mi-4 'Hounds' in Soviet naval service, a version of the Mi-8 'Hip' with a boat-like hull was developed as the **Mi-14 'Haze'**.

The prototype of the series, which was designated **V-14**, flew for the first time in 1973, to be followed by the initial production **Mi-14PL 'Haze-A'** ASW helicopter.

Improvements incorporated during production included more powerful engines and the switching of the tail rotor from the starboard to the port side for increased controllability.

New variants

The latest 'Haze-A' aircraft have revised and updated equipment which includes a repositioned MAD system and are designated **Mi-14PLM**.

From 1983, trials were carried out with the **Mi-14BT 'Haze-B'** minesweeper. The helicopter has various airframe changes for its role and as primary equipment uses a towed mine sled. Although Mi-14BTs have been used on international mine-clearing operations, few were built. Russian forces prefer to use surface minesweepers, while some of the six BTs delivered to East Germany passed to the

Above: The boat hull of the 'Haze' allows operations in Sea States 3-4, or for planing at up to 60 km/h (37 mph). Note the sponson-mounted flotation bags and tail float of this Russian navy Mi-14PS.

Below: The Mi-14BT lacks a towed MAD 'bird', the aft fuselage instead housing mine countermeasures towing equipment. Only 25-30 examples were built, including a pair for Bulgaria's Naval Air Arm (illustrated).

SPECIFICATION

Mil Mi-14PL 'Haze-A'
Type: ASW helicopter
Powerplant: two Klimov (Isotov) TV3-117A turboshafts each rated at 1268 kW (1,700 shp) in early helicopters; or two TV3-117MT turboshafts each rated at 1434 kW (1,923 shp) in late helicopters
Performance: maximum level speed 'clean' at optimum altitude 230 km/h (143 mph); maximum cruising speed at optimum altitude 215 km/h (133 mph); initial rate of climb 468 m (1,535 ft) per minute; service ceiling 4000 m (13,123 ft); range 925 km (575 miles) with standard fuel
Weights: empty 8902 kg (19,625 lb); maximum take-off 14000 kg (30,864 lb)
Dimensions: rotor diameter, each 21.29 m (69 ft 10¼ in); length overall, rotors turning 25.32 m (83 ft 1 in); height 6.93 m (22 ft 9 in); main rotor disc area 356 m² (3,832.08 sq ft)
Armament: one AT-1 or APR-2 torpedo, or one 'Skat' nuclear depth bomb, or eight depth charges

Luftwaffe as SAR helicopters, before emerging as civilian water bombers.

The final production 'Haze' variant was the **Mi-14PS 'Haze-C'** SAR helicopter. Built primarily for the AV-MF, 'Haze-C' was also exported to Poland.

A few non-standard Mi-14 versions and designations have also appeared. **Mi-14PL 'Strike'** was a variant proposed for attack missions with AS-7 'Kerry' ASMS. **Mi-14PW** is the Polish designation for the Mi-14PL, while the **Mi-14PX** is one Polish Mi-14PL stripped of ASW gear and used for SAR training. Other Mi-14s have been converted for civilian use.

Kamov Ka-25 'Hormone' Naval helicopter family

Designed to meet a 1957 Soviet navy requirement for a new shipborne ASW helicopter, the first member of the Ka-20/25 family was the **Ka-20 'Harp'**, which initially flew during 1960. The production **Ka-25BSh 'Hormone-A'** was of near identical size and appearance, but was fitted with operational equipment and uprated GTD-3F turboshaft engines (from 1973 these were replaced by GTD-3BMs). The helicopter entered service in 1967.

Although the lower part of the fuselage is sealed and watertight, the Ka-25 is not intended for amphibious operations, and flotation bags are often fitted to the undercarriage for use in the event of an emergency landing on the water. The cabin is adequate for the job, but is not tall enough to allow the crew to stand upright. Progressive additions of new equipment have made the interior even more cluttered.

Primary sensors for the ASW mission are the I/J-band radar (ASCC/NATO 'Big Bulge'), OKA-2 dipping sonar, a downward-looking 'Tie Rod' electro-optical sensor in the tailboom and a MAD sensor, either in a recess in the rear part of the cabin or in a fairing sometimes fitted below the central of the three tailfins. A box-like sonobuoy launcher can also be scabbed on to the starboard side of the rear fuselage. Dye-markers or smoke floats can also be carried externally. Comprehensive avionics, defensive and navigation systems are also fitted as standard.

Armament is not normally carried, although the helicopter can be fitted with a long 'coffin-like'

weapons bay which runs along the belly from the radome back to the tailboom, and small bombs or depth charges can be carried on tiny pylons just aft of the nosewheels. The underfuselage bay can carry a variety of weapons, including nuclear depth charges. When wire-guided torpedoes are carried, a wire reel is mounted on the port side of the forward fuselage.

It has been estimated that some 260 of the 450 or so Ka-25s produced were 'Hormone-As', but only a handful remains in Russian and Ukrainian service, mostly fulfilling secondary roles. Small numbers of Ka-25BShs were exported to India, Syria, Vietnam and former Yugoslavia, and most of these aircraft remained in use in mid-2003.

'Hormone' variants

The second Ka-25 variant identified in the West was given the NATO reporting name **'Hormone-B'**, and is designated

Above: This Ka-25BSh 'Hormone-A' (displaying the flag of the Soviet navy) is bereft of flotation gear, fuel tanks and all the usual ASW equipment. In this configuration, the Ka-25 could carry a useful load of freight or 12 passengers, enabling it to perform an important secondary ship-to-shore transport role.

Ka-25K. This variant is externally identifiable by its bulbous (instead of flat-bottomed) under-nose radome and small datalink radome under the rear fuselage. Ka-25K was used for acquiring targets and providing mid-course missile guidance, for ship- and submarine-launched missiles. On the 'Hormone-B' only, the four undercarriage units are retractable and can be lifted out of the scanning pattern of the radar.

The final version of the military Ka-25 is the **Ka-25PS 'Hormone-C'**. A dedicated SAR and transport helicopter, the Ka-25PS can carry a practical load of freight or up to 12 passen-

SPECIFICATION
Kamov Ka-25BSh 'Hormone-A'

Type: ASW helicopter
Powerplant: two OMKB 'Mars' (Glushenkov) GTD-3F turboshafts each rated at 671 kW (898 shp) in early helicopters, or two GTD-3BM turboshafts each rated at 738 kW (900 shp) in late helicopters
Performance: maximum level speed 'clean' at optimum altitude 209 km/h (130 mph); normal cruising speed at optimum altitude 193 km/h (120 mph); service ceiling 3350 m (10,990 ft);

range 400 km (249 miles) with standard fuel
Weights: empty 4765 kg (10,505 lb); maximum take-off 7500 kg (16,534 lb)
Dimensions: rotor diameter, each 15.74 m (52 ft 7¾ in); fuselage length 9.75 m (32 ft); overall 5.37 m (17 ft 7½ in); main rotor disc area 389.15 m² (4,188.93 sq ft)
Armament: provision for torpedoes, conventional or nuclear depth charges and other stores up to a maximum of 1900 kg (4,190 lb)

gers, making it a useful ship-to-ship or ship-to-shore transport and vertrep platform. A quadru-ple Yagi antenna ('Home Guard') fitted to many aircraft is report-edly used for homing on to the personal locator beacons carried by aircrew. Most Ka-25PSs also have searchlights, and a 300-kg (660-lb) capacity rescue winch. Ka-25PS has largely been replaced by Ka-27.

Kamov Ka-27, Ka-29, and Ka-31 'Helix'
Naval helicopter family

Ka-29TB is a formidable assault and attack helicopter. It mounts a sizeable weapons load on braced fuselage outriggers.

Work on the **Ka-27** family of naval helicopters began in 1969. The Ka-27 retains Kamov's well-proven contra-rotating co-axial rotor configuration, and has dimensions similar to those of the Ka-25.

With more than double the power of the Ka-25, the Ka-27 is a considerably heavier helicopter with a larger fuse-lage, but nevertheless offers increased performance with improved avionics and a more modern flight-control system.

The first production variant was the **Ka-27PL 'Helix-A'** basic ASW version, which entered service in 1982. The Ka-27PL's fuselage is sealed over its lower portions for buoyancy,

while extra flotation equipment can be fitted in boxes on the lower part of the centre fuse-lage. Ka-27 is extremely stable and easy to fly, and automatic height hold, automatic transition to and from the hover and auto-hover are possible in all weather conditions. Ka-27PL has all the usual ASW and ESM equipment, including dipping sonar and sonobuoys as well as Osminog (octopus) search radar.

SAR and planeguard
The main SAR and planeguard Ka-27 variant is the radar-equipped **Ka-27PS 'Helix-D'**. This usually carries external fuel tanks and flotation gear, and is equipped with a hydraulically-

operated, 300-kg (661-lb) capac-ity rescue winch.

Ka-28 'Helix-A' is the export version of the Ka-27PL ordered by China, India, Vietnam and Yugoslavia and with a revised avionics suite.

Assault and transport
The **Ka-29TB** (**Transportno Boyevoya**) is a dedicated assault transport derivative of the Ka-27/32 family, intended especially for the support of Russian navy amphibious operations and featuring a substantially changed airframe. The first example was seen by Western eyes on the assault ship *Ivan Rogov* in 1987, the type having entered service in 1985, and the **Ka-29TB** was initially assumed to be the Ka-27B, resulting in the allocation of the NATO reporting designation **'Helix-B'**. Many of the new variants went unnoticed, and the Ka-29TB was initially thought to be a minimum-change version of the basic Ka-27PL without radar. In fact the Ka-29TB features an entirely new, much widened forward fuselage, with a flight deck seating three members of the crew side-by-side, one of

these crew members acting as a gunner to aim the various types of air-to-surface unguided rocket carried on the four hard-points of the helicopter's pair of strut-braced lateral pylons, and the trainable machine-gun hidden behind an articulated door on the starboard side of the nose. In addition, the two-piece curved windscreen of the Ka-27 has given way to a five-piece unit.

An air data boom projects from the port side of the nose, which also carries an EO sensor to starboard and a missile guidance/illuminating and TFR pod to port.

The basic Ka-29TB served as the basis for the **Ka-31**, which was originally known as the **Ka-29RLD** (**Radiolokatsyonnogo Dozora**, or radar picket helicopter). This AEW type helicopter first flew in 1988, and was first seen during carrier trials aboard *Kuznetsov*. All four landing gear units are retractable, making space for the movement of the E-801E Oko (eye) surveillance radar's antenna, which is a large rectangular planar array that rests flat under the fuselage when inactive.

SPECIFICATION

Kamov Ka-27PL 'Helix-A'
Type: three-crew shipborne anti-submarine and utility helicopter
Powerplant: two Klimov (Isotov) TV3-117V turboshaft engines each rated at 1633 kW (2,190 shp)
Performance: maximum speed 250 km/h (155 mph) at optimum altitude; cruising speed 230 km/h (143 mph) at optimum altitude; service ceiling 5000 m (16,404 ft); hovering ceiling 3500 m (11,483 ft) out of ground effect; range 800 km (497 miles) with auxiliary fuel
Weights: empty 6100 kg (13,448 lb);

maximum take-off 12600 kg (27,778 lb)
Dimensions: rotor diameter, each 15.9 m (52 ft 2 in); length, excluding rotors 11.27 m (37 ft 11¾ in); height to top of rotor head 5.45 m (17 ft 10½ in); rotor disc area, each 198.5 m² (2,136.6 sq ft)
Armament: up to 200 kg (441 lb) of disposable stores, generally comprising four APR-2E homing torpedoes or four groups of S3V guided anti-submarine bombs
Payload: up to 5000 kg (11,023 lb) of freight

Kaman SH-2 Seasprite Multi-role naval helicopter

The **H-2 Seasprite** was conceived in response to a 1956 USN requirement for a high-speed, all-weather, long-range SAR, liaison and utility helicopter. The first of four **YHU2K-1** (from 1962 **YUH-2A**) service test prototypes made its maiden flight on 2 July 1959, and the type entered production as the **HU2K-1** (**UH-2A**). Later variants were progressively improved and updated, gaining a second engine (for a greater safety margin for ship-based operations), dual mainwheels and a four-bladed tail rotor. Manufacture stopped after the delivery of the last **UH-2B**. The helicopter was first used in the ASW role in October 1970, when the USN selected the **SH-2D** as an interim **LAMPS I** (**Light Airborne Multi-Purpose System Mk I**) platform.

LAMPS I

The SH-2D introduced an under-nose Litton LN-66 search radar radome, an ASQ-81 MAD on the starboard fuselage pylon and a removable sonobuoy rack in the port side of the fuselage. Twenty were produced as conversions from **HH-2D** armed-SAR standard, entering service in 1972.

Deliveries of the definitive **SH-2F**, which also bore the LAMPS I designation, began in May 1973. The primary role of the SH-2F was the generation of a major extension of the protected area

Above: ASW was just one of the tasks assigned to US Navy Seasprites, like this SH-2F.

provided by the outer defensive screen of a carrier battle group. It introduced T58-GE-8F engines, an improved main rotor, and strengthened landing gear including a tailwheel relocated farther forward. The SH-2F also featured an improved Marconi LN-66HP surface search radar, ASQ-81(V)2 towed MAD bird and a tactical navigation and communications system. Some 88 machines were converted from earlier variants, and 16 SH-2Ds were also modified.

New production

The Seasprite was reinstated in production during 1981, when the USN placed an order for the first of an eventual 60 new-build SH-2Fs. From 1987 some 16 SH-2Fs received a package of modifications to allow them to operate in the Persian Gulf. During the 1991 Gulf War, the

SH-2F tested the ML-30 Magic Lantern laser sub-surface mine detector.

Continued development of the Seasprite resulted in the appearance of the **SH-2G Super Seasprite**. The prototype **YSH-2G** first flew on 2 April 1985, as an SH-2F conversion with T700 engines. The new type entered service in 1991, but the end of

the Cold War reduced the USN's requirement to 23 machines and the Seasprite has left US Navy service. Kaman has sold rebuilt surplus SH-2Fs to Egypt, which received **SH-2G(E)** helicopters from October 1997. In June 1997 the Royal Australian Navy and Royal New Zealand Navy ordered a total of 15 SH-2Gs rebuilt to an improved standard from SH-2F airframes. The rebuilt **SH-2G(NZ)** helicopters for New Zealand entered service in 2001, while the **SH-2G(A)** machines for Australia have been delayed by avionics problems and will not become operational until 2004.

Left: Australia and New Zealand (illustrated) bought their Seasprites to equip their new 'Anzac'-class multi-role frigates. Australia may purchase further SH-2G(A)s.

SPECIFICATION

Kaman SH-2G Super Seasprite
Type: three-crew shipborne ASW, missile defence, SAR and utility helicopter
Powerplant: two General Electric T700-GE-401/401C turboshaft engines each rated at 1285 kW (1,723 shp)
Performance: maximum speed 256 km/h (159 mph) at sea level; cruising speed 222 km/h (138 mph) at optimum altitude; initial climb rate 762 m (2,500 ft) per minute; service ceiling 7285 m (23,900 ft); hovering ceiling 6340 m (20,800 ft) in ground effect and 5485 m (18,000 ft) out of ground effect; radius 65 km (40 miles) for a patrol of 2 hours 10 minutes with one torpedo

Weights: empty 3483 kg (7,680 lb); maximum take-off 6123 kg (13,500 lb)
Dimensions: main rotor diameter 13.51 m (44 ft 4 in); length overall 16.08 m (52 ft 9 in) with rotors turning; height 4.58 m (15 ft ½ in) with rotors turning; main rotor disc area 143.41 m² (1,543.66 sq ft)
Armament: provision for two 0.3-in (7.62-mm) M60 trainable lateral-firing machine-guns on optional pintle mounts in the cabin doors, plus up to 726 kg (1,600 lb) of disposable stores
Payload: (with sonobuoy system removed) provision for up to four passengers, or two litters, or 1814 kg (4,000 lb) of freight carried as a slung load

---

Sikorsky S-61/H-3 Sea King ASW and multi-role helicopter

One of the most important helicopter families yet developed, and once a mainstay of the Western world's shipborne anti-submarine forces, the **Sikorsky SH-3 Sea King** series began life as the **HSS-2** anti-submarine helicopter for the US Navy. The prototype of this helicopter first flew on 11 March 1959, and the aircraft, which has the company designation **Sikorsky S-61**, was the first which could carry all the sensors and weapons needed for ASW missions without external help (though the US Navy policy developed to regard the aircraft as an extension of the ASW surface vessel from which it operates, so that helicopter-carried sensors detect the hostile submarine before the warship is called in for the kill).

Sea King features

New features included an amphibious boat hull with retractable tailwheel landing gear, twin turboshaft engines (for power, lightness, reliability and single-engine flight capability) above the cabin and an unobstructed tactical compartment for two sonar operators whose sensors included a dipping sonobuoy lowered through

Below: US Navy squadron HC-2 remained a Sea King operator in 2003. Its UH-3H utility helicopters were produced by conversion from SH-3H standard.

Right: The US Navy produced its 150-strong SH-3H (illustrated) fleet by converting earlier SH-3A, SH-3D and SH-3G aircraft. Even a pair of ex-USAF CH-53Bs was consumed.

a keel hatch. Above the extensive avionic systems was an attitude-hold autopilot and a sonar coupler which maintained exact height and station in conjunction with a radar altimeter and Doppler radar. Over 1,100 **H-3** type helicopters were built, the ASW models being SH-3s in four basic models.

ASW variants

The **SH-3A** was the original model with 933-kW (1,260-shp) T58-GE-8B turboshafts, the **SH-3D** is the upgraded version; the **SH-3G** is the utility version; and the **SH-3H** is the multi-role model fitted with dipping sonar and MAD gear for ASW and search radar for the detection of incoming anti-ship missiles. Single examples of the SH-3D and SH-3G, plus 50 SH-3Hs remained in US Navy service in mid-2003.

Licence-production

Agusta has built the Sea King under licence in Italy as the **AS-61/ASH-3**, some variants being equipped with Marte anti-ship missiles. Mitsubishi built 55 Sea Kings in three versions, all retaining the original HSS-2 designation, for the JMSDF. By far

the most important overseas manufacturer, however, has been Westland in the UK. Westland-built aircraft are powered by Rolls-Royce H.1400 Gnome-series engines and have much UK-sourced equipment. The initial **Sea King HAS.Mk 1** made its first flight on 7 May 1969 and was little more than a re-engined SH-3D. Subsequent ASW variants for the Royal Navy have included the **HAS.Mk 2**, **HAS.Mk 5** and **HAS.Mk 6**. To fill the massive gap that became apparent in the RN's airborne AEW coverage during the Falklands War, the **Sea King AEW.Mk 2A** was produced by conversion from HAS.Mk 2 standard. Later, HAS.Mk 5 aircraft were converted to **AEW.Mk 5**

Above: Italy will replace its ASH-3D (illustrated) and ASH-3H helicopters with the EH 101. The Sea Kings are flown from the Italian navy's larger vessels and the aircraft-carrier Garibaldi.

and **AEW.Mk 7** standard. **Sea King HAR.Mk 3** and **Mk 3A** SAR helicopters have been built for the RAF and many Westland Sea Kings, including the **Sea King International**, have been built for export.

Sikorsky exported its Sea Kings to many countries, including Canada, where the aircraft is designated **CH-124**. Specialised US SH-3 variants included the **RH-3** minesweeper, while the **VH-3** executive transport remains in service.

SPECIFICATION	
Sikorsky SH-3D Sea King	(21,500 lb)
Type: ASW helicopter	**Dimensions:** main rotor diameter
Powerplant: two 1044-kW	18.9 m (62 ft); fuselage length
(1,400-shp) General Electric T58-10	16.69 m (54 ft 9 in); height 5.13 m
turboshafts	(16 ft 10 in); main rotor disc area
Performance: maximum speed 267	280.5 m² (3,019.10 sq ft)
km/h (166 mph); range with	**Armament:** external hardpoints for a
maximum fuel and 10 per cent	total of 381 kg (840 lb) of
reserves 1005 km (625 miles)	weapons, normally comprising two
Weights: empty 5382 kg (11,865 lb);	Mk 46 torpedoes
maximum take-off 9752 kg	

Sikorsky S-70/H-60 Seahawk ASW and multi-role helicopter

A derivative of the US Army's UH-60 Black Hawk, the **Sikorsky SH-60B Seahawk** (originally produced under the company designation **S-70L**, later **S-70B**) won the US Navy's LAMPS (Light Airborne Multi-Purpose System) III competition in September 1977. A complex and extremely expensive machine, the SH-60B was designed for two main missions: ASW and ASST (anti-ship surveillance and targeting). The ASST mission involved the aerial detection of incoming sea-skimming AShMs, and the provision of radar-derived data for similar weapons launched from US warships. Secondary missions included SAR, medevac and vertrep (vertical replenishment). The basic airframe differs from that of the UH-60 in being marinised, with a sealed tail-boom, having its tailwheel moved and inflatable bags for emergency buoyancy fitted, and having an electrically-folding main rotor and pneumatically-folding tail (including upward-hinged tailplanes). Other modifications are greater fuel capacity and the removal of cockpit armour for the pilot and co-pilot. The type is also fitted with haul-down equipment to facilitate recovery onto small platforms on pitching and rolling ships in heavy seas. Under the nose is the large APS-124 radar and on the left side of the fuselage is a large vertical panel with tubes for launching sonobuoys.

On the right of the rear fuselage is a pylon for a towed MAD

Above: Mitsubishi has built SH-60Js (illustrated) and UH-60Js for the JMSDF. In 2003 SH-60Js were still being funded and a KAI upgrade programme is underway.

'bird'. The first prototype flew on 12 December 1979 and a total of 181 was built for the USN.

Subsequent variants for US Navy service have included the **SH-60F Ocean Hawk**, equipped with dipping sonar for inner-zone ASW cover around aircraft-carriers; the **HH-60H Rescue Hawk** for ship-borne SAR, plane guard and special forces missions and the **MH-60R** multi-mission helicopter. The latter were to be

SPECIFICATION
Sikorsky SH-60B Seahawk

Type: multi-role shipboard helicopter

Powerplant: (aircraft delivered from 1988) two 1417-kW (1,900-shp) General Electric T700-GE-401C turboshafts

Performance: dash speed at 1525 m (5,000 ft) 234 km/h (145 mph); operational radius 92.5 km (57.5 miles) for a 3-hour loiter

Weights: (for the ASW mission) empty 6191 kg (13,648 lb); mission take-off 9182 kg (20,244 lb)

Dimensions: main rotor diameter 16.36 m (53 ft 8 in); fuselage length 15.26 m (50 ft ¾ in); height overall, rotors turning 5.18 m (17 ft); main rotor disc area 210.05 m^2 (2,262.03 sq ft)

Armament: normally two Mk 46 torpedoes, or Penguin AShMs

Above: Easily identified by the two windows in its portside cabin door, this HH-60H is shown performing a vertrep mission.

Right: The many roles now tackled by the SH-60 family are shown here by an HH-60H taking off for a plane guard sortie.

produced by conversion from SH-60B/F/HH-60H helicopters, but 243 new-build helicopters will now be bought for delivery from 2005. They will join 237 **MH-60S** utility aircraft which combine much of the UH-60's airframe with SH-60 systems and began replacing Boeing-Vertol CH-46 Sea Knights in February 2002. Other, non-navy, versions include the US Coast Guard's **HH-60J Jayhawk**, while naval variants have been widely exported and built under licence in Australia and Japan.

Harbin SH-5 (PS-5) Multi-role flying boat

Known to the West as the PS-5, the SH-5 was in service in the early part of 2003 to the extent of no more than four examples.

Developed in China on the basis of the wings and powerplant of the Y-8 (Chinese-built An-12 'Cub') combined with the empennage of the Be-12 'Mail' and a new fuselage/hull combination clearly owing much to that of the Japanese US-1A, the **SH-5** (**Shuihong**, or **Shuishang Hongzhaji**, or maritime bomber; **PS-5** in Westernised form) is a substantial flying-boat of all-metal construction with a single-step hull and retractable tricycle beaching gear with single-wheel main units and a twin-wheel nose unit. The wing has a flat, constant-chord centre section that includes the inner two engines, and then increasing anhedral on the two tapered outer panels on each side.

Multi-role 'boat

The type first flew in April 1976 but entered service only in 1986 as the Chinese navy's dedicated maritime reconnaissance/anti-submarine flying-boat with a flight crew of five, a mission crew of three (expandable when required) or, in the 'boat's secondary transport role, passengers and/or freight. The type's development was seriously delayed by the Cultural Revolution, which explains in part why a type that entered service comparatively recently has an elderly engine type and unpressurised accommodation. This last is no hindrance in the SH-5's low-altitude patrol regime, but means that transit flights between base and any

distant operational area have to be flown at comparatively low altitude and therefore reduced speed. It is thought that perhaps only seven of the type were completed and the in-service fleet appears to be diminishing.

SPECIFICATION

Harbin SH-5
Type: eight-crew maritime reconnaissance flying-boat with anti-submarine, anti-ship, air/sea rescue and transport capabilities
Powerplant: four Dongan (DEMC) Wojiang-5A1 turboprop engines each rated at 2349 kW (3,150 hp)
Performance: maximum speed 555 km/h (345 mph) at optimum altitude; cruising speed 450 km/h (280 mph) at optimum altitude; patrol speed 230 km/h (143 mph) at optimum altitude; service ceiling 10250 m (33,630 ft); range 4750 km (2,951 miles); endurance between 12 and 15 hours on two engines

Weights: empty less than 25000 kg (55,115 lb) equipped for the SAR and transport roles, or 26500 kg (58,422 lb) for the ASW role; maximum take-off 45000 kg (99,206 lb)
Dimensions: wing span 36 m (118 ft 1¼ in); length 38.9 m (127 ft 7½ in); height 9.8 m (32 ft 2 in); wing area 144 m² (1,550.05 sq ft)
Armament: two 23-mm Type 23-1 trainable rearward-firing cannon in a power-operated dorsal turret, plus up to 6000 kg (13,228 lb) of disposable stores carried in a lower-fuselage weapons bay and on four underwing hardpoints
Payload: passengers or 10000 kg (22,046 lb) of freight

Breguet Atlantic 1 and Dassault Atlantique 2 Specialised maritime patrol aircraft

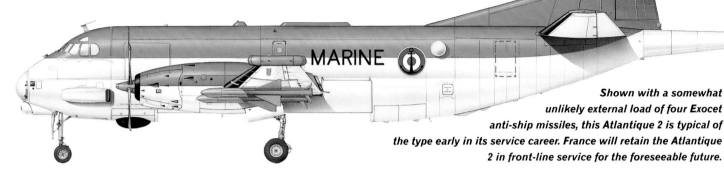

Shown with a somewhat unlikely external load of four Exocet anti-ship missiles, this Atlantique 2 is typical of the type early in its service career. France will retain the Atlantique 2 in front-line service for the foreseeable future.

Above: With its 'dustbin' radome in the retracted position, an 86° Gruppo Antisomergibili, 30° Stormo Atlantic returns to its base after a maritime patrol sortie.

NATO selected the **Breguet Br.1150** for production to satisfy its long-range maritime patrol aircraft requirement at the end of 1958. The aircraft was called **Atlantic**, later altered to **Atlantic 1** after development of the **Atlantique 2**.

The Atlantic was the first combat aircraft to be designed and built as a multi-national project. The responsibility for production was given to the specially created SECBAT (Société d'Etudes et de Construction du Breguet Atlantic).

The original consortium members, led by Breguet, comprised Sud-Aviation, the Belgian ABAP grouping, Dornier in Germany and Fokker in the Netherlands. Italy joined in 1968, with some of the work then being allocated to Aeritalia.

A similar multi-national organisation was set up to build the Rolls-Royce Tyne turboprop engine. The Atlantic incorporates a 'double-bubble' fuselage with a pressurised upper deck and a MAD boom extending rearward from the tail, a conventional tail unit with an ECM pod at the tip of the fin and two Tynes in wing-mounted nacelles.

Atlantic roles

Suitable for anti-ship, coastal recce, SAR, fleet escort, logistic support, freight and passenger transport and minelaying roles, the Atlantic was designed primarily for the ASW role.

As such, it is equipped with sonobuoys and Thomson-CSF search radar. For attack, the Atlantic carries bombs, depth charges and homing torpedoes in its weapons bay; additional capability is provided by the carriage of ASMs or rockets on underwing attachments. The Atlantic's crew of 12 includes no less than seven specialists to co-ordinate and direct the aircraft's operations.

The first prototype made its maiden flight on 21 October 1961 and the first of 40 aircraft for the French navy was delivered in July 1965, followed by 20 aircraft for the German navy. A second production batch of aircraft included nine for the Netherlands navy and 18 for Italy. Three of those supplied to France were later transferred for service in Pakistan.

The Atlantic's sensors are mainly of Thomson-CSF manufacture, and are computer-integrated on display and control panels in the tactical compartment. Useful updating has been achieved within the limitations of the 1950s-vintage electronics, but the Atlantic can now only be regarded as obsolescent; the French started to retire their aircraft as early as 1992.

Five of the German naval air arm's 15 survivors were extensively converted as Sigint aircraft, with E-Systems Peace Peek mission equipment installed by Vought and based on a Loral ESM suite with antennas in wing-tip pods. The Italian aircraft were upgraded by Aeritalia with improved radar and navigation systems, as well as the Selenia ALR-730 ESM system.

New generation

Originally called the **ANG** (**Atlantic Nouvelle Génération**, or new-generation Atlantic), the **Dassault Atlantique 2** was planned as a multi-national programme to replace the Atlantic 1. However, France has remained the sole customer, with a 30-aircraft order. After very prolonged studies, the Atlantique 2 was designed as a minimum-change type with totally new avionics, systems and equipment, packaged into an airframe differing from that of the original model only in ways to increase service life, reduce costs and minimise maintenance.

SPECIFICATION	
Dassault Atlantique 2 **Type:** 10/12-crew long-range maritime patrol and ASW/anti-ship aircraft **Powerplant:** two Rolls-Royce Tyne RTy.20 Mk 21 turboprop engines each rated at 4549 ekW (6,100 ehp) **Performance:** maximum speed 648 km/h (402 mph) at optimum altitude; patrol speed 315 km/h (196 mph) between sea level and 1525 m (5,000 ft); initial climb rate 884 m (2,900 ft) per minute; service ceiling 9145 m (30,000 ft); operational radius 3333 km	(2,071 miles) for a 2-hour patrol in the anti-ship role with one AM39 Exocet missile; endurance 18 hours **Weights:** empty 25600 kg (56,437 lb); maximum take-off 46200 kg (101,852 lb) **Dimensions:** wing span 37.42 m (122 ft 9¼ in) including wing-tip ESM pods; length 31.62 m (103 ft 9 in); height 10.89 m (35 ft 8¾ in); wing area 120.34 m² (1,295.37 sq ft) **Armament:** up to 6000 kg (13,228 lb) of disposable stores

The Atlantique 2's sensors include the Thomson-CSF Iguane frequency-agile radar, a SAT/TRT Tango FLIR in a chin turret, over 100 sonobuoys in the rear fuselage, a new Crouzet MAD receiver and the ARAR 13 ESM installation. The main weapons bay can accommodate all NATO-standard bombs and depth charges, as well as other weapon types including two ASMs or AShMs, up to eight Mk 46 torpedoes or seven Franco-Italian MU39 Impact advanced torpedoes. The Atlantique has a rarely used secondary transport function, and could also be used in a limited overland electronic reconnaissance role.

The first Atlantique 2 flew in May 1981 and production deliveries began in 1989.

Above: Of the 18 Atlantics remaining in German service, the 14 standard machines (illustrated) fly long-range recce for aerial patrols and ASW missions.

Left: Differences between the Atlantique 2 (illustrated here) and the Atlantic include the former's wing tip ECM pods, nose-mounted Tango FLIR turret, prominent cooling intakes below the cockpit and re-shaped fin top, housing an ECM aerial.

ShinMaywa PS-1, US-1 and SS-2 Military seaplanes

The **ShinMaywa** (up to 1992 **Shin Meiwa**) SS-2 family is one of the few modern flying-boat series in service anywhere in the world. The first member of the family to enter service with the Japan Maritime Self-Defence Force was the **PS-1**, a capable ASW machine. The origins of the SS-2 can be discovered in a JMSDF requirement issued in

While on patrol the PS-1 was designed to make repeated landings and take-offs, dipping its sonar after alighting. This could be accomplished in seas with up to 3-m (10-ft) waves.

the early 1960s, and the first of two prototypes made its maiden flight on 16 October 1967. Trials revealed excellent STOL performance largely as a result of the wing's high-lift devices (outboard leading-edge slats and

Left: The 71st Koku-tai at Iwakuni has operated the US-1 since 1976, and the original batch of 12 aircraft was augmented by at least five further aircraft. The US-1/1A was returned to production in 1992.

Right: The original PS-1 was a dedicated ASW flying-boat, optimised for very long-range patrol duties. The prototype and two pre-production aircraft were followed by 20 production aircraft. The type served from 1971 to 1989, when it was replaced by land-based Lockheed P-3 Orions.

trailing-edge flaps) and a boundary layer control system on the flaps, rudder and elevators powered by a T58 gas turbine in the fuselage.

PS-1 described

Production was completed in 1979 with the 23rd machine, and the type was withdrawn from first-line service in 1989. The PS-1 had accommodation for a flight crew of three and a mission crew of seven. The armament comprised up to 2000 kg (4,409 lb) of disposable stores carried in a lower fuselage weapons bay and on two underwing and two wing-tip hardpoints. The weapons bay could carry four 150-kg (331-lb) depth bombs, the underwing hardpoints could each accommodate two Mk 46 torpedoes, and the wing-tip hardpoints could each accept three 127-mm (5-in) rockets. The PS-1's electronics included APS-80N search radar, HQS-101C dunking sonar, HSQ-10A MAD, the 'Julie' active ranging system with 12 charges, AQA-3 'Jezebel' passive detection system with 20 sonobuoys and the HLR-1 ECM system.

The **US-1** is a SAR variant of the PS-1 with retractable wheeled landing gear to turn the type into an amphibian. It has a crew of nine, and its cabin can accommodate three additional crew members as well as 20 survivors, or 12 litters or, in the transport role, 69 passengers. The first example of the US-1 (company designation **SS-2A**) variant flew in October 1974, and production totalled six 'boats before the line switched to the improved **US-1A** standard, to which the US-1s were later raised. The last 12 US-1 'boats were delivered as US-1As, with an uprated powerplant of four 2605-kW (3,493-ehp) T64-IHI-10J engines supplied with fuel from an enlarged internal capacity.

The **US-1A KAI** is the updated version of the US-1A with the powerplant of four 3355-kW (4,400-shp) Rolls-Royce AE2100J turboprop engines driving six-bladed propellers, a fly- by-wire control system, improved cockpit avionics, and a pressurised fuselage to permit a higher cruising altitude within the context of a service ceiling increased to 7620 m (25,000 ft) and a range boosted to more than 5003 km (3,109 miles). It is planned that all seven surviving US-1As will be upgraded to the US-1A KAI standard and supplemented by three 'boats built to this standard. The first US-1A KAI should fly in 2003 and enter service in 2005.

SPECIFICATION	
ShinMaywa PS-1	
Type: ASW flying-boat	**Dimensions:** wing span 33.14 m (108 ft 8¾ in); length 33.5 m (109 ft 11 in); height 9.71 m (31 ft 10¼ in); wing area 135.82 m² (1,462 sq ft)
Powerplant: four 2282-ekW (3,060-ehp) General Electric T64-IHI-10 turboprops (made under licence by IHI)	
Performance: maximum speed 547 km/h (340 mph); range at low altitude with maximum weapons 2168 km (1,347 miles)	**Armament:** internal weapons bay for four 149-kg (328-lb) AS bombs and extensive search gear, two underwing pods for four Mk 44 or Mk 46 homing AS torpedoes and triple launcher under each wing tip for 127-mm (5-in) rockets
Weights: empty 26300 kg (57,982 lb); maximum 43000 kg (94,799 lb)	

Left: Withdrawal of the PS-1 did not mark the end of the ShinMaywa flying-boat, since an amphibious SAR derivative had already been designed, under the designation US-1 (foreground).

Fokker F27 Maritime and Maritime Enforcer/50 Maritime Mk 2 and Maritime Enforcer Mk 2

ASW/maritime patrol aircraft

First flown in 1955, the F27 exceeded Fokker's expectations in terms of sales, becoming one of the world's most successful twin-turboprop airliners, and leading to the new-generation Fokker 50. Fokker also developed military transport and special missions versions of both the F27 and F50.

F27MPA Maritime

In 1975 Fokker completed definition of a specialised maritime patrol version of the F27 as the **Fokker F27MPA Maritime**. Intended for all forms of coastal surveillance, SAR and environmental control missions, the Maritime has a crew of up to six and can mount 12-hour patrols. It is equipped with Litton APS-504 search radar in an underfuselage radome, nose-mounted Bendix weather radar and fully comprehensive navigation systems, as well as a fully equipped tactical compartment, crew rest areas and bulged observation windows to the flight deck and rear of the cabin. This **F27-200MPA** version was sold to Angola, the Netherlands and Peru (where it is no longer operated) and is currently in use with the air forces of Spain (three) and Thailand (three).

Maritime Enforcer

Thailand's aircraft are armed, but otherwise not to the **F27MPA Maritime Enforcer** standard.

This latter variant is tasked with armed surveillance, ASW, anti-ship attack and other combat roles, and is equipped with LAPADS (lightweight acoustic processing and display system) for active and passive sonobuoys, a magnetic anomaly detector (MAD), and comprehensive electronic support measures (ESM) equipment and infra-red (IR) detection systems, plus an optional underwing searchlight.

F50 Maritime Mk 2

The **F50 Maritime Mk 2** was to have been a considerably developed version of the Maritime, with a flightcrew of two or three, a mission crew of between two and four, and a mission suite that included an IR detection system and the Texas Instruments APS-134 surveillance radar with its antenna in a ventral radome.

Enforcer Mk 2

The F50 Maritime Enforcer Mk 2 is a considerably developed version of the F27MPA Maritime Enforcer, based on the airframe and powerplant of the F50. It has basically the same airframe as the F27MPA Maritime Enforcer but with aerodynamic refinements, flight deck improvements, and a powerplant of two PW125B turboprops. The avionics suite is basically an improved version of

Above: Spain bought three F27 Maritime aircraft fitted with APS-504 search radar in belly blisters. The aircraft's endurance of over 12 hours allows long-range SAR and patrol missions.

that which would have been carried by the F50 Maritime Mk 2. The weapons capability was increased to 3930 kg (8,664 lb) of disposable stores carried on eight hardpoints (two under the fuselage and six under the wings), allowing the carriage of up to eight torpedoes and/or depth bombs, or two or four AGM-84 Harpoon or AM.39 Exocet anti-ship missiles, or a mixed load of torpedoes and missiles; more typical loads might be four torpedoes, or two anti-ship missiles. Singapore was the only customer for the type, buying five.

As well as the Maritime Mk 2 and Maritime Enforcer Mk 2, a range of special-purpose F50 variants was proposed, based for the most part on equipment fits originally proposed on the F27. These variants included the **Black Crow 2** Comint/ Elint version with an ARCO Sigint system; the **Kingbird Mk 2** for airborne early warning (AEW) with phased array radar; and the **Sentinel Mk 2** with synthetic aperture radar, side-looking airborne radar (SLAR), and a podded electro-optical imaging system for surveillance and reconnaissance.

Below: Thailand's maritime aircraft carry a range of armament, including the depth charges and torpedoes illustrated here.

SPECIFICATION	
Fokker 50 Maritime Enforcer Mk 2 **Type:** ASW and anti-ship aircraft **Powerplant:** two Pratt & Whitney Canada PW125B turboprop engines each flat-rated at 1864 kW (2,500 shp) **Performance:** normal cruising speed 298 mph (480 km/h) at optimum altitude; service ceiling 7620 m (25,000 ft); operational radius 2224 km (1,382 miles) with a 1814-kg (4,000-lb) mission payload	**Weights:** operating empty 13314 kg (29,352 lb); maximum take-off 21545 kg (47,500 lb) **Dimensions:** wing span 29 m (95 ft 1¾ in); length 25.25 m (82 ft 10 in); height 8.32 m (27 ft 3½ in); wing area 70 m² (753.50 sq ft) **Armament:** provision for up to 3930 kg (8,664 lb) of disposable stores including AShMs, depth charges and torpedoes

Ilyushin Il-38 'May' Maritime patrol and ASW aircraft

The Il-38 is characterised by its prominent underfuselage radome and MAD 'tail sting'. The aircraft bears some similarity in configuration to the Lockheed P-3 Orion.

The **Il-38**, which has the NATO reporting designation **'May'**, was derived from the Il-18 airliner. The Il-38 resulted from a 1959 AV-MF requirement for a long-range maritime patrol and ASW aircraft, and the prototype first flew on 27 September 1961. There followed a pre-production prototype and 57 production aircraft delivered from 1968 (although some sources quote a figure of about 100 aircraft delivered in 1965-68).

Il-38 changes

The changes involved in the evolution of the basic Il-18 into the Il-38 were the lengthening of the fuselage by about 4.00 m (13 ft 1½ in) and the forward movement of the wing by some 2.75 m (9 ft ¼ in), probably to compensate for the effect of the new role equipment on the type's centre of gravity. Most of the original cabin windows were removed, and the remainder were mostly reduced in size. The Il-18's original passenger entry doors were all removed, to be replaced by a new door on the starboard side at the rear of the cabin in the location of the Il-18's service door.

Other structural alterations to the Il-38 included the provision of a MAD stinger projecting rearward from the tailcone, and a pair of internal weapons bays fore and aft of the wing carry-through structure.

The standard **Il-38 'May-A'** has weather radar in the nose, with a large search radar ('Wet Eye') in a bulged radome below the forward fuselage, immediately to the rear of the nosewheel bay. The otherwise smooth skin is disrupted by a handful of antennas and heat exchanger outlets, and there are large heat exchanger pods and cable ducts ahead of the wing.

'May' in service

Most of the former Soviet Il-38s remain in use with the AV-MF (naval air arm), although some were passed to the Ukraine. The only export customer was the Indian navy. Il-38s encountered over the Mediterranean in Egyptian markings during the early 1970s were Soviet aircraft operating from Egyptian bases and wearing 'flag of convenience' markings.

An upgrade programme, with the aim of keeping Russian Il-38s viable into the 21st century, was mooted around 2000 by the Leninets Holding Company. This upgrade, known as Sea Dragon, was initially to be applied to Indian Il-38s. However, India lost two of its four Il-38s in a collision at an airshow in September 2002, and may not now upgrade its depleted fleet. The Russian aircraft are likely to have their airframes modified for at least a further 10 year's service, but the future of the Sea Dragon programme was still undecided late in 2002.

Below: New engines may be fitted to the Il-38 and airframe, as well as avionics improvements are also being considered. With the demise of the Tu-95RTs in the 1990s, the Il-38 was increasingly tasked with surface reconnaissance missions in addition to its ASW tasking.

Below: Airframe modifications developed for the Il-18 airliner could easily be applied to Russian Il-38s and the related Il-20 command post.

SPECIFICATION	
Ilyushin Il-38 'May-A'	**Weights:** empty 35500 kg
Type: seven/eight-crew medium-/long-range maritime patrol and anti-submarine warplane	(78,263 lb); maximum take-off 66000 kg (145,503 lb)
Powerplant: four ZMDB Progress (Ivchyenko) AI-20M turboprop engines each rated at 3169 ekW (4,250 ehp)	**Dimensions:** wing span 37.42 m (122 ft 9¼ in); length 40.19 m (131 ft 10¼ in); height 10.17 m (33 ft 4½ in); wing area 140 m² (1,507 sq ft)
Performance: maximum speed 722 km/h (448 mph) at 6400 m (21,000 ft); patrol speed between 320 and 400 km/h (199 and 248 mph) between 100 and 1000 m (330 and 3,280 ft); service ceiling 11000 m (36,090 ft); range 7500 km (4,660 miles) with maximum fuel	**Armament:** up to 8400 kg (18,520 lb) of disposable stores carried in two lower-fuselage weapons bays, and generally comprising 216 RGB-1 sonobuoys or 144 RGB-2 sonobuoys as well as two AT-1 torpedoes, or 10 PLAB-250-120 depth charges, or eight AMD-2-500 mines, or one nuclear depth bomb

Tupolev Tu-142 'Bear-F' Long-range ASW/MP aircraft

The lengthened cabin of the Tu-142 series had no effect on fuselage length. Aircraft like this 'Bear-F Mod. 3', which is illustrated as it would have appeared in the 1980s, were potentially formidable ASW assets.

Development of a Tu-95 variant optimised for ASW duties was officially initiated in 1963. Based on the airframe of the Tu-95RTs, the **Tu-142** introduced a search and track system and an ASW weapon system. The new aircraft carried a sophisticated and accurate navigation system that was also part of the weapons system targeting hardware. Tupolev's earlier attempts at an ASW platform based on the 'Bear' (the **Tu-95PLO** proposed in the early 1960s) had been rendered abortive by the lack of such a powerful sensor system.

The Tu-142 was also equipped for electronic reconnaissance, utilising Kvadrat-2 and Kub-3 EW systems. In accordance with Soviet military doctrine, the Tu-142 was required to be capable of operations from unprepared airstrips: as a result the aircraft incorporated a new undercarriage with six wheels on each main unit, accommodated in increased-size nacelles.

Further refinements included a larger-area wing housing new rigid metal fuel tanks, and a defensive ECM suite. From the second prototype onwards, the cabin was lengthened by 1.50 m (3 ft 5 in), providing space for new systems.

RTs commonality

The prototype Tu-142 first flew on 18 July 1968. Compared to the Tu-95RTs, with which it retained much commonality, the Tu-142 had the ventral and dorsal cannon turrets removed, and the large dielectric radome of the RTs replaced by a smaller fairing for an IR system. New antennas

were positioned in fairings on the horizontal stabiliser tips, replacing the Arfa system carried by the Tu-95RTs 'Bear-D'.

During May 1970 the first production Tu-142s were delivered for operational test and evaluation by Soviet navy ASW units.

After the successful completion of trials and the completion of testing of the Berkut-95 search radar, the Tu-142 was declared operational in December 1972.

Operational aircraft

Attaining initial operational capability was hampered by slow deliveries, and the 12 aircraft received (of 36 ordered) by the AV-MF in 1972 were fitted with the original 12-wheel main undercarriage units, as carried by the first prototype. In service, the Tu-142's rough-field capability was found to be of limited utility. Furthermore, the aircraft's performance was hampered by its weight, and these two factors were consequently dealt with by the introduction of a modification plan.

The modified Tu-142 introduced a crew rest area for long-duration flights, and the main landing gear units were replaced by lighter examples, resulting in a 3,630 kg (8,000 lb) weight reduction and improved flight characteristics. This modified aircraft received no new designation (only 18 Tu-142s were built before production switched to the **Tu-142M**) but received the reporting name **'Bear-F Mod. 1'**). In 1972 the Kuibyshev facility produced its last Tu-142, and this became the standard configuration for pro-

Above: All maritime 'Bears' are equipped with IFR probes. A single inflight-refuelling typically increases range by some 2000 km (1,250 miles). This is a 'Mod. 3' aircraft.

duction aircraft, which were now to be delivered as the **Tu-142M** (**'Bear-F Mod. 2'**) from the Taganrog plant. The Tu-142M was equipped with the extended cockpit and new undercarriage, but other equipment remained unchanged compared to earlier aircraft. As a result of their similarity with the final Tu-142s delivered from Kuibyshev, the Taganrog- built aircraft were known by the AV-MF as Tu-142s, despite their Tu-142M factory designation.

New threats

Development of more 'stealthy' submarines, together with operational experience, indicated that conventional sonobuoys were becoming less effective. Instead,

sonobuoys with explosive sound sources would have to be used. The **Tu-142MK** (**'Bear-F Mod. 3'**) therefore combined improved sonobuoy equipment with a Korshun target acquisition system. The first example successfully completed its first flight on 4 November 1975. The new Korshun radar, avionics suite and ASW equipment proved problematic, and it seemed likely that it could become obsolete even before it entered service.

As a result, in July 1979, a year before the Korshun-equipped Tu-142MK entered service, it was declared that the aircraft needed substantial upgrading. Regardless, production of the Tu-142MK began during 1978, superseding that of the baseline

SPECIFICATION	
Tupolev Tu-142M ('Bear-F') **Type:** long-range ASW and maritime reconnaissance aircraft **Powerplant:** four 11033-kW (14,795-shp) Kuznetsov NK-12MV turboprops **Performance:** maximum speed 850 km/h (528 mph); service ceiling 10700 m (35,100 ft); range with maximum load 12000 km (7,460 miles)	**Weight:** maximum take-off 185000 kg (407,850 lb) **Dimensions:** wing span 50 m (164 ft); length, overall 48.17 m (158 ft ½ in); height about 12.12 m (39 ft 9¼ in); wing area 289.90 m² (3,121 sq ft) **Armament:** two NR-23 23-mm self-defence cannon in tail turret, plus depth charges, bombs and torpedoes

Right: Russia retains the 'Bear-F Mod. 3' (illustrated) in service alongside the Tu-142MZ.

Tu-142M, although the AV-MF elected to use its own designation system to identify the new model. Aircraft equipped with the new ASW system became known as Tu-142M machines, while older 'Bears' remained Tu-142s.

Improved capability

The first three Tu-142MKs entered service in November 1980, introducing a magnetic anomaly detector (MAD), a new navigation system, and improved ECM.

The Tu-142 continued to be updated and improved throughout the course of its long production run. The ultimate ASW 'Bear' variant is the **Tu-142MZ 'Bear-F Mod. 4'** with a more sophisticated ASW system, further improved ECM and new engines and APU.

The Tu-142MZ's additional equipment effectively doubled its efficiency. After state acceptance trials beginning in 1987, the last Tu-142MZ 'Bear-F Mod. 4' was declared fully operational during 1993.

The only Tu-142 export customer was the Indian Air Force, which received eight **Tu-142MK-A** aircraft. These have slightly down-graded avionics compared to the Tu-142MK. Following the loss of two of its Il-38s, India may take ex-Russian 'Bears' to bolster its maritime aircraft fleet.

Dassault Atlantique 2 ASW, ASV and maritime patrol aircraft

Originally called the **ANG** (**Atlantic Nouvelle Génération**, or new-generation Atlantic), the **Dassault Atlantique 2** was originally planned as a multinational programme to replace the Atlantic (now known as the Atlantic 1) with its various users. France has remained the sole customer, however, although its requirement for 30 aircraft (originally 42) made the project viable even if the rate of manufacture is too low for competitive costings.

After very prolonged studies, the Atlantique 2 was designed as a minimum-change type with totally new avionics, systems and equipment, packaged into an airframe differing from that of the original model only in ways to increase service life, reduce costs and minimise maintenance. In addition, an Astadyne gas-turbine auxiliary power unit is fitted, and production machines are fitted with Ratier/BAe propellers with larger composite blades.

Sensors and weapons

The Atlantique 2's sensors include the Thomson-CSF Iguane frequency-agile radar with a new interrogator and decoder, a SAT/TRT Tango FLIR in a chin turret, over 100 sonobuoys in the rear fuselage,

a new Crouzet MAD receiver in the boom, extending rearward from the tail, and the Thomson-CSF ARAR 13 ESM installation with frequency analysis at the

Above: A key sensor of the 'Nouvelle Génération' Atlantique 2 is the Thomson-CSF Iguane radar, housed in a retractable 'dustbin' radome. Here it is seen deployed on the first production aircraft.

top of the fin and D/F in the new wingtip nacelles. All processors, data buses and sensor links are of standard digital form, navaids include an inertial system and Navstar satellite receiver, and every part of the

avionics and communications has been upgraded. The main weapons bay can accommodate all NATO standard bombs and depth charges, as well as other

weapon types including two air-to-surface or anti-ship missiles, up to eight Mk 46 torpedoes or seven Franco-Italian MU39 Impact advanced torpedoes. The

SPECIFICATION	
Dassault Atlantique 2	(2,071 miles) for a 2-hour patrol in the ASV role with one AM39 Exocet missile
Type: 10/12-crew long-range maritime patrol and ASW/ASV aircraft	
Powerplant: two Rolls-Royce Tyne RTy.20 Mk 21 turboprop engines each rated at 4549 ekW (6,100 ehp)	**Weights:** empty 25600 kg (56,437 lb); maximum take-off 46200 kg (101,852 lb)
Performance: maximum speed 648 km/h (402 mph) at optimum altitude; patrol speed 315 km/h (196 mph) between sea level and 1525 m (5,000 ft); initial climb rate 884 m (2,900 ft) per minute; service ceiling 9145 m (30,000 ft); operational radius 3333 km	**Dimensions:** wing span 37.42 m (122 ft 9¼ in) including wingtip ESM pods; length 31.62 m (103 ft 9 in); height 10.89 m (35 ft 8¾ in); wing area 120.34 m² (1,295.37 sq ft)
	Armament: up to 6000 kg (13,228 lb) of disposable stores carried as 2500 kg (5,511 lb) internally and 3500 kg (7,717 lb) externally

Atlantique has a rarely used secondary transport function, and could also be used in a limited overland electronic reconnaissance role.

The first Atlantique 2 flew in May 1981 and production deliveries began in 1989.

Proposed variants of the Atlantique 2 have included a BAe Nimrod replacement for the RAF, with additional turbofan engines in pods under the wing and with either Allison T406 or General Electric T407 turboprop engines replacing the Tynes; an **Atlantique 3** with further improvements; and the

Europatrol, a derivative aimed at replacing NATO's Lockheed P-3 Orions. A Tyne upgrade has also been proposed.

Above: The most noticeable differences between the Atlantique 2 and the Atlantic are the former's wingtip ECM pods, nose-mounted Tango FLIR turret, the prominent cooling intakes below the cockpit and the re-shaped fin top, housing an ECM aerial.

Hawker Siddeley/BAe/BAE Systems Nimrod
Turbofan-powered maritime patrol aircraft

This Nimrod MR.Mk 2P is shown in the Hemp over Light Aircraft Grey scheme. This was replaced by an overall Camouflage Grey scheme as standard by 2003.

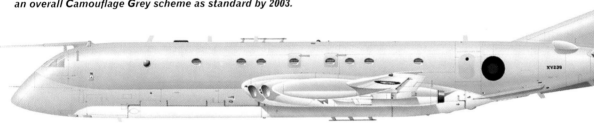

The type now known as the **BAE Systems Nimrod** began life as the **Hawker Siddeley HS.801**, which was created on the basis of the de Havilland Comet's airframe as a maritime reconnaissance aircraft to replace the ageing, piston-engined Shackleton in service with the RAF's Coastal Command. Development began in 1964, and two unsold Comet 4Cs were converted as prototypes. A MAD 'stinger' was added to the tailcone, a search radar was added in the nose, a fin-tip radome ('football') was fitted to accommodate ESM equipment, and a new ventral weapons pannier was added beneath the cabin, giving a distinctive 'double-bubble' cross-section. These changes necessitated an increase in fin area. The first prototype was powered by the production

Nimrod's intended powerplant of four Spey turbofan engines and made its maiden flight on 23 May 1967, serving as an aerodynamic test bed and for airframe/engine integration. The second conversion retained the Comet's original Avon turbojets and recorded its first flight on 31 July, then serving as the avionics development aircraft.

Nimrod variants

The first of 46 examples of the production type, known as the **Nimrod MR.Mk 1**, flew on 28 June 1968, and the type entered service with No. 236 OCU in October 1969, eventually equipping five operational squadrons including one based overseas at RAF Luqa, Malta. The British withdrawal from Malta rendered the last batch of eight Nimrods surplus to requirement, although they could usefully have been

used to spread hours more evenly across the fleet, extending the Nimrod's life. Five were delivered to the RAF, and the others were retained by BAe for trials, but their useful life was short, seven of them being selected for conversion to **Nimrod AEW.Mk 3** standard, along with four earlier Nimrod MR.Mk 1s. All of these airframes were effectively wasted, since the Nimrod AEW.Mk 3 never entered productive service and all but one were scrapped, the survivor becoming an instructional airframe.

From 1975 the 35 remaining MR.Mk 1s were upgraded to **Nimrod MR.Mk 2** standard, the first MR.Mk 2 being redelivered to the RAF in August 1979. The Nimrod MR.Mk 2 introduced a completely new avionics and equipment suite, in which all major sensors and equipment

items were changed. The aircraft received a new GEC central tactical system, which was based on a new computer and three separate processors for navigation systems, radar and acoustic sensors. The old ASV.Mk 21D radar was replaced by Thorn EMI Searchwater equipment with a colour display. The acoustics system was made compatible with modern sonobuoys, including the BARRA, SSQ-41 and SSQ-53, TANDEM and Ultra active and passive types. The aircraft's communications equipment was similarly upgraded.

Combat additions

The addition of an inflight-refuelling probe (initially to 16 aircraft for participation in Operation Corporate, the UK's campaign to regain the Falkland Islands in 1982) created the

Nimrod MR.Mk 2P – the 'P' was subsequently dropped in the late 1990s – and this change also necessitated the addition of tiny swept finlets on the horizontal tail surface. The Falklands war also resulted in the first operational use of the Nimrod's underwing hardpoints, giving the ability to carry AIM-9 Sidewinders for self-defence, or Harpoon anti-ship missiles, Stingray torpedoes, bombs or depth charges for offensive purposes. The planned wing-tip Loral ARI.18240/1 ESM pods were added later, these requiring larger rectangular finlets. All the aircraft were then revised with both refuelling probes and ESM pods. For operations from

Seeb in Oman, during Operation Desert Storm, to drive the Iraqi occupying forces from Kuwait, a number of aircraft were drawn from Nos 120 (lead), 42 and 206 Sqns to form the Nimrod MR Detachment. Several of the aircraft were modified to what was unofficially known as **Nimrod MR.Mk 2P(GM)** standard, the **Gulf Modification** involving the addition of an underwing FLIR turret on the starboard wing, BOZ electronic countermeasures pods and a TRD (Towed Radar Decoy).

Nimrod MRA.Mk 4

During the mid-1990s, BAe was selected to create a radically updated and revitalised force of

Above: The Nimrod fulfils three primary roles in RAF service: anti-submarine warfare (ASW), anti-surface unit warfare (ASUW) and search and rescue (SAR). In addition to these roles the Nimrods also assist civil agencies such as HM Customs or the Department for Environment, Food and Rural Affairs when requested.

21 Nimrods after winning the Ministry of Defence's Maritime Patrol Aircraft competition. Due to re-enter service between 2002 and 2007, but now likely to be 2005 at the earliest, after virtually total reconstruction to the so-called **Nimrod 2000** standard, the **Nimrod MRA.Mk 4** retains only the pressure hull, keel, weapons bay, tailcone and fixed tail surfaces of its predecessor. The rest of the airframe is essentially new, and the powerplant is changed to a quartet

of Rolls-Royce BR.710 turbofan engines each rated at 66.73 kN (15,000 lb st) to provide undiminished performance despite a 20 per cent increase in maximum take-off weight to 105598 kg (232,800 lb), which also requires beefed-up landing gear units. A new generation of mission avionics is also being provided by a Boeing-led team to maintain the MRA.Mk 4's maritime reconnaissance, anti-ship and anti-submarine capabilities at a very high level.

Left: Nimrod MRA.Mk 4 has been beset by development problems and cost overruns, but should emerge as the world's most capable MR platform.

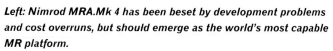

SPECIFICATION

Hawker Siddeley (BAe) Nimrod MR.Mk 2
Type: 12-crew maritime reconnaissance, anti-submarine and anti-ship aircraft
Powerplant: four Rolls-Royce Spey RB.168-20 Mk 250 turbofan engines each rated at 54 kN (12,140 lb st)
Performance: maximum speed 926 km/h (575 mph) at optimum altitude; cruising speed 880 km/h (547 mph) at optimum altitude; patrol speed 370 km/h (230 mph)

at low altitude; service ceiling 12800 m (42,000 ft); range 9266 km (5,758 miles); endurance 19 hours with one inflight refuelling
Weights: empty 39010 kg (86,000 lb); maximum take-off 87091 kg (192,000 lb)
Dimensions: wing span 35 m (114 ft 10 in); length 38.63 m (126 ft 9 in); height 9.08 m (29 ft 8½ in); wing area 197.04 m² (2,121 sq ft)
Armament: up to 6124 kg (13,500 lb) of disposable stores carried internally and externally

Lockheed P-3 Orion Maritime patrol aircraft

This P-3C Update III is shown as it appeared with VP-4 'Skinny Dragons' at Kaneohe Bay, Hawaii. All of the Orion units previously operating at MCAS Barber's Point transferred to this new location in July 1999. VP-4 was active during Desert Storm, flying from Masirah.

In August 1957 the US Navy issued Type Specification No. 146 calling for a new anti-submarine aircraft to replace the P-2 Neptune. The Lockheed proposal was based on the L-188 Electra airliner, and in May 1958 the company was awarded a contract for the new type.

It modified the third Electra airframe as the prototype, with a tail-mounted MAD boom and a ventral bulge simulating a weapons bay. Following extensive adaptations (including a shortening of the fuselage), the aircraft made a successful maiden flight as the **YP3V-1** (later redesignated as the **YP-3A**) on 25 November 1959. The USN ordered an initial batch of seven in October 1960, and the first of these flew in April 1961. In 1962 the type was redesignated as the **P-3A Orion**.

The P-3A entered service in the summer of 1962 with 3355-kW (4,500-eshp) T56-A-10W turboprops and, from the 110th aircraft, the DELTIC (DELayed TIme Compression) acoustic data-processing system that doubled sonobuoy information-processing capability and also

incorporated redesigned avionics. Within a short time most existing aircraft had also been retrofitted. In the summer of 1965, after the delivery of 157 P-3As, Lockheed began production of the **P-3B**. This was fitted with more powerful T56-A-14 engines and was heavier than its predecessor, mainly through having provision for the AGM-12 Bullpup ASM, but retained basically the same electronics fit. The P-3B secured the first export orders for the type, and became operational with New Zealand and Norway (five aircraft each) and also with Australia (10 aircraft). From 1977 the USN's P-3Bs were updated with improved navigation and acoustic-processing equipment, and with provision for the AGM-84 Harpoon missile. P-3B production ended in 1969 after the completion of 144 aircraft (125 of them for the US Navy).

Surplus P-3As were later converted to **RP-3A** standard (three aircraft) for oceanographic reconnaissance, and to **WP-3A** standard (four aircraft) for weather reconnaissance. Six early aircraft were refitted as

Above: VP-9 'Golden Eagles' was deployed with its P-3Cs to Misawa, Japan, when this photograph was taken in February 2003.

staff transports under the **VP-3A** designation, while a handful entered service as **TP-3A** aircrew trainers. Several early Orions were converted for utility transport duties as **UP-3A** and **UP-3B** machines. Four P-3As were transferred to the US Customs Service under the **P-3A(CS)** designation with APG-63 nose radar to complement four **P-3B AEW** aircraft with the APS-138 surveillance radar using an antenna in a rotodome above the rear fuselage.

Upgrades and orders

New Zealand's aircraft received an avionics upgrade (the first by Boeing and the other five by Air

New Zealand) to become **P-3K** machines: the sixth of these aircraft was an ex-Australian P-3B. Norway acquired two P-3Bs in 1979 and one of these, plus one original aircraft, were adapted to **P-3N** standard for pilot training and fishery protection. The other five were transferred to Spain to replace four P-3As leased from the USN and to augment the surviving two of three P-3As purchased by Spain. The six surviving Australian aircraft were upgraded to **P-3C** standard as **P-3P** machines and subsequently transferred to Portugal in 1986. Australia later purchased three surplus USN P-3Bs for use as trainers with the designation **TAP-3**. Later customers for ex-USN P-3As and P-3Bs include Argentina (eight P-3Bs), Greece (six P-3Bs) and Thailand (two P-3As and one **UP-3T**).

Left: Many JMSDF P-3Cs (a VP-2 aircraft is illustrated) carry a dorsal radome for SATCOMs.

Above: No. 92 Wing of the RAAF maintains two operational squadrons (10 – illustrated – and 11) and one training (292) squadron of P-3Cs at RAAF Edinburgh.

Right: The RNZAF was the first export customer for the Orion, receiving five P-3B DELTIC aircraft for service with No. 5 Squadron at Whenuapai in 1966 to replace Sunderlands. In the 1980s the fleet was enhanced under the Rigel programme, resulting in the P-3K variant with APS-134 imaging radar and an infrared turret. Another upgrade programme, known as Sirius, was cancelled in 2000, but a a new upgrade was being implemented in 2003.

Ultimate ASW Orion

The P-3C is now the USN's primary land-based ASW patrol aircraft. It retains the airframe/powerplant combination of the P-3B, and the first service-test **YP-3C** was a P-3B conversion that first flew on 18 September 1968. Since then, the P-3C has also been exported to Australia, the Netherlands, Norway, Japan, Pakistan and South Korea. The baseline P-3C has APS-115B search radar, ASQ-81 MAD and the AQA-7 DIFAR (Directional Acoustics-Frequency Analysis and Recording) system, as well as an integrated ASW and navigation system.

The P-3C entered service in 1969, and 118 baseline aircraft were followed by about 247 of various **Update** versions for the USN and export, of which the last was a machine delivered to South Korea in September 1995

from a newly established production line.

The **P-3C Update I** (31 built) introduced a seven-fold increase in computer memory and Omega navigation in place of the original LORAN. The **P-3C Update II** (37 built for delivery from August 1977) featured an advanced sonobuoy reference system, provision for the AGM-84 and the AAS-36 IRDS (Infra-Red Detection System). The **P-3C Update II.5** (24 aircraft) has a more reliable nav/comms suite, MAD compensation, standardised pylons and other improvements. The definitive P-3C Orion variant is the **P-3C Update III**, fitted with an entirely new IBM UYS-1 Proteus acoustic signal processor and a new sonobuoy communications link. These enable the aircraft to monitor twice the number of sonobuoys, as can the Update II.5 version. The Update III was the last production version and was first delivered in May 1984. Most baseline P-3C Orions were later modified to the **P-3C Update III Retrofit** standard.

Exports of the P-3C included 10 Update II aircraft for Australia with the Anglo-Australian Barra acoustic data processor and indigenously developed Barra passive directional sonobuoys. Australia's second 10-aircraft batch comprised P-3C Update II.5 machines, but these are known locally by the designation **P-3W**. Ten Australian aircraft later received an Elta-developed ESM suite, and were then upgraded to **AP-3C** standard in a Raytheon-led programme including the Elta EL/M-2022 radar,

Canadian UYS-503 acoustic processing system and improved nav/comm systems. The Netherlands and Japan also received Update II.5s. The P-3Cs operated by Norway and South Korea are Update IIIs. Japan received three aircraft, plus a further five in component knocked-down kit form for assembly before Kawasaki switched to complete manufacture of the balance of the 110 aircraft required. Iran received six baseline P-3C aircraft to the **P-3F** standard with a receptacle for inflight refuelling. The **CP-140 Aurora**, which resembles the P-3C externally, was built to Canadian specification with different avionics, and the 18 such aircraft were complemented by three **CP-140A Arcturus** aircraft with no ASW equipment, which were therefore used for training and economic zone protection.

SPECIFICATION

Lockheed P-3C Orion
Type: 10-crew long-range maritime patrol and anti-submarine aircraft
Powerplant: four Rolls-Royce T56-A-14 turboprop engines each rated at 3661 kW (4,910 ehp)
Performance: maximum speed 761 km/h (473 mph) 'clean' at 4575 m (15,000 ft); maximum climb rate 594 m (1,950 ft) per minute; service ceiling 8625 m (28,300 ft); radius 2494 km (1,550 miles) with 3 hours on station
Weights: empty 27890 kg (61,491 lb); maximum take-off 64410 kg (142,000 lb)
Dimensions: wing span 30.37 m (99 ft 8 in); length 35.61 m (116 ft 10 in); height 10.27 m (33 ft 8½ in); wing area 120.77 m² (1,300 sq ft)
Armament: up to 9072 kg (20,000 lb) of disposable stores carried in a lower-fuselage weapons bay and on 10 underwing hardpoints; including 10/20-kiloton B57 nuclear weapons; 1,000-lb (454-kg) Mk 52 mines; 2,000-lb (907-kg) Mk 55 or Mk 56 mines; Mk 54 and Mk 101 depth bombs; Mk 82 and Mk 83 bombs; Mk 38 and Mk 40 destructors; Mk 46 and Mk 50 Barracuda torpedoes; AGM-84 Harpoon AShMs, AGM-65 Maverick ASMs; AIM-9L Sidewinder AAMs and rocket pods

US Navy Orions today

In the post-Cold War era, the Orion has been adapted to perform a number of new missions, mostly concerned with war in the 'littorals'.

A series of modification programmes has been applied to the P-3C Update III fleet to improve its capabilities, especially in the non-USW (undersea warfare) world. Although traditional 'blue-water' USW is still an important part of the Orion's operations, the decrease in Russian submarine activity (and changed political situation) has lessened the emphasis in this area. However, a concurrent rise in operations in the littoral ('white-water') regions has seen a whole new range of sensors and systems developed for the Orion, culminating in the current AIP/AIMS modification, which is being applied to most of the fleet.

In the late 1980s the Orion underwent the Command Survivability Program, which added a host of defensive measures, the most obvious of which was a change to the TPS (Tactical Paint Scheme), a grey camouflage. IR detectors and chaff/flare dispensers were also added.

Under the Outlaw Hunter programme, a single Orion was fitted with APS-137 inverse synthetic aperture radar (ISAR) which could image vessels or submarine periscopes. The aircraft also received GPS navigation and a new, highly accurate ESM suite. This turned it into a capable stand-off over-the-horizon targeting system. Outlaw Hunter was extremely successful in the 1991 Gulf War, guiding US Navy attack aircraft on numerous occasions. Three more Orions were subsequently updated, the programme having been rechristened OASIS (Over-the-horizon Airborne Sensor Information System).

Anti-drug operations

Another role which became an important task for the Orion community was fighting drug smugglers in the Caribbean, for which detachments were, and are, maintained at a number of locations. A special sensor package, dubbed CDU (Counter Drug Update) was developed, consisting of a roll-on, roll-off system including an APG-66 fire-control radar (from the F-16) for tracking small airborne targets, and a Cluster Ranger long-range electro-optical sensor.

Thirty P-3s were modified to take the CDU package, and are widely used in tracking boats and aircraft used by smugglers. Cluster Ranger imagery can be transmitted in real time to intercepting agencies. Further EO systems have been used, including Cast Glance. These early systems peered out from the rear observer station, requiring the port outer engine to be shut down during use so that the jet efflux would not interfere with the sensor. A partial solution was found with the AVX-1 camera, which is mounted in the port forward (Tacco) station. However, this makes the station very cramped.

AIP

Elements of the CDU and OASIS improvements were incorporated into the AIP (Anti-surface warfare Improvement Program), which is being applied to most Orions. This brings together the GPS and ISAR of the OASIS with the AVX-1 camera of the CDU, plus new equipment such as ALR-66C(V)5 ESM (with underfuselage radome), new displays, new mission computer and additional Satcoms. Weapons capability includes Maverick, Harpoon, SLAM, SLAM-ER and, most likely, JASSM.

From 1999 AIP P-3s began to appear with the Wescam

Above: The Orion has always had a limited surface attack capability through the use of rockets. In recent times precision-guided weapons such as Maverick, Harpoon and SLAM have become available, although the P-3 can still employ unguided weapons. Such a capability is demonstrated here by a pair of VP-45 Orions firing 5-in (12.7-cm) Zuni rockets.

AIMS turret under the nose, which includes a long-range electro-optical sensor to replace the cumbersome AVX-1 system, and freeing space at the Tacco station. AIPs first went to war during the Kosovo campaign, in the course of which a number of SLAMs was fired at coastal targets, and numerous coastal reconnaissance/battle damage assessment missions were flown.

With AIP/AIMS, the Orion is fully equipped for the missions it faces in the first part of the 21st century, many of which are aimed at coastal patrol. However, the airframes are getting old, and a SLAP (Service Life Assessment Program) is under way which may lead to structural improvements. In the longer term, a replacement is sought under a programme dubbed MMA (Multi-mission Maritime Aircraft). Little funding is available for this, but the solution is likely to be a combined crewed aircraft/UCAV buy.

P-3C Orion

P-3C BuNo. 159511, an early production example, is depicted here in as-built condition and in the markings of Patrol Squadron Nineteen (VP-19), based at NAS Moffett Field, California.

Radar
Specially developed for the Orion, the I-band, frequency-agile Texas Instruments APS-115 was the standard radar in the P-3C. Two antennas provide 360° coverage. One is located in the nose radome and the other faces aft from the tailcone. Under the AIP (Anti-surface Improvement Program) selected P-3Cs are being fitted with the APS-137(V)5 radar, a version of the radar introduced by the S-3B Viking.

Crew
While the flight deck houses the two pilots and the flight engineer, most of the Orion's standard 10 crew are situated in the main cabin of the aircraft. These comprise seven mission specialists: the nav/comms operator, a tactical co-ordinator and three sensor operators (one non-acoustic and two acoustic), all in the forward part of the cabin. In the rear of the cabin are the inflight technician and ordnanceman, who both double as observers.

Powerplant
The P-3C is powered by four Allison (now Rolls-Royce) T56 turboprops, the common T56-A-14s each being rated at 3424 kW (4,591 shp) for take-off, or 3661 ekW (4,910 ehp) when jet thrust is taken into consideration. The T56 is one of the true classics of aero-engine design, having first flown in the nose of a B-17 testbed in 1954. A single-shaft turboprop with a 14-stage axial compressor and four-stage turbine, the T56 runs at a speed of 13,820 rpm. The T56-A-10W (P-3A) and -14 (P-3B/C) differ from other military-spec T56s by having the gearbox mounted below the drive shaft (as opposed to above, as in the E-2 and C-130), resulting in the P-3's distinctive nacelle shape. The civilian-spec Allison 501 engine, as used in the Electra and Convair CV-580, also employed this configuration.

Undernose cameras and FLIR
The P-3's photographic capabilities were enhanced by the addition of two new camera systems, including KA-74A surveillance cameras. This was located in an undernose fairing with four glass panels. Mounted on a gimbal, this camera could rotate through forward, left or right, and 30° down horizontal views. This was replaced during the extensive P-3C Update II programme by the Texas Instruments (now Raytheon) AAS-36 FLIR, as the Infra-Red Detection System (IRDS). Housed in a retractable ball-turret and located under the aircraft's nose, the IRDS is provided for passive thermal detection of surface vessels and for battle damage assessment. The IRDS operates through fog, smoke and haze and is an undetectable sensor. Operating through fog and smoke will show general shapes of 'hot versus cold', but no detail, so it is not as reliable under those conditions. Moreover, the IRDS is sensitive to humidity, which can fog the display beyond use.

Weapons bay
The shallow but useful weapons bay under the forward fuselage can accommodate 500-lb (227-kg) class bombs/depth charges/mines or three larger weapons (including, at one time, B57 nuclear depth charges, which are no longer in service). Up to eight Mk 46 torpedoes or six Mk 50 Barracuda torpedoes can also be carried.

Right: P-3C BuNo. 161329 of VP-65 peels away from the camera during a mission over the Pacific in 1997. The first P-3s reaching the extent of their fatigue lives will be retired in the period 2002-2004. The Orion's intended successor, known as the MMA, might join the fleet some time during the mid-2010s, but its future is uncertain. Several MMA options have been considered, including a Boeing 737-700 derivative and the possibility of re-opening the P-3 production line with a re-engined variant.

Enhanced capability
Building on an integrated ASW system first conceptualised in 1960, the P-3C represented a quantum leap in overall ASW capabilities and made the Orion one of the most advanced maritime patrol aircraft ever to fly. Termed the A-NEW ASW Avionics Systems Program, the P-3C designation integrated all of the aircraft's sophisticated sensors through a centralised computer processor, thereby reducing the amount of time air crews needed to spend making paper records, called paper grams.

Mission system
The P-3C Update III's core system is the IBM UYS-1 Proteus, with a plethora of processing computers, sonobuoy signal receivers and recording systems. Data is displayed on ASA-66 (pilot), ASA-70 (Tacco – Tactical Co-ordinator) or USQ-78 (Senso – Sensor operator – 1 and 2) displays. Search and attack patterns are commanded on the pilot's display, as directed by the Tactical Co-ordinator. The system has been the subject of continuing improvements and additions, although these have not been implemented fleetwide, with the result that there are many Orion system configurations existing in the force. The Navy is working to achieve an Update III Common Configuration, including the continued upgrading of Update II/II.5 aircraft under the BMUP ('Block Mod') programme.

Above: This No. 10 Sqn, Royal Australian Air Force P-3C is finished in the latest low-viz scheme applied to the type by the RAAF. Australia was an early export customer for the Orion, taking delivery of the first of 10 P-3Bs in 1968, two years after the first foreign user, New Zealand, received five similar Orion aircraft.

MAD
The 'tail sting' houses an ASQ-81 Magnetic Anomaly Detector which detects submarines by sensing distortions in the Earth's magnetic field caused by large metal objects. Though an important system in the past, MAD is used only rarely by Orions in service in 2003, and then usually in the final prosecution of a submarine attack to verify the location of the vessel.

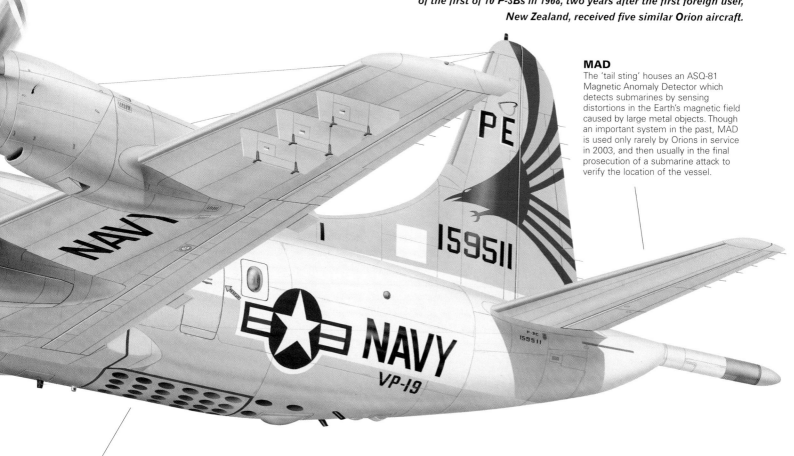

Sonobuoys
The P-3 carries a variety of sonobuoys for detecting underwater vessels. These fall into two main categories: active and passive. Active buoys, typified by the SSQ-62 DICASS (Directional Command-Active Sonobuoy System) generate their own noise to give range, bearing and velocity data, but their noise emissions also alert the submarine to the fact that it is being watched. Passive buoys simply receive and interpret underwater noise.

Right: Lockheed initially developed the P-3 AEW&C for the international market, marrying the Hawkeye's APS-125 radar with the P-3 airframe. An aerodynamic prototype first flew on 14 June 1984 with the APA-171 rotodome fitted, but was later fully equipped with systems. It subsequently became the first aircraft delivered to the Customs Service and was joined by three further examples, including N148CS seen here.

Index